lonely planet

Lake Tahoe, Yosemite & Central California

Suzie Dundas, Esther Carlstone,
Ashley Harrell, Helena Smith

FROM LEFT: SUZIE DUNDAS, SUZIE DUNDAS

Kings Beach (p120)

CONTENTS

Plan Your Trip

The Guide

Snowshoeing, Truckee (p127)

Toolkit

Storybook

Land Acknowledgement

Lonely Planet respectfully acknowledges that California is the traditional territory of 110 federally recognized tribes, as well as more than 80 others who are seeking recognition. We gratefully honor the communities with ancestral ties to the land on which we travel, specifically the Ahwahneechee people, also known as the Southern Sierra Miwok (Yosemite Valley) and the Washoe Tribe also known as Wá·šiw (Lake Tahoe Basin). During your travels, we encourage you to learn about these communities and reflect upon their histories.

SUZIE DUNDAS

Northstar California (p129)

LAKE TAHOE, YOSEMITE & CENTRAL CALIFORNIA

THE JOURNEY BEGINS HERE

I grew up on the central East Coast, far removed from California. Everything I knew about California was based on TV shows and movies, and I thought it was all surfers, palm trees and big cities. But in my early teens, we took a family trip to Lake Tahoe, and I learned that a whole other side of California exists. We stayed in some generic budget hotel on the South shore, and despite being in the peak of my jaded teen years, the one day we spent driving round the lake convinced me that it was the prettiest place I'd ever been.

Suzie Dundas

@hikeupyourskirt

Suzie is a journalist, author and editor based in Truckee. Her work focuses on adventure travel, the outdoors and issues related to mountain living and tourism. She wrote the Lake Tahoe chapter.

My favorite experiences are any on my mountain bike, when cruising down a Tahoe trail feels like a twisting roller coaster ride where I get to drive. Northstar California's bike park (p129) is an ideal place to hone your skills.

WHO GOES WHERE

Our writers choose the places which, for them, define Lake Tahoe, Yosemite & Central California.

VENEMAMA/GETTY IMAGES

Nevada City (pictured; p85) was a charming surprise, with its historic buildings and sense of community fellowship. Ingredients straight from local farms combined with some gorgeous hikes make it a must-visit in my book. I can't wait to see it at Christmas, when it's covered in cheer and twinkle lights.

Esther Carlstone

@familyfieldtrip

Esther is a travel and lifestyle writer with a focus on family travel. She wrote the Gold Country chapter.

WIRESTOCK CREATORS/SHUTTERSTOCK

The lesser-traveled **Eastern Sierra** (pictured; p168) feels like a jaunt through a Tim Burton dream, with eerie beauty oozing from every crevice. No matter how many times I drive Hwy 395, I'll always be mesmerized by its surreal desertscapes.

Ashley Harrell

@where_smashley_went

Ashley is the national parks bureau chief at SFGATE and co-author of the National Geographic book 100 Beaches of a Lifetime. *She wrote the Yosemite & the Sierra Nevada chapter.*

CASSIOHABIB/SHUTTERSTOCK

Entering **Sacramento** (pictured; p44), I always feel, paradoxically, that I'm entering both a city and a forest at once. The city has more than a million trees, cooling walkers on summer days, meeting in grand arches over the streets and framing the 1920s Craftsman homes and flamboyant midtown Victorians.

Helena Smith

@helenasmithpix

Helena loves to write about eco-travel, community and the outdoors. She wrote the Sacramento & the Central Valley chapter.

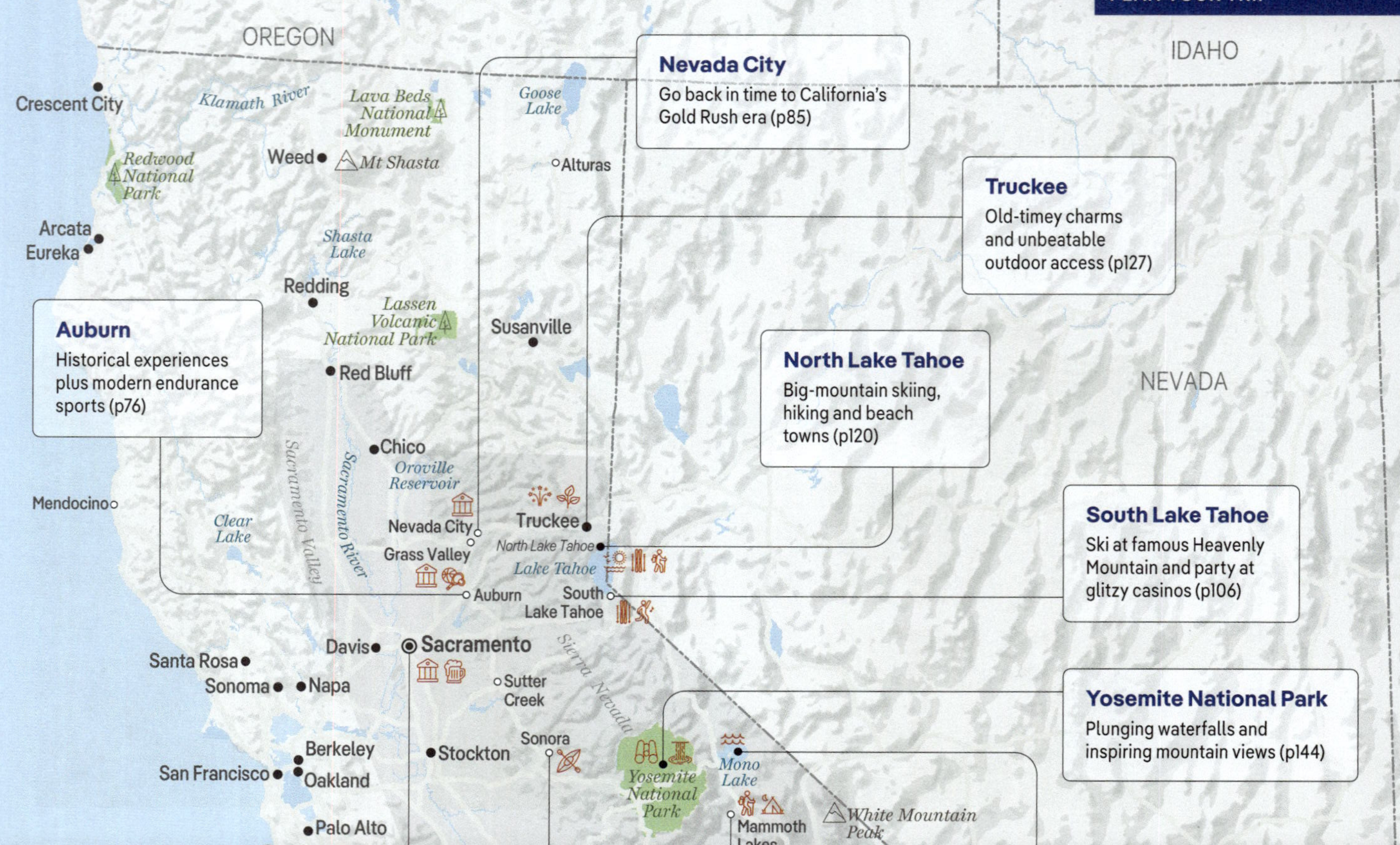
OREGON
IDAHO
NEVADA
Nevada City
Go back in time to California's Gold Rush era (p85)
Truckee
Old-timey charms and unbeatable outdoor access (p127)
North Lake Tahoe
Big-mountain skiing, hiking and beach towns (p120)
South Lake Tahoe
Ski at famous Heavenly Mountain and party at glitzy casinos (p106)
Yosemite National Park
Plunging waterfalls and inspiring mountain views (p144)
Auburn
Historical experiences plus modern endurance sports (p76)
Crescent City
Klamath River
Lava Beds National Monument
Goose Lake
Redwood National Park
Weed
Mt Shasta
Alturas
Arcata
Eureka
Shasta Lake
Redding
Lassen Volcanic National Park
Susanville
Red Bluff
Chico
Oroville Reservoir
Sacramento Valley
Sacramento River
Mendocino
Clear Lake
Nevada City
Grass Valley
Truckee
North Lake Tahoe
Lake Tahoe
Auburn
South Lake Tahoe
Davis
Sacramento
Sierra Nevada
Santa Rosa
Sonoma
Napa
Sutter Creek
Berkeley
San Francisco
Oakland
Stockton
Sonora
Yosemite National Park
Mono Lake
Mammoth Lakes
White Mountain Peak
Palo Alto

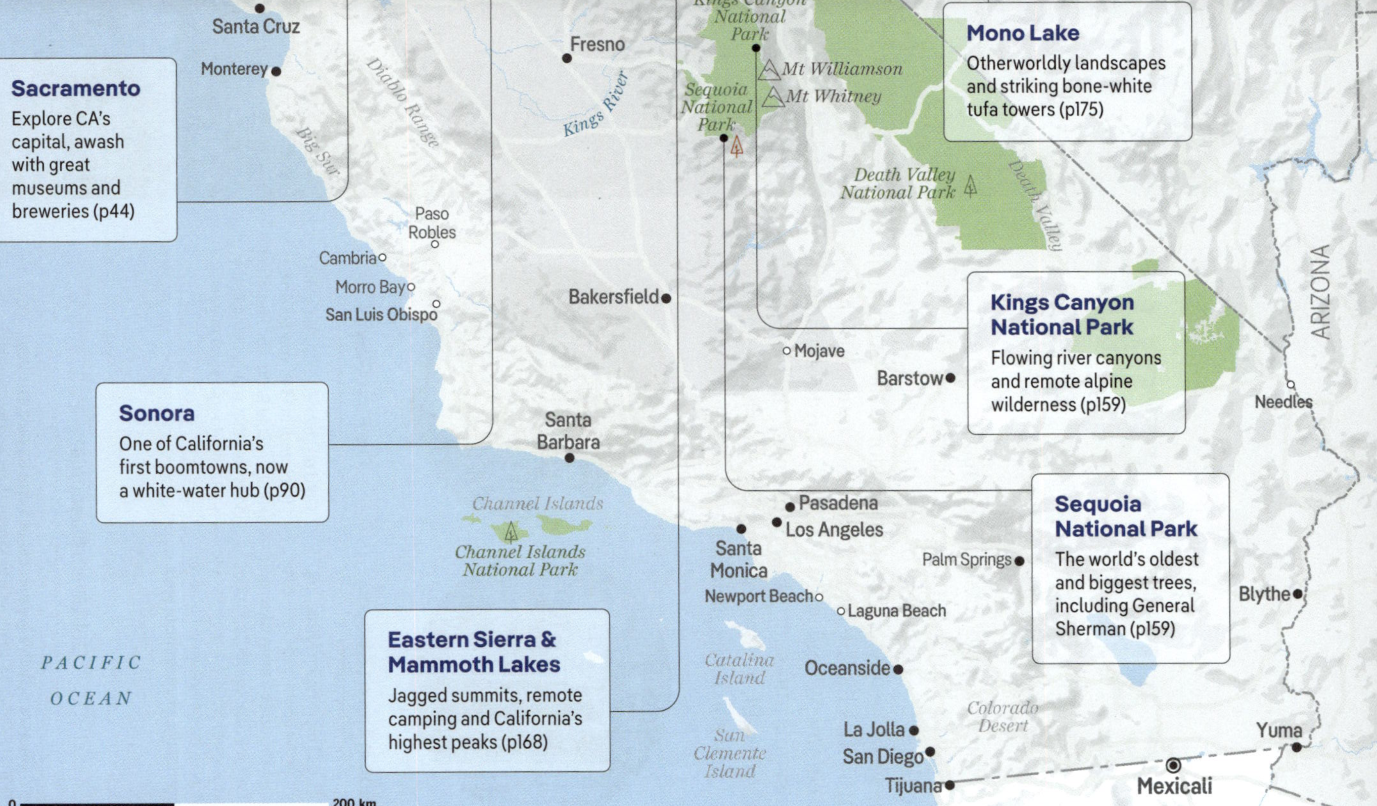
Sacramento
Explore CA's capital, awash with great museums and breweries (p44)
Sonora
One of California's first boomtowns, now a white-water hub (p90)
Eastern Sierra & Mammoth Lakes
Jagged summits, remote camping and California's highest peaks (p168)
Mono Lake
Otherworldly landscapes and striking bone-white tufa towers (p175)
Kings Canyon National Park
Flowing river canyons and remote alpine wilderness (p159)
Sequoia National Park
The world's oldest and biggest trees, including General Sherman (p159)
Santa Cruz
Monterey
Big Sur
Diablo Range
Paso Robles
Cambria
Morro Bay
San Luis Obispo
Fresno
Kings River
Bakersfield
Santa Barbara
Channel Islands
Channel Islands National Park
Sequoia National Park
Mt Williamson
Mt Whitney
Death Valley National Park
Death Valley
Mojave
Barstow
Pasadena
Los Angeles
Santa Monica
Newport Beach
Laguna Beach
Palm Springs
Catalina Island
San Clemente Island
Oceanside
La Jolla
San Diego
Tijuana
Colorado Desert
Mexicali
Yuma
Blythe
Needles
ARIZONA
MEXICO
PACIFIC OCEAN
0 200 km
0 100 miles

HEART OF THE GOLD RUSH

Before the Gold Rush, California was inhabited mostly by Native American cultures and Mexican settlers. The discovery of gold in 1848 kicked off a series of events that would transform the West and turn cities like SF and Sacramento into major hubs for commerce and culture. Today, ghost towns, mine museums and state parks remember the Gold Rush era. After all, it's not the constant sunshine that gives California its nickname: the Golden State.

Boom Towns Abound

They call them boom towns, but really, they're boom-and-bust towns. They sprang up overnight when gold or silver was discovered, and dried up just as quickly. Often, they were so short lived that there wasn't time for minor details, like sheriffs or laws.

The First Flakes

Gold discovered at Sutter's Mill (pictured) in 1848 sparked the California Gold Rush, and launched industries that would reshape the Sierra, like logging and railroads.

Gold Rush Museums

This era is such a key part of the Sierra Nevada's history that nearly every museum (and many bars and restaurants) are packed with Gold Rush memorabilia.

FROM LEFT: ARNE BERULDSEN, GERALD PEPLOW/SHUTTERSTOCK, ALEXANDER HOWARD/LONELY PLANET

Flume Trail (p133)

BEST GOLD RUSH EXPERIENCES

Hike the ❶ **Flume Trail** (p133) in Lake Tahoe, so named for its inventive transport system to carry logs to the mines in Virginia City.

Walk through ❷ **Virginia City** (p126; pictured far left), a still-populated Gold Rush town with 1860s-era saloons and mine shafts hidden under floorboards.

Explore ❸ **Donner Memorial State Park** (p128), site of the infamous Donner Party tragedy, now housing a packed museum.

Make the dusty drive to ❹ **Bodie** (p186), one of the best-preserved ghost towns in the West, complete with hundreds of buildings – many still furnished.

See Gold Rush artifacts and art at the ❺ **Mariposa Museum & History Center** (p154) focused on the lives of California gold rushers.

HIGH-ELEVATION ADVENTURES

Nowhere in California hurts for outdoor recreation, but it's hard to beat the diversity and scale of the adventures awaiting in California's mountains. Unparalleled adventures await in the peaks here; summit the (literally) breathtaking Mt Whitney, raft narrow river canyons, stand in the shadow of a 1500-year-old sequoia or paddle between boulders on the dazzlingly clear water of Lake Tahoe. It's more than you could fit into one lifetime, let alone one vacation.

Spring Snowmelt

If you're hoping to get out on the water, choose the season carefully. Snowmelt feeds rivers in the spring and early summer, creating large rapids, raising water levels and causing occasional flooding. It's better for whitewater, but beaches are smaller.

Bring Snowshoes

Low-elevation hiking trails in Gold Country and the Yosemite Valley may be accessible year-round, but most in the mountains around Tahoe and the Eastern Sierra will be covered in snow from November to May.

Plan Ahead

Yosemite and Tahoe have some of the coolest campgrounds in California, but you'll need to plan ahead. State and national park campgrounds almost always require reservations, which can fill months in advance.

FROM LEFT: HAYK_SHALUNTS/SHUTTERSTOCK, CK FOTO/SHUTTERSTOCK, SUZIE DUNDAS

Tahoe Rim Trail (p122)

BEST ADVENTURE EXPERIENCES

Go white-water rafting through ❶ **Yosemite National Park** (p144) on the Merced River, or climb the park's famous granite cliffs with Yosemite Mountaineering School.

Paddleboard or kayak on the crystal-clear water of Lake Tahoe's ❷ **Sand Harbor State Park** (p131).

Send it on the 16-mile ❸ **Downieville Downhill** (p88) mountain bike trail north of Nevada City in Downieville. Several companies provide shuttles and rentals; you should be at least intermediate or above.

Explore caves in Sequoia National Park, including the recently reopened ❹ **Crystal Cave** (p161).

Hike a section of the ❺ **Tahoe Rim Trail** (p122), a high-elevation hiking trail encircling Lake Tahoe with epic Sierra Nevada views.

WHERE MOUNTAINS MEET DESERT

It's California's coastal regions that get most of the attention, but the landscapes in the eastern part of the state are among the country's most unique. In Tahoe, massive mountains ring sparkling alpine lakes, and around Mammoth, the jagged peaks of the Eastern Sierra reveal the state's geologic power. Fortunately, it's a region well suited to road tripping, with plenty of free Bureau of Land Management (BLM) camping and no shortage of parks and landmarks to entice you to pull over.

Know Your Roads

Hwy 395 (pictured) is the only north-to-south route through the Eastern Sierra – but what a drive it is. On the western side, you'll have more options for meandering mountain roads. Going east, both Hwy 50 and Hwy 80 connect Sacramento to Tahoe.

Nature or History?

Cruising to the west of the Sierra Nevada offers more Gold Rush history and historic towns, while the eastern route (pictured) is more about sprawling views and open skies, with fewer places to sleep and eat.

Loop Around the Lake

You can drive a full loop around Lake Tahoe's shoreline (p98) in a day. Leave plenty of time to stop at beaches, historic sites and lakefront parks and restaurants.

BEST ROAD TRIP EXPERIENCES

Tie together three national parks on a road trip between ❶ **Yosemite** (p144), **Kings Canyon** and **Sequoia National Parks** (p159).

See the highest point in the continental US (excluding Alaska): ❷ **Mt Whitney** (p168) stands 14,505ft above sea level.

Beat the heat with a quick weekend trip from Sacramento to ❸ **Auburn** (p76) and Nevada City, then loop down Tahoe's West shore, stopping at an Apple Hill farmstand on your way back to Sac.

Stroll the shore of ❹ **Mono Lake** (p175), where lanky, statuesque tufa towers emerge from the lake, formed by calcium carried up by springs beneath the lake.

Detour to ❺ **Malakoff Diggins State Historic Park** (p89), a ghost town and mine once inhabited exclusively by French miners, now turned into a walkable state park.

HIT THE SLOPES

The best ski resorts in California are scattered between Lake Tahoe and Mammoth Lakes, including Palisades Tahoe, famous for hosting the 1960 Winter Olympics. Winter may bring dicey driving, but the trade-off is fresh snow and an indescribable sense of excitement in ski village bars and restaurants. And the best part about skiing in California? If it's not snowing, it's sunny – so pack your sunscreen, unless you're going for that trendy goggle tan.

BEST SKI EXPERIENCES

Don your T-shirt (and sunscreen) for a day of spring skiing at ❶ **Mammoth Mountain** (p174), which stays open into June and occasionally July.

Get in a clean top-to-bottom run under ❷ **Palisades Tahoe** (p124)'s KT-22 lift, or watch pros throw front flips off the Fingers or the Nose while you cheer from the lift.

Enjoy a beer or wine tasting at ❸ **Diamond Peak** (p124)'s lakeview Snowflake Lodge, then ski down after the lifts have closed during the resort's Last Tracks events.

Explore backcountry lines off Tioga Pass Road near Yosemite, or ski inside a national park at Yosemite's ❹ **Badger Pass** (p153).

Cross-country ski at ❺ **Granlibakken Resort** (p117) in Tahoe City – the region's first recreation area – opened in 1922 (when it was known as Ski Canyon).

FROM LEFT: DAVID A LITMAN/SHUTTERSTOCK, ALISA_CH/SHUTTERSTOCK

Don't Slip & Slide

Winter driving demands patience. Have snow chains or 4WD with wire-rated tires, and be prepared for heavy traffic and road closures, especially on Hwy 395 and around Lake Tahoe's Emerald Bay.

Account for Elevation

Mammoth Mountain tops out at just over 11,000ft, while Tahoe's Heavenly Resort (pictured) is just over 10,000ft. Stay hydrated, wear sunscreen and expect leg and muscle fatigue.

Buy in Advance

The priciest way to go skiing is to walk up to the window and buy a ticket that morning. Buying a single-day lift ticket via EpicPass at least a month out can be the cheapest way to ski the Vail resorts, while Tahoe's other resorts usually offer discounts if you're buying online at least a week in advance.

NURPHOTO SRL/ALAMY

Victorian Christmas market, Nevada City (p85)

BEST FESTIVAL EXPERIENCES

Celebrate foothills wine at the ❶ **Big Crush Harvest Festival** (p82), held in Amador County.

See the Bard's works in a spectacular setting at the ❷ **Lake Tahoe Shakespeare Festival** (p133), at Sand Harbor State Park.

Attend the ❸ **Bracebridge Dinner** (p153), a tradition that transforms the historic Ahwahnee Hotel's dining room into a 17th-century Christmas castle.

Party at ❹ **Truckee Thursdays** (p127) in summer, when Downtown becomes an all-ages free summer concert and street fair.

Celebrate Gold Discovery Day at the ❺ **Marshall Gold Discovery State** (p79) and Sutter's Mill state historic parks.

PARTY IN THE MOUNTAINS

Sierra Nevada venues may not be on an A-list star's tour circuit, but California's mountain towns know how to party. And they're not just limited to music, with lively theatre performances, historical celebrations and community-wide events that welcome locals and visitors alike. Most ski resorts host summer festivals, and jam-band fans will find no shortage of ways to fill their weekends.

Ski Resort Happenings

Ski towns like Tahoe, Mammoth and even Sacramento draw more year-round tourists with busy summer event schedules, generally running from Memorial Day to Labor Day.

Local Traditions

Some festivals are holdovers from days gone by, like the Bishop Mule Fest, Sacramento Greek Festival and Nevada City Victorian Christmas. One-of-a-kind celebrations offer a taste of what locals are most proud of.

Rubicon Trail (p115)

NATIONAL & STATE PARKS

The Sierra Nevada's three national parks are among the park system's most dazzling. But its state parks deserve just as much consideration, with many that rival the national parks in natural beauty. State parks offer camping on granite cliffs above Lake Tahoe, hikes beneath towering sequoias and a wealth of historic sites – not to mention much smaller crowds.

Majestic Mountain Loop

The region's big three parks – Yosemite, Kings Canyon and Sequoia – are easy to connect in one trip, called the Majestic Mountain Loop *(majesticmountainloop.com)*; the website has winter and summer itineraries.

Plan Ahead

A reservation system helps control tourism in Sierra state parks. You may need a reservation for parking, camping or hiking. Book as early as possible on ReserveCalifornia.com, and cancel if plans change.

BEST PARK EXPERIENCES

Walk the ❶ **Yosemite Valley Loop** (p147), a mostly flat trail that passes famous sites like Half Dome, El Capitan and Yosemite Falls.

Hike from Emerald Bay State Park to DL Bliss State Park along the ❷ **Rubicon Trail**, (p115) hugging one of Tahoe's prettiest shorelines.

Tour one of the largest gold mines in the state – and the mine owner's former mansion – at ❸ **Empire Mine State Historic Park** (p87).

Stand in front of the largest tree in the world: ❹ **General Sherman** (p161), protected in Sequoia National Park.

Explore the undeveloped beaches of ❺ **Lake Tahoe–Nevada State Park** (p134), stretching the length of Lake Tahoe's northeastern shore.

NATURAL WONDERS

The Sierra Nevada formed over millions of years of tectonic instability, volcanic activity and ongoing uplifts of massive swaths of earth. While it's a little more stable now, that geologic action left behind wildly unique natural wonders you'll find few other places in the US.

FROM LEFT: EB ADVENTURE PHOTOGRAPHY/SHUTTERSTOCK, CHAD MCDERMOTT/SHUTTERSTOCK

Take a Dip

The ongoing subterranean action under the mountains means the wilderness areas along 395 are covered in hot springs, some easier to find than others. If you visit, leave no trace and read up on hot spring etiquette.

Keep it Clean

Many of the region's natural draws are at risk from overtourism. Follow regulations around permits, fire restraints, wildlife and backcountry camping. When hiking, carry out any trash you find on trails.

Be Prepared

Hiking into California's wilderness isn't the same as a walk in a national park. Always have an offline map downloaded or printed, and carry more food than you think you'll need. Portable water filters are inexpensive, and a great way to ensure against dehydration on most trails.

BEST NATURAL WONDER EXPERIENCES

Peer into Kings Canyon, deeper than the Grand Canyon in some places. The ❶ **Kings Canyon Scenic Byway** (p163) passes many of the most scenic points.

Soak in undeveloped hot springs like ❷ **Travertine** (p174) and **Buckeye** (p174), roughly an hour north of Mammoth Lakes.

Marvel at ❸ **Devils Postpile** (p175), a natural wall of geometric basalt (columns that formed after a volcanic eruption about 100,000 years ago).

Hike into ❹ **Emerald Bay** (p114), where an ancient glacier carved a dramatic inlet surrounded by towering granite walls.

Go underground at ❺ **Mercer Caverns** (p95), where stalactites and stalagmites show the evidence of eons of erosion and geologic activity.

REGIONS & CITIES

Find the places that tick all your boxes.

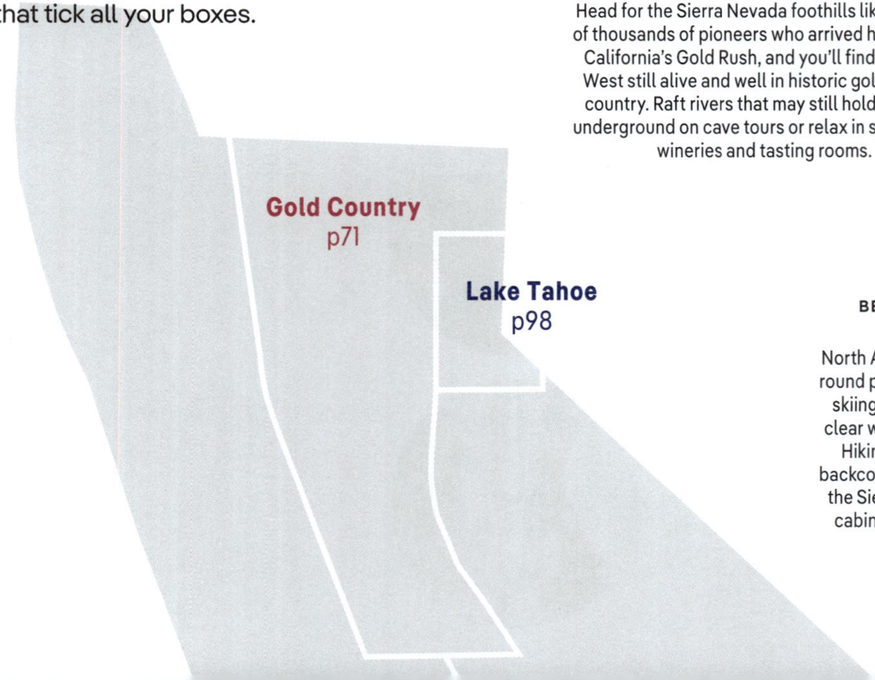

Gold Country
p71

Lake Tahoe
p98

Gold Country

LOVELY TOWNS FILLED WITH HISTORY

Head for the Sierra Nevada foothills like the tens of thousands of pioneers who arrived here during California's Gold Rush, and you'll find the Wild West still alive and well in historic gold-mining country. Raft rivers that may still hold gold, go underground on cave tours or relax in small-town wineries and tasting rooms.

Lake Tahoe

BEACHES, SKIING, MOUNTAINS AND CASINOS

North America's largest alpine lake is a year-round playground. Come for Olympic-worthy skiing and boarding in winter, and crystal-clear water and beachside parks in summer. Hiking and mountain biking through the backcountry takes you to the wildest sides of the Sierras. Charming towns, cozy lakeside cabins, great festivals and flashy casinos round things out.

Sacramento & the Central Valley p38

Yosemite & the Sierra Nevada p139

Sacramento & the Central Valley

GRITTY, WIDE OPEN AND SOULFUL

Arrive in California's often-overlooked capital in summer for epic farmers markets, or better yet, the California State Fair, then cool off in nearby swimming holes on the Sacramento River Delta. With easy access to both Tahoe and Yosemite, plus a growing culinary and arts scene, it's worthy of a day or two of your vacation time.

Yosemite & the Sierra Nevada

FORMIDABLE AND EXQUISITE ADVENTURER'S WONDERLAND

Nowhere in California's mountains lacks beauty, but the area around Yosemite kicks everything up a notch. It's shockingly stunning and brimming with superlatives: the world's biggest and oldest trees, the highest waterfall in North America, and both the highest and lowest points in the Lower 48.

YIMING CHEN/GETTY IMAGES

Tioga Road (p149)

ITINERARIES

An Eastern Sierra Stunner

Allow 8 days **Distance** 255 miles

The driving along 395 is one of California's most rewarding routes, shooting straight down the dramatic eastern side of the Sierra, where the peaks are jagged and the valleys are vast. The landscapes shift from pine-covered peaks to desert basins, with a stop in Yosemite National Park via stunning Tioga Pass Rd (closed between November and May) before ending at the highest peak in the Lower 48.

1

NORTH LAKE TAHOE 1 DAY

Try to get to Tahoe's **North shore** early in the morning to give yourself a full day to take in the lake's alpine beauty. Cycle from **Palisades Tahoe** (p124) to **Tahoe City** (p134) or hit one of many public beaches. In Tahoe City, swing by the Gatekeepers Museum to learn about the Sierra's Indigenous summer residents.

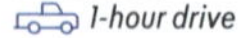
1-hour drive

2

SOUTH LAKE TAHOE 1 DAY

On your second day, give yourself all morning to drive the East shore to **South Lake Tahoe** (p106). Kayak and paddleboard around Sand Harbor State Park, hike to hidden beaches like Skunk Harbor or stretch your legs on a hike to a 'floating' lake 1000ft above Lake Tahoe. Spend the evening on the South shore at one of the town's best restaurants. *2½-hour drive*

3

JUNE LAKE 1 DAY

From Tahoe, head down to **June Lake** (p173), a small town with an old-timey quality. The main strip is mostly vintage motor lodges and stores, with excellent swimming and camping. Just before June Lake, stop at otherworldly Mono Lake (p175), for photo ops with tufa towers. *40-min drive*

Detour Stop at ***Bodie State Historic Park*** *(p176) if you're visiting between late May and early October and spend half a day walking through the fantastically preserved boom town.* *1-hour*

FROM LEFT: SIMON MATIN/SHUTTERSTOCK, SUZIE DUNDAS, 4KCLIPS/SHUTTERSTOCK

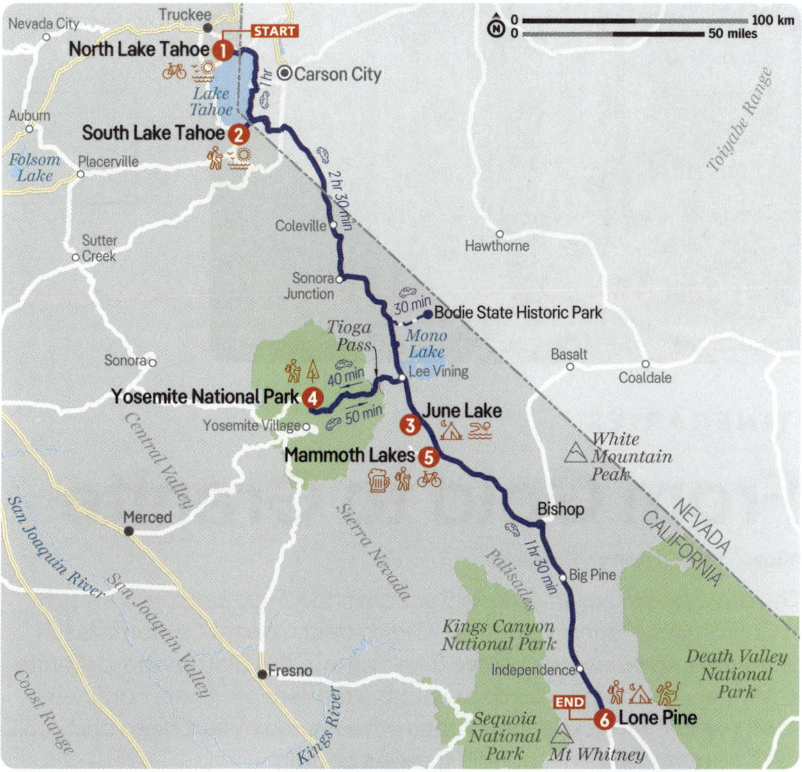

4

YOSEMITE NATIONAL PARK 2 DAYS

Open from late spring to late fall, Tioga Pass Rd is one of the prettiest drives in the Sierra, connecting 395 with the **Yosemite Valley** (p147). Whether you hike or not, leave plenty of time for roadside stops like Tuolumne Meadows, Tenaya Lake, Olmstead Point and the Tuolumne sequoia grove. From 395, it's about a 1½-hour drive to the Yosemite Valley, where you can check out the Ahwahnee Village, Yosemite Museum and historic Ansel Adams Gallery. *50-min drive*

5

MAMMOTH LAKES 2 DAYS

Swap the stark surrounds of Mono Lake for the forested surrounds of **Mammoth Lakes** (p173). Spend time in the downhill bike park, or hike a section of the famous John Muir Trail. Devil's Postpile is a quick shuttle ride away, and Mammoth's lineup of summer festivals will fill your evenings, as will its breweries and beer gardens. *1½-hour drive*

Detour *Stop in Bishop to visit the* ***Eastern California Museum*** *(p172), with a native plant garden and exhibits on Indigenous, Gold Rush and WWII history.*

6

LONE PINE 1 DAY

End in **Lone Pine** (p172), a town beloved by rock climbers but with more than enough to entertain outdoorsy types. Hike and explore around Alabama Hills (pictured), where piles of unusually round boulders have served as movie sets for many a Hollywood western, camp in the desert for a late-night stargazing session, or snag a permit to summit Mt Whitney.

FROM LEFT: KONOPLYTSKA/SHUTTERSTOCK, ROBERT PATTON/SHUTTERSTOCK, MIMI DITCHIE PHOTOGRAPHY/GETTY IMAGES

KEVIN CASE/SHUTTERSTOCK

Sequoia National Park (p159)

ITINERARIES

From Gold to Granite

Allow 6 days **Distance** 315 miles

The drive from Sacramento to Sequoia and Kings Canyon is a study in California's vertical extremes. Cruise past Central California's flat orchards and vineyards before climbing into the Sierra, where granite towers and plunging falls dominate the landscape. Then, continue south, where Kings Canyon plunges thousands of feet deep and you'll pass as many ancient sequoia trees as people.

1 SACRAMENTO 1 DAY

Whether you're flying into Sacramento or just passing by, spend a day and night here to give yourself time to have an indulgent meal, stock up on road trip snacks and explore the city's many museums, such as the California State Railroad Museum (pictured).

1-hour drive

2 SUTTER CREEK 1 DAY

Taste the best of foothills wine in and around **Sutter Creek** (p83) and Amador City, where you can venture to the vines themselves or walk between downtown tasting rooms. History buffs can also check out several worthwhile museums, including the Kennedy Gold Mine and Amador County Museum.

2¼-hour drive from Sutter Creek to Mariposa / 98 miles via CA-49

Detour *En route to Yosemite, stop at Mercer Caverns for a guided cave tour.*

3 MARIPOSA & YOSEMITE NATIONAL PARK 2 DAYS

Yosemite's Arch Rock Entrance is both the closest to the valley and the easiest to access year-round, making the town of **Mariposa** (p154) an appealing pit stop for a few days. Spend both days exploring Yosemite, or split your time with a day in **Yosemite** (p144) and a day outside park boundaries, perhaps marveling at the California State Mining and Mineral Museum or rafting on the Merced River. *2½-hour drive from Mariposa to Kings Canyon / 126 miles via CA-41*

FROM LEFT: RITU MANOJ JETHANI/SHUTTERSTOCK, JEFFREY B BANKE/SHUTTERSTOCK, SRONGKROD/GETTY IMAGES/GETTY IMAGES

START
Sacramento 1
1hr
2 Sutter Creek
2hr 15 min
3 Mariposa & Yosemite National Park
2hr 30 min
Kings Canyon National Park 4
1hr 40 min
5 Sequoia National Park
END
Placerville
Coleville
Walker Lake
Hawthorne
Sonora Junction
NEVADA
CALIFORNIA
Suisun Bay
Stockton
Sonora
Yosemite National Park
Mono Lake
Lee Vining
Basalt
Coaldale
Central Valley
San Joaquin River
Modesto
Yosemite Village
Mammoth Lakes
Benton
Palo Alto
San Jose
White Mountain Peak
Merced
Sierra Nevada
Palisades
Big Pine
Santa Cruz
Los Banos
San Joaquin Valley
Death Valley National Park
Monterey Bay
Salinas
Monterey
Fresno
Mt Whitney
Lone Pine
Salinas River
Coast Range
Kings River
Visalia
Santa Lucia Range
Big Sur
Tulare
Porterville
Owens Valley
Isabella Lake
Searles Lake
Paso Robles
Cambria
Ridgecrest
PACIFIC OCEAN
Morro Bay
San Luis Obispo
Bakersfield
Buena Vista Lake
Mojave
0 100 km
0 50 miles

4

KINGS CANYON NATIONAL PARK ⏱ 1 DAY

Kings Canyon (p159) and Sequoia's close proximity (and co-management) makes it easy to visit both in one trip. Stop in at the Kings Canyon Visitors Center to grab a map, then drive the Kings Canyon Scenic Byway. It's a 100-mile out-and-back drive from the visitors center, ending at gorgeous 'roads end' and passing must-see sights along the way, like the General Grant Tree and Grizzly Falls (pictured).

1hr 40min drive

5

SEQUOIA NATIONAL PARK ⏱ 1 DAY

Leave Kings Canyon via the Generals Hwy, the scenic artery connecting both parks and passing trailheads. Consider touring **Crystal Cave** (p161; pictured), a sparkling cave system formed from a massive block of marble, which reopened in 2025.

Detour *Consider heading south from* ***Sequoia National Park*** *to Sequoia National Forest and Death Valley National Park, which is less than an hour from* ***Lone Pine*** *(p172). From here, you can follow the Eastern Sierra itinerary (p20) from south to north, ending in North Lake Tahoe to fly home from Reno or Sacramento.*

WHEN TO GO

Summer and winter are both huge draws, but offer vastly different experiences, with little overlap between the two.

In the Sierra Nevada, winter typically begins in December, with snowpack not melting until May or June. Despite the lingering snow, spring often brings sunny days warm enough to ski in the morning and hit the beach in the afternoon. In winter, trails around Tahoe, Mammoth and the higher elevations of Yosemite are inaccessible, but ski resorts are in full swing.

Prepare for winter driving conditions. Four-wheel drive or all-wheel drive vehicles are all but mandatory – except during frequent periods of highway chain control, in which case they're fully mandatory. Expect slow travel and icy roads throughout the season.

By early June, most trails reopen, and wildflowers are in full bloom, marking the start of the hiking season. Memorial Day to Labor Day is considered the unofficial summer season, with many rental and guiding companies operating only during this window. September and October can be a bit slower, though it's arguably the best season for hiking, climbing and mountain biking. For non-ski activities in winter, head to lower-elevation destinations such as Yosemite Valley, Gold Country and Sacramento. Just remember that the foothills can be unbearably hot in peak summer.

I LIVE HERE

ENDLESS SUMMER

Wedding photographer and Tahoe local Mark Steinlein shares why he loves the first hot days of summer. *@marksteinleinphoto*

Though winter brought me to Tahoe, it was summer that truly won me over. There's something about long, sun-filled days that makes everything feel possible, from early morning paddle board sessions on calm, glassy water to mountain bike rides through the pines. Afternoons are made for floating down the river or catching an outdoor concert. Summer here means adventure, connection and endless ways to soak up the beauty of the Sierra – just sunshine, the open trail and time to roam.

FROM LEFT: EMILY C MCCORMICK/SHUTTERSTOCK, BILL45/SHUTTERSTOCK

Sierra Nevada

BLIZZARD CONDITIONS

Snowfall is no joke in the Sierra Nevada. Mammoth Mountain averages 400in (about 33ft) of snowfall per year, and during the Donner Party disaster of 1846–7, snow at Donner Lake is thought to have been 20ft deep.

Weather through the year in South Lake Tahoe

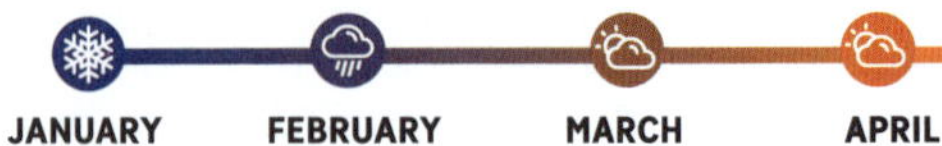

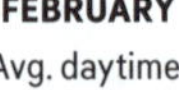

JANUARY	FEBRUARY	MARCH	APRIL	MAY	JUNE
Avg. daytime max: **43°F**	Avg. daytime max: **45°F**	Avg. daytime max: **49°F**	Avg. daytime max: **54°F**	Avg. daytime max: **63°F**	Avg. daytime max: **62°F**
Days of snowfall: **10**	Days of snowfall: **10**	Days of snowfall: **13**	Days of snowfall: **11**	Days of snowfall: **8**	Days of snowfall: **4**

SUNNY SACRAMENTO

Love sunny days? Then skip the SoCal coast, notorious for all-day ocean fog, and head to Sacramento. It's regularly ranked as the sunniest city in California, and sometimes the entire world, averaging 14 hours of sunshine per day on a yearly basis.

Music in the Mountains

The Mammoth Village gets packed to the gills with music festivals every weekend in the summer, from classic rock to reggae to jazz and even a 'country music extravaganza.' **June to August**

Tahoe City's sprawling **Commons Beach** (p119) fills with music fans every summer Sunday for free, family-friendly concerts. **June to August**

Aftershock is the biggest rock-focused music festival on the West Coast, with three-days of A-list headliners keeping Sacramento's Discovery Park lively. **October**

On nights without stage performances, the **Tahoe Shakespeare Festival** (p133) hosts live concerts, ranging from classical orchestras to David Bowie tribute bands. **July and August**

Quirky California

Bishop Mule Days celebrates the animals that made living in the region possible, with Wild West shows, country music and more. **May**

Don your newsboy cap for a weekend at the Great Gatsby Festival, with jazz performances, a fashion show, afternoon tea and more at the **Tallac Historic Site** (p110). **August**

The weekly Progression on Pedals event at **Northstar California** (p129) is a women-focused evening mountain bike session, with group coaching and good deals on lift tickets. **July and August**

The Western States Endurance run is the world's oldest 100-mile footrace, starting in north Lake Tahoe and ending with a celebration in Auburn. **June**

I LIVE HERE

AUTUMN JOY

Chris Van Leuven is a journalist based in Mariposa. He's the founder of *YosemiteEbiking.com.*

I moved to Yosemite right after high school in the mid-90s and have called this area home ever since. I love climbing the towering walls of Yosemite in late autumn when the rock is cool to the touch. I ride my e-bike then, too. Mariposa offers endless hilly dirt roads, fire roads and narrow, winding pavement traveled by few cars, making riding here safe, scenic and oh-so-fun for everyone.

Autumn, Yosemite National Park (p144)

ALWAYS PACK A PUFFY

Truckee holds the record for the lowest temperature ever recorded in California (-45°F). It also has some of the biggest day-to-night temperature swings; summer temperatures can drop 40°F or more after the sun sets.

JULY	AUGUST	SEPTEMBER	OCTOBER	NOVEMBER	DECEMBER
Avg. daytime max: **79°F**	Avg. daytime max: **79°F**	Avg. daytime max: **72°F**	Avg. daytime max: **63°F**	Avg. daytime max: **50°F**	Avg. daytime max: **43°F**
Days of snowfall: **2**	Days of snowfall: **1**	Days of snowfall: **3**	Days of snowfall: **7**	Days of snowfall: **9**	Days of snowfall: **13**

FROM LEFT: JUANCAT/SHUTTERSTOCK, PHOTO 12/ALAMY

Eastern Sierra (p168)

GET PREPARED
FOR LAKE TAHOE, YOSEMITE AND CENTRAL CALIFORNIA

Useful things to load in your bag, your ears and your brain

Clothes

Warm outer layers Wild temperature swings are common in the mountains, so you're going to want an insulated or puffy jacket, even in summer. It's very unusual to have a night in Tahoe or Mammoth so warm that you can comfortably wear shorts late into the evening.

Rain jacket Rain is uncommon in the mountains, but is frequent in foothill towns when winter storms roll in off the coast. Have a water-resistant layer if you're visiting places like Nevada City or Mariposa in the fall or winter.

Footwear You don't need fancy hiking boots, but a shoe with good traction will serve you well. National park trails tend to be the most well maintained, but state park, forest service and wilderness trails can be muddy, rocky and loose.

Manners

Hiking etiquette in California: always pack out what you pack in, and avoid blasting music – it's disruptive to wildlife and fellow hikers. On multi-use trails, horses have the right of way, followed by hikers, then bikers. Uphill travelers have priority, but it's courteous to step aside if you're on foot when bikes come by. Locals are generally friendly, though conversations about wildfire policy or corporate ski resort takeovers can spark strong opinions. So tread lightly, on both the trail and in discussions.

Sunglasses You'll want sunglasses year-round. In the mountains, it's usually sunny when it's not snowing, and the summer sun around Sacramento and Gold Country towns can dry your eyes during long days.

READ

Wild (Cheryl Strayed; 2012) A much-lauded tale of one young woman's unexpected experiences on the Pacific Crest Trail.

The High Sierra: A Love Story (Kim Stanley Robinson; 2022) A fascinating account of the Sierra Nevada's human and natural history.

The Age of Gold: The California Gold Rush and the New American Dream (HW Brands; 2003) An in-depth nonfiction account of the fortunes won and lost in the California Gold Rush.

We Are the Land: A History of Native California (William Bauer, Jr; 2021) A telling of California's history through the eyes of Indigenous and Native groups.

Words

In California, language goes way beyond 'dude' (which is gender-neutral, by the way). The foothills are more diverse than mountain towns, and you'll find many languages spoken, some of which include English, Spanish and Chinese. Most tourist destinations in the mountains have original Indigenous names, including *De-ek Wadapush* (Cave Rock, p133), *Tesa'ak* (Half Dome, p151) and *Da ow a ga* (Lake Tahoe, p98). The word 'Tahoe' comes from a mispronunciation of the latter.

WATCH

Free Solo (Elizabeth Chai Vasarhelyi and Jimmy Chin; 2018) This Oscar-winning film chronicles pro climber Alex Honnold's attempt to climb Yosemite's famous El Capitan – without ropes.

The Godfather, Part II (Francis Ford Coppola; 1975) The famous opening scene of this beloved series was filmed at Tahoe's Fleur de Lac waterfront estate (though it's now been turned into private condos).

The National Parks: America's Best Idea (Ken Burns; 2009) Episodes 1 and 2 of this gorgeous documentary chronicle the establishment of Yosemite and the changes to the park's Hetch-Hetchy Valley.

Django Unchained (Quentin Tarantino, 2012; pictured) Scenes from this violent but well-received western were filmed among the boulder piles of Lone Pine (as were other recent films like *The Lone Ranger* and *Gladiator*.)

LISTEN

Washoe (Dead Winter Carpenters; 2016) The most recent album from north Lake Tahoe's Americana/bluegrass band is the perfect backdrop for desert vistas and open roads.

California Stars (Billy Bragg & Wilco; 2001) Though not set specifically in the Sierra Nevada, this indie hit evokes the freedom of California's wide-open spaces and skies.

Folsom Prison Blues (Johnny Cash; 1955) After Cash released this song, prisoners from around the country asked him to play for them (which he did, at Folsom Prison, in 1968).

Yosemite (Molly Tuttle feat Dave Matthews; 2023) A folk-tinged, rootsy ballad reflecting on a couple's road trip to Yosemite.

JEFFREY B BANKE/SHUTTERSTOCK

Amador County (p82)

THE FOOD SCENE

What the mountains lack in locally grown fruits and veggies, they make up for in unique breweries and coffee shops. Don't miss out on visiting a few foothills wineries either.

While much of the Sierra Nevada is too cold, dry and rocky for significant agriculture, the mountains have fostered a different kind of bounty: a thriving culture of craft breweries and independent roasters and coffee shops that serve as community hubs. Breweries like Mammoth Brewing in Mammoth Lakes and the Gold Wolf in Truckee embrace the Sierra spirit by using local ingredients in beers ranging from foraged juniper to spring water, while youthful coffee shops like Tahoe's Drink Coffee, Do Stuff specialize in high-elevation coffee beans.

Foodies who travel to the foothills can benefit from the region's Mediterranean-like growing conditions by visiting some of the region's wineries. Multiple wineries around Jackson do full tasting for under $20, and Amador County is known for its Old World–style reds – especially zinfandels, which once accounted for nearly all its vines.

Elevated American cuisine generally reigns supreme, though you'll find local specialties if you know where to look. Old-timey saloons in towns like Placerville and Virginia City are quirky places to grab a bite, and Cornish pasties are common in Nevada City – a lingering holdover from a time when many of the region's miners hailed from the county of Cornwall in England.

Don't Call it Happy Hour

There's no such thing as happy hour. Well, there is – but in most of the Sierra Nevada,

Best Sierra Nevada dishes

CORNISH PASTIES
Small baked hand pies, filled with either sweet or savory fillings.

BREAKFAST BURRITO
The perfect grab-and-go breakfast for skiers. Try it California-style, with french fries in the mix.

BANANA CREAM PIE
Frank Fat's in downtown Sacramento is the place to try the city's famous dessert: a banana- and custard-filled pie topped with meringue.

it's called après-ski, or just après. And it happens year-round, regardless of how much snow is on the ground. Après runs from roughly 3pm to 6pm and is never formal, so feel free to roll up to just about any mountain bar in dirty bike shorts or wet ski pants. (But don't walk inside in ski boots).

Alcohol-free and gluten-free beers are available at nearly all convenience and grocery stores, and most bars won't blink an eye at making mocktails. In fact, many may have their own mocktail menus equally as appealing as the cocktails.

Vegans & Vegetarians

California is very friendly to plant-based eaters, and this region is no exception. There are a handful of restaurants specializing in meat-free meals throughout the Sacramento region, and nearly all restaurants will have multiple veggie options beyond just salads and a veggie burger.

Oenophiles on a Budget

While tastings in regions like Napa and Sonoma can easily be $60 or $70, Gold Country's wineries are far more affordable. The Sierra Foothills AVA covers parts of eight counties, concentrated in towns like Murphys, Sutter Creek, Jackson and Amador. Tastings are often no more than $15, with fees frequently waived if you buy a bottle.

Sacramento's Culinary Bounty

Sacramento is by far the best destination for foodies in the region. It's surrounded by agricultural lands, allowing even inexpensive restaurants to practice farm-to-table principles. Farmers markets run year-round (the Midtown Farmers Market is especially noteworthy, with more than 200 vendors every Saturday), and multiple food tours await inside the city. Just outside of Sac, agro tourism experiences are both growing and relatively accessible, including tours of farms and working cattle ranges.

Farmers market, Sacramento (p44)

Black Velvet Coffee

FROM LEFT: JULIA E HEATH/SHUTTERSTOCK, YVETTE CARDOZO/ALAMY

THE BEST BEANS

Mountain towns run on coffee, especially when you're waking up at 5am to be in line for first chair on a powder day. A whole host of high-elevation coffee roasters have sprung up around the region, sourcing beans grown on mountain summits. The threshold is usually 4000ft above sea level, where cooler temperatures and harsher growing conditions bear sugarier and more acidic beans, giving it what many coffee aficionados consider a more complex flavor profile. Notable local purveyors include Drink Coffee, Do Stuff, owned by a former professional snowboarder in Tahoe, and Black Velvet Coffee in Mammoth Lakes.

HANGTOWN FRY

Omelet with bacon and oysters popularized during Placerville's Gold Rush days.

BRANDY FRIED CHICKEN

Unique sweet-and-crunchy Chinese-American dish that originated in the Sacramento area.

CHEESE SKIRT BURGER

Burger with extra cheese oozing past the bun; you'll find it on many a Sacramento menu.

APPLE CIDER DONUTS

A must-try in Apple Hill, especially in the harvest season.

Local Food Experiences

Food & Adventure Pairings

Hop aboard the Tahoe Dixie for an on-the-water dinner cruise from Lake Tahoe's **Zephyr Cove** (p133).

Backpack through Yosemite with **Echo Adventure Cooperative** (p158), whose guides provide expertly cooked backcountry meals and snacks.

Step through the snow on a mid-mountain snowshoe dinner, hosted a few times each year at **Alpine Meadows** (p124) in Tahoe.

Cycle or e-bike between wineries on country roads around Murphys or **Sutter Creek** (p83).

Dine Like the Olden Days

Grab breakfast or bites and a brew at the surprisingly vegetarian-friendly **Hideout Saloon** (p156), a Gold Rush-era original

Ahwahnee Hotel

Watch the sun set over Truckee from the deck of **Cottonwood** (p129), a memorabilia-covered bar inside one of California's oldest ski lodges.

Grab a beer after a long hike at **Iron Door Saloon** (p157), Groveland's pub from the 1850s, still with a tin roof, granite walls and, yes, an iron door.

Dine under the lofted ceilings of the historic Dining Room at **Ahwahnee Hotel** (p153) in Yosemite, one of the finest examples of 20th-century 'parkitecture' still standing.

HIGH-ELEVATION COOKING

Renting a home with a kitchen? Don't forget to adjust your recipes, unless you like flat and crumbly cookies. For cooking or baking above 3000ft, you'll need to make the oven hotter and knock five to 10 minutes off your baking time. You'll also want to decrease the baking soda or powder so your scones don't rise too fast and collapse. And just like you'll want to drink more water in higher elevations, you'll also want to add more moisture to your baked goods, lest your cookies turn out dryer than a Tahoe August afternoon.

THE YEAR IN FOOD

SPRING

Local chefs and restaurants start rolling out lighter spring menus, usually using local seasonal crops like strawberries and asparagus.

SUMMER

Berries, peaches, pepper, herbs – take your pick: it all grows in California and is all readily available at the region's many weekly farmers markets.

AUTUMN

The bounty of harvest season is spread throughout the mountains, with harvest festivals in the foothills, you-pick farm stands aplenty, and more than a dozen varieties of apple around Apple Hill.

WINTER

The mountains are all about hot toddies and indulgent après-ski bites, while Gold Country restaurants lean into seasonal crops like root veggies and hearty greens.

TOP: FRANCISCO BLANCO/SHUTTERSTOCK; FROM LEFT: SADESSHUTTERS/SHUTTERSTOCK, EMMACOS/SHUTTERSTOCK, LASZLO PODOR/GETTY IMAGES, BRANNON_NAITO/SHUTTERSTOCK

CHRIS ALLAN/SHUTTERSTOCK

MS *Dixie II*, Lake Tahoe (p104)

FROM LEFT: THINKSTOCK/GETTY IMAGES, CASSIOHABIB/SHUTTERSTOCK

Snowmobiling, Lake Tahoe (p98)

THE OUTDOORS

Save perhaps for surfing, the Sierra Nevada has nearly every type of outdoor recreation available in California, most set against the backdrop of some of the prettiest vistas in the West.

It's challenging both to sum up the breadth of recreation available between the Sierra foothills and the summits, and to describe the feeling of pure bliss when you're skiing down a lakeview run or climbing a granite wall towering over the Yosemite Valley. Outdoor experts flock to this region by the vanful every summer to backpack the Pacific Crest Trail, hike through national parks and mountain bike massive peaks, but the vastness of the outdoor recreation sector in this part of California means even beginners and first-timers in any sport will find an enticing nature-focused adventure.

Backpacking

Backpackers could spend a whole summer in Sierra without touching pavement (well, except to pick up resupply shipments). This region is home to nearly 400 miles of the Pacific Crest Trail, the 211-mile John Muir Trail through Yosemite and the jaw-droppingly beautiful Tahoe Rim Trail. High elevations demand a certain level of fitness, and backpackers will need to take note of restrictions around party size, campfires, bear precautions, campsite selection and more.

Most backpacking trails in the Sierra Nevada will require backpacking permits, and scoring them can be competitive. All trails on federally managed land use recreation.gov to manage reservations, with each trail and agency having different (and seasonally shifting) rules around party size, permit quotas and reservation dates.

Embracing Snow Season

SLEDDING

Ask your hotel where the best local sledding hill is if you're around Tahoe or Mammoth – and see if they have a sled you can borrow, too.

SNOWMOBILING

Bump up the adrenaline on a snowmobile tour or jump line session on the snowmobile track in South Lake Tahoe.

BACKCOUNTRY SKIING

Shred Yosemite's backcountry pow on a tour with an expert ski guide from the **Yosemite Mountaineering School** (p150).

FAMILY ADVENTURES

Float the Truckee River (p104) on a leisurely inner-tube ride from Tahoe City, where you'll always go the right way, even if you don't do that much paddling.

Ride in an open-air tram on a Yosemite Valley Floor Tour, led by park rangers.

Take a white-water rafting trip (p81) on the South Fork of the American River, which maxes out at Class III rapids; best for families with older kids.

Enjoy **stroller-friendly walks**, which are especially interesting at historic sites like Tahoe's **Tallac Historic Site** (p110) and **Rabe Meadows** (p133), or Sequoia National Park's **General Sherman** (p161) and Tall Trees trails.

Hit the slopes without fear at smaller, family-friendly ski resorts like **Sierra-at-Tahoe** (p111) or **June Mountain** (p173), where kids under 12 ski free if their parent has a pass.

Venture beneath the earth on a cave tour, like those at **Mercer Caverns** (p95) in Murphys or **Boyden Cavern** (p162) in Kings Canyon.

Hiking

Day hiking is accessible throughout the region, whether that means a quick jaunt to Tahoe's Lake Aloha, a full-day leg burner to Yosemite's Vernal and Nevada falls, or a birding adventure on Sonora's short Dragoon Gulch Trail. The draw for most trails here is sheer natural beauty, but many state parks and popular forest service areas have interpretive trails with historical signage along the way, as well as self-guided history hikes.

In national and state parks, trails are well maintained, easy to find and follow, and usually patrolled by rangers. Outside of parks, most of the region's trails are on Bureau of Land Management or National Forest Service land, with varying degrees of maintenance and signage. Apps like AllTrails or Gaia can help you plan your hikes and ensure you're making the right turns.

ACTION AREAS
See p34

Vernal Fall (p149)

Cycling & Mountain Biking

Mountain biking is popular here, and experts should dedicate days to ride trails like the Downieville Downhill (Downieville) or Mr Toad's Wild Ride (South Lake Tahoe). However, it's also home to California's two biggest lift-serviced bike parks at Mammoth and Northstar, with a collective 100-plus trails for riders of all skill levels. For more relaxed rides, e-bike rentals are available at nearly all bike shops, whether you want to pack on the miles or just rent a beach cruiser for moving between parks and activities.

Cyclists exploring the area's trails should always wear helmets, which bike shops should provide with rentals. Cell service can be spotty on some trails, so it's useful to use bike trail apps that work offline and are based on location services, like Strava or Trailforks.

For more relaxed downhill mountain biking, consider booking a group shuttle. They'll drive you to the top of a trail, so you can bike back to the starting point without an uphill pedal. Popular shuttle options include the Flume Trail *(flumetrailtahoe.com; from $22)* in Lake Tahoe or the Mount Hough shuttle *(yubaexpeditions.com; from $40)* in Quincy, both suitable for advanced beginners.

SNOWSHOEING & CROSS-COUNRY SKIING

Cross-country ski or snowshoe through South Lake Tahoe's undeveloped **Hope Valley** (p111), or through the wooded forests around Tahoe City.

WALKING IN THE SNOW

Walk through a snow-covered old-timey wonderland at the annual Victorian Christmas celebration, complete with costumed carolers, held in **Nevada City** (p85) throughout December.

SKIING

Ski big lines, deep powder and wide-open bowls at resorts like **Palisades Tahoe** (p124), **Mammoth Mountain** (p174) or Heavenly Resort, where you can ski between two states.

ACTION AREAS

Where to find Lake Tahoe, Yosemite and Central California's best outdoor activities.

Walking & Hiking
1 Desolation Wilderness (p112)
2 Half Dome (p151)
3 High Sierra Trail (p161)
4 Ancient Bristlecone Pine Forest (p171)
5 The Rim Trail (p122)
Kayaking, Canoeing & Rafting
1 Tahoe's West Shore (p118)
2 South Fork of the American River (p81)
3 Mono Lake (p173)
4 Mammoth Lakes (p173)
5 Tenaya Lake (p145)
Vineyards & Wineries
1 Mt Vernon Winery (p82)
2 Idle Hour Winery & Kitchen (p157)
3 Ironstone Vineyards (p95)
4 Miraflores Winery (p82)
5 PaZa Winery (p82)
Santa Cruz
Fresno
Kings Canyon National Park
Sequoia National Park
Mt Williamson
Mt Whitney
Death Valley National Park
Kings River
Diablo Range
Paso Robles
Cambria
Morro Bay
San Luis Obispo
Bakersfield
Mojave
Santa Barbara
Pasadena
Los Angeles
Santa Monica
Channel Islands
Channel Islands National Park
PACIFIC OCEAN
0
200 km
0
100 miles

LAKE TAHOE, YOSEMITE & CENTRAL CALIFORNIA

THE GUIDE

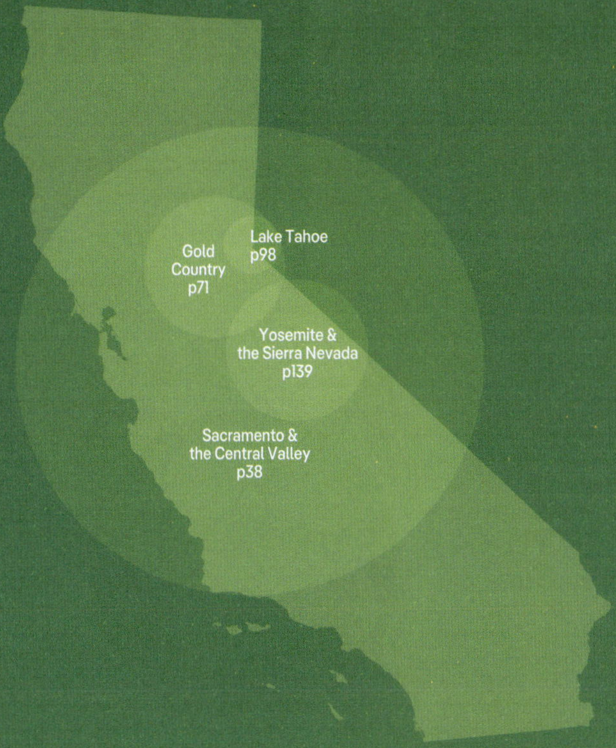

Chapters in this section are organized by hubs and their surrounding areas. We see the hub as your base in the destination, where you'll find unique experiences, local insights, insider tips and expert recommendations. It's also your gateway to the surrounding area, where you'll see what and how much you can do from there.

Yosemite Falls (p147)
DANESPRINTSHOP/SHUTTERSTOCK

Researched by Helena Smith

Sacramento & the Central Valley

GRITTY, WIDE OPEN AND SOULFUL

Explore the region that put the 'western' in country-and-western music. Discover genial small towns, endless almond groves and the state's likeable capital.

The Central Valley is a vast, flat expanse between the Sierra Nevada and Pacific Ocean, divided into the Sacramento Valley in the north and the San Joaquin Valley in the south. For millennia, the rivers cutting through here flooded seasonally, creating extremely fertile soil. Today, those waterways are tamed by mighty public works projects that support massive agricultural endeavors and human life itself in thirsty Southern California. Half the produce in the US is grown here – including almost every almond, olive and tomato.

Most travelers just pass through, zipping along the freeways to more popular parts of the state. But those who pause are rewarded with compelling historical spots, thriving craft beer and wine scenes, uniquely scenic byways and quirky small towns. It's a vast region for driving – get lost in the expansive flatlands that can be both bleak and inspirational. (The crop duster scene in Hitchcock's *North by Northwest* was shot northwest of Bakersfield.)

Attractive state capital Sacramento mixes history and culture with great food and drink. Every nonglitzy aspect of California is celebrated at the annual California State Fair. Wine is foundational to the valley's produce and you can enjoy fine vintages in the vast vineyards around Lodi.

Bust the flatland cliché by hitting world-class white-water on the rushing Kern River. Driving the valley's byway, Hwy 99, you'll find outstanding Mexican food at nearly every exit.

MIERCAT PHOTOGRAPHY/SHUTTERSTOCK

THE MAIN AREAS

SACRAMENTO
Historic, lively and leafy state capital.
p44

SACRAMENTO VALLEY
Farmlands and appealing towns like Chico.
p57

SAN JOAQUIN VALLEY
Gritty heart of California.
p60

For places to stay in Sacramento & the Central Valley, see p69

Left: Antelope Valley California Poppy Reserve (p67); Above: Sacramento (p44)

Find Your Way

The Central Valley covers an enormous swath of California: from Red Bluff to Bakersfield is over 400 miles. The wide open spaces here are awe-inspiring and are easily reached from the rest of the state.

Sacramento Valley, p57

Bounteous farmland gives way to enticing roads into the Sierras and nearby national parks. Chico makes a good stop for zesty nightlife.

Sacramento, p44

The state's capital is awash in history. Explore its shady streets to learn more about California and enjoy excellent places to eat and drink.

CAR

Convertible, rugged pickup or electric cruiser – pick your vehicle of choice for the wide-open roads, many running arrow-straight across table-flat lands where the distant horizon never seems to draw closer. The Kern Valley detour demands your own wheels.

TRAIN

The Central Valley has an excellent train service. The main cities of the San Joaquin Valley, such as Fresno and Bakersfield, are linked to Sacramento and the Bay Area by fast and frequent Amtrak trains. Combining trains with car rental reduces driving stress.

BUS

Buses provide bare-bones service across the valley. Amtrak buses provide important links out of the region to Lake Tahoe, the Gold Country, Yosemite and LA. Local buses in larger cities like Sacramento will get you around and to some nearby attractions.

San Joaquin Valley, **p60**

The heart of the Central Valley is a string of cities linked by scrappy Hwy 99. Look for historical and outdoor adventures around its edges.

Plan Your Days

Relax on the upper deck of an Amtrak train or get behind the wheel. You could drive the length of this region in one long day on Hwy 99, but it's best to go slow and explore.

CHRIS LABASCO/SHUTTERSTOCK

Sacramento (p44)

If You Only Have One Day

- Head to Sacramento via the **Sacramento Delta** (p52) with its sinuous drives through a lost California of fading historic towns such as **Locke** (p53). In the state capital, drop by the **California Museum** (p46), which celebrates Californians of all stripes. Walk the gorgeous gardens of the imposing **State Capitol building** (p46) alongside hurried legislators and hangers-on and ID some of the city's mighty trees.

- Wander **Old Sacramento** (p47), squinting so you can see the 1800s authenticity amid the tourist clutter. Take an underground tour to explore the city's origins and feel the enormous might of the historic trains in the **California State Railroad Museum** (p47). Laze away your evening in the **Midtown neighborhood** (p50), dotted with funky restaurants and funkier bars and venues.

Seasonal Highlights

The valley comes alive in a rainbow of spring colors. Summer gets blazingly hot – cool off with fresh-fruit ice cream. The vineyards turn radiant with fall colors.

MARCH

California's golden poppies turn entire hillsides a brilliant safety-vest orange; other wildflowers add dashes of color, from purple to yellow.

APRIL

The **Red Bluff Round-Up** (p59) rowdily celebrates ranch life. Stockton's huge **San Joaquin Asparagus Festival** (p56) honors the vegetable. Fresno's **Tower Porchfest** (p64) brings free live music to the streets.

JUNE

Modesto takes to the streets for **Graffiti Summer** (p62), a carnival of classic cars, cruising and oldies music. Join a **Juneteenth Block Party** in Sacramento.

Three Days to Travel Around

● Spend your first day as suggested in **Sacramento** (p44). Then hit the open road on historic Hwy 99, the asphalt spine of the Central Valley. Head south for a root beer at a historic stand in **Modesto** (p62). Explore visionary subterranean citrus groves at **Forestiere Underground Gardens** (p63) on the edge of Fresno, then look for vinyl and vintage clothes in the city's Tower District.

● Satisfy lunch cravings at one of the excellent Mexican restaurants that line Hwy 99. Detour to **Kingsburg** (p64) with its unexpected Swedish heritage: yes, that includes cinnamon pastries. At night in Bakersfield, have a filling **Basque dinner** (p68), then feel the passion of the Bakersfield country sound at **Buck Owens' Crystal Palace** (p65).

If You Have More Time

● Head north up the Sacramento Valley to the beer heaven that is pretty **Chico** (p57). Watch for migrating birds in the vast marshes and open plains. To the south, make time for experiences beyond Central Valley cliches. Seek out **Colonel Allensworth State Historic Park** (p65), an African American pioneer town, now abandoned and preserved. Continue south to the outdoor spring spectacle that is the **Antelope Valley California Poppy Reserve** (p67).

● East of Bakersfield, seek out the **white-water adventure** (p66) of your dreams in the rugged high country around Kernville. Finally, drop down to **César E Chávez National Monument** (p63) and learn about the man and the movement that radically changed the Central Valley and its people.

JULY

One of the state's biggest parties, Sacramento's **California State Fair** (p51) showcases agriculture, thrill rides, improbable junk food and more.

AUGUST

Farmers markets across the valley burst with waves of bounty as peak seasons for many fruits and vegetables converge: it all started in **Davis** (p55).

SEPTEMBER

Old Sacramento comes alive in early September for **Gold Rush Days** (p47), with horse races, historic costumes, music and gold panning.

NOVEMBER

The end of the growing season sees the **Pomegranate Festival** in Madera near Fresno, with cooking contests and a focus on dried fruits and nuts.

Sacramento

HISTORIC AREA | URBAN FOREST | GREAT NIGHTLIFE

TOP TIP

Get to know the grid. Sights and nightlife are spread throughout the city. Numbered streets run north-south and lettered streets run east-west. Old Sacramento is at the west end of the grid. Distances from here to Midtown in the east are long.

Sacramento is a former cow town where the SUVs of state legislators go bumper-to-bumper with the muddy, half-ton pickups of local farmers at rush hour. It has sprawling suburbs aplenty, but also new lofts and upscale boutiques squeezed in between aging mid-century storefronts. Its sights range from rows of gold-rush-era historical buildings to cutting-edge art museums.

The people of 'Sac' are a resourceful lot that have fostered energetic food, art and nightlife scenes. Numerous breweries keep the city well stocked with award-winning beers and farmers markets and farm-to-fork fare are another point of pride, as well as city celebrations, from the State Fair to Juneteenth block parties. In this city of a million trees, leafy relief from the often intense heat is provided by an impressive urban forest canopy.

Sacramento sits at the crossroads of Interstates 5 and 80, roughly halfway between San Francisco and Lake Tahoe.

GETTING AROUND

Sacramento International Airport has plenty of flights and is the nearest major option for those traveling to Yosemite National Park. Trains and buses from the station next to Old Sacramento serve Lake Tahoe, the Central Valley south to Bakersfield and the Bay Area. It's a stop for the distance *Coast Starlight* (Seattle to LA) and the *California Zephyr*, which links the Bay Area to Chicago via the spectacular run through the Sierras on the original route of the Transcontinental Railroad.

Sacramento Regional Transit buses cover the center and SacRT also runs a trolley between Old Sacramento and downtown.

HIGHLIGHTS
1 California Museum
2 Golden 1 Center

SIGHTS
3 California State Capitol
4 California State Railroad Museum
5 Crocker Art Museum
6 Harlow's
7 Old Sacramento State Historic Park
8 Sacramento History Museum
9 State Indian Museum
10 Sutter's Fort State Historic Park
11 Tower Bridge

ACTIVITIES
12 Sac Brew Bike

SLEEPING
13 Citizen Hotel
14 Delta King
15 Family Laundry & Spa
16 HI Sacramento Hostel

EATING
17 Aioli Bodega Espanola
18 Kin Thai Street Eatery
19 Localis
20 Rick's Dessert Diner
21 Saigon Alley Kitchen + Bar
22 Tower Cafe
23 Veg Café & Bar

DRINKING & NIGHTLIFE
24 58 Degrees and Holding Co
25 Bike Dog Broadway Taproom
26 Fieldwork Brewing Company
27 Flamingo House Social Club
28 Old Soul
29 Ruhstaller BSMT
30 Torch Club

ENTERTAINMENT
31 Gold Rush Days
32 Tower Theatre

SHOPPING
33 Midtown Farmers' Market

SACRAMENTO'S EARLY HISTORY

Sacramento embodies much of California's history. Native peoples fished the rivers, harvested acorns and thrived before waves of colonists began arriving and the Native communities were decimated by disease. In 1840, John Sutter came seeking fortune and built a fortified **outpost** (p48) in what was then Mexico. After the US annexed the territory in 1848, Sutter lost his land and gold rushers stampeded to the fast-growing town, now christened Sacramento. It became the state capital in 1850. In the following decades, a quarter of a million Chinese people arrived in California, many working as indentured servants. They built much of the Central Pacific Railroad, which began construction in Sacramento in 1863 and connected to the Union Pacific in Promontory, UT, in 1869.

VICTORIA DITKOVSKY/SHUTTERSTOCK

California State Capitol

Face to Face at the California Museum

Celebrate Golden State achievements

The eclectic, modern **California Museum** *(californiamuseum.org; adult/child $10/8; closed Sun and Mon)* has rotating exhibits that focus on the contributions of the state's diverse residents, from Chinese gold-rush immigrants to the early Native American population to progressive legislators and union activists. Interactive elements encourage you to get involved, both with the museum and with social issues. It's also home to the photographic California Hall of Fame where you can encounter César Chávez, Serena Williams, Steve Jobs and many others.

California's Historic State Capitol

Monumental building and grounds

The gleaming dome of the **California State Capitol** *(capitolmuseum.ca.gov; free)* is Sacramento's most recognizable structure. The renovated ground floor functions as a working museum and important offices have been restored to their period glory. Outside, **California State Capitol Park** is an alluring and eclectic mix of elaborate gardens and memorials.

EATING IN SACRAMENTO: OUR PICKS

Localis: A relaxed Midtown temple to Central Valley produce and California cuisine. Book ahead, especially for patio tables. *5-8:15pm Wed-Sat* $

Kin Thai Street Eatery: Busy Midtown cafe with a vibe like an Asian street market. *11am-3pm & 4.30-9pm Mon-Fri, 11am-9pm Sat, noon-9pm Sun* $

Rick's Dessert Diner: This 1950s-inspired diner specializes in sweet treats, from boat-like banana splits to mile-high tortes. *8am-midnight Sun-Thu, to 1am Fri & Sat* $

Saigon Alley Kitchen & Bar: A modern spin on Vietnamese cuisine – try Pho-rench Dip, flaky bahn mi dipped in pho broth. *11am-8pm Sun-Thu, 11am-9pm Fri & Sat* $

Take time to read the labels on the myriad trees as they show the state's vast range of species, from date palms to coast redwoods. The Capitol is closed on weekends and holidays.

Explore Old Sacramento

Historic center with fascinating museums

The historic river port next to downtown, **Old Sacramento** *(oldsacramento.com; free)* is the city's top visitor draw. If you're walking here from town you need to enter the area on K St to avoid the deafening junction of roads. The kitschy gold-rush-era atmosphere makes it good for a stroll and California's largest concentration of buildings on the National Register of Historic Places is found here. However, the massive reconstructions do give Old Sacramento an odd film-set artificiality. A great time to visit is during September's **Gold Rush Days** festival, when you can pan for gold amid costumed characters and horses.

Of the 100 buildings, 35 are mostly original to the gold-rush era (get a guide from the visitor center). If you ignore the tatty gift shops, fudgeries and tourist-trap eateries, you can get an engaging sense of the past. Join the underground tour run by the on-site **Sacramento History Museum** *(sachistorymuseum.org; adult/child $12/6, underground tour $30/25)*, which explores the tunnels that date from the time before everything had to be raised 18ft due to floods. The museum is open daily.

The top sight is the **California State Railroad Museum** *(csrmf.org; adult/child $12/6)*, which re-creates the completion of the Transcontinental Railroad and has a huge collection of restored and notable locomotives and cars. On many days (weather permitting) you can go for a train ride along the river, which gives the riverfront a lively air, all in the shadow of the iconic **Tower Bridge** (featured in 2017's Oscar-winning *Lady Bird*). The Railroad Museum is open daily.

Get Arty at the Crocker Museum

Contemporary Californian and international artworks

Housed in the ornate Victorian mansion of a railroad baron (with sprawling contemporary additions), the **Crocker Art Museum** *(crockerartmuseum.org; adult/child $15/8)* has excellent collections. Works by California painters and European masters hang alongside a dynamic array of contemporary art and installations.

CALIFORNIA'S NOTABLE GOVERNORS

Sacramento has been home to California's governors since 1850. The state has elected many colorful characters, none more notorious than its first governor, Peter Burnett. An avowed racist, he played a significant role in the genocide of California's Native peoples. In contrast, the 30th governor, Earl Warren (1943–53), went on to serve as the chief justice of the US, presiding over landmark decisions that liberalized civil rights.

Former actor Ronald Reagan (1967–75) used the office as a springboard to the presidency. Jerry Brown transformed the state during two terms: as the state's youngest governor (1975–83), then as its oldest (2011–19). California's 38th governor, Arnold Schwarzenegger (2003–11), was notable for his intemperate statements and huge budget deficits.

EATING IN SACRAMENTO: OUR PICKS

Aioli Bodega Espanola: Spanish tapas in a garden near the Capitol, plus a long wine list. *11am-10pm Mon-Sat, 3-9pm Sun* $$

Veg Café & Bar: Veg enchants with a modern boho space and beautifully presented vegan dishes like cauliflower momo. *11.30am-9pm Tue-Sat, 11am-3pm Sun* $$

Tower Café: Best bet for big breakfasts; it's next to the iconic art deco movie theater. *8am-3pm Mon & Tue, 8am-8pm Wed-Sun, to 9pm Fri & Sat* $$

The Kitchen Restaurant: This cozy dining room in the northeast 'burbs is the pinnacle of Sacramento's food experience. *reserve 2 months in advance* $$$

BEER HEAVEN

In the past few years, Sacramento has developed one of California's best craft beer scenes. A number of excellent breweries are clustered on the Grid and some of the most promising newer spots are just a bit further afield. In total there are some 50 breweries and taprooms in the city, many of the brews concocted from farm-fresh local ingredients. Taking a lead from the restaurant scene, several breweries produce seasonal beers, infused with spring flowers, figs and even pumpkins in the fall.

If you want to taste all that Sacramento has to offer, pedal your way from one brewery to the next on a 15-person human-powered contraption from **Sac Brew Bike**.

It's recommended to spent at least two hours here, perhaps with a break at the soothing museum cafe or a stroll in tree-studded Crocker Park. The collection of light-flooded Californian art from 1945 onward is exceptional, from abstract expressionist works by bold Bay Area artists to pop art and painterly realism. Elsewhere, you'll find geometric-patterned basketry alongside more modern Native American pieces, a ceramic collection that spans the centuries, Old Master drawings collected by the museum's founders, as well as African, Oceanic, Asian and ancient American art. Be sure to make time for the thoughtfully curated photography gallery. The Crocker is closed Mondays and Tuesdays.

The City's Colonial Origins

Dig into John Sutter's historic fort

Originally built by Swiss immigrant John Sutter, the mostly reconstructed site of **Sutter's Fort State Historic Park** *(parks.ca.gov; adult/child $5/3)* was once the only white settlement for hundreds of miles. Established in 1840 as part of the Mexican province of Alta California, you can today stroll within the fort's whitewashed adobe walls, where displays of furniture, medical equipment and a working blacksmith shop re-create life in the 19th century. If John Sutter's name sounds familiar, that's because he also established **Sutter's Mill**, the saw mill where California's first gold flakes were discovered in 1848. Sutter's Fort is open daily.

Sutter was an entrepreneur, a con artist and itinerant debtor – qualities that survive to this day

THE LONG ROAD TO SUTTER'S FORT

Sutter's Fort was the goal of the stranded **Donner Party**, a group of blizzard-hit pioneers who turned to cannibalism in the winter of 1846–47. Only half of them survived to complete the desperate journey.

KIT LEONG/SHUTTERSTOCK

Sutter's Fort State Historic Park

in Silicon Valley. He enslaved the local Native American population to create his fortune, which was lost after the United States annexed California and gold-seekers swamped his lands. This story is sensitively told in the introductory video, which reframes the hero pioneer tale into one of destruction and trauma. Visit the neighboring State Indian Museum to learn about the culture that Sutter helped destroy.

Ponder California's Indigenous History

Appreciate the state's Native cultures

It's with some irony that the small **State Indian Museum** *(parks.ca.gov; adult/child $5/3)* sits in the shadow of Sutter's Fort. The excellent exhibits and handicrafts on display – including the intricately woven and feathered baskets of the Pomo – are traces of cultures nearly stamped out by the immigration fervor ignited by the discovery of gold at Sutter's Mill. Ceremonial garments and objects are displayed alongside mesmerizing historic photos of the ceremonies. A moving section comprising photographs and fragile artifacts documents the life of Ishi, thought to be the last of the Yahi tribe.

A new iteration of the museum – an ambitious replacement across the river from Old Sacramento – is in the works and promises to be a collaboration between Native Americans and the parks department. In the meantime, the current museum is open daily.

Cheer on the Sacramento Kings

Root for the underdog

The local professional basketball team has a passionate following in Central California despite having sixteen consecutive losing seasons from 2006 to 2022. Games are played

LIVE MUSIC IN MIDTOWN

Jen Moore, owner of *@rivercitymarketplace*, introduces the city's music scene.

Midtown Sacramento's vibrant, eclectic music scene pulses with creativity and community. From soulful acoustic sets and indie rock to energetic, funk, jazz and hip hop, every genre has a home in this lively urban hub. On any given night, music spills from cozy clubs, open-air patios and bustling taprooms, creating a rich tapestry of sound that reflects the city's diversity. The neighborhood's walkability makes it easy to explore multiple shows in one evening, whether you're catching a rising local artist or a surprise touring act. With events ranging from intimate performances to full-blown music festivals, it's more than music – it's the heartbeat of Sacramento.

IAN DAGNALL/ALAMY

Midtown

in the glitzy **Golden 1 Center** *(golden1center.com),* which is built from local materials, powered by solar and cooled by five-story airplane hangar doors that swing open to capture the delta breeze.

Savor Farmers Markets

Reap the rewards of rich agriculture

Sacramento lies at the center of some of the continent's most fertile farmlands, so you're never far from a mind-blowing year-round farmers market in the city (check out *market locations.com*). Most will have food trucks, excellent morning coffee vendors and street performers. One of the best in the entire country is the **Midtown Farmers' Market** *(exploremidtown.org/midtown-markets),* where 200 vendors array their delicious fare on Saturday mornings on 20th St.

Wine & Dine Downtown

Sacramento's best eating and nightlife districts

Lively **Midtown** begins east of 17th St and comprises an appealing mix of older buildings, huge shade trees and a zesty assortment of shops, restaurants, bars and music venues. A cruise up J St and nearby parallel streets passes a number

SINK A DRINK IN SACRAMENTO

Fieldwork Brewing Company: Bustling brewpub in Midtown. Over 20 rotating taps of excellent draft beer; hoppy IPAs are the specialty. *Times vary*

Torch Club: Long-established bar where everyone will soon know your name. Fabulous live music. *5pm-midnight Mon-Sat, from 3pm Sun*

Ruhstaller BSMT: This cozy basement bar on the Kay serves up red ales and Kolsch alongside experimental brews. *3-9pm Wed-Sat*

Harlow's: Quality jazz, R&B and the occasional salsa or indie act. Beware of the potent martinis. *5pm-midnight*

of creative-but-affordable restaurants where tables spill onto the sidewalks in the summer.

On K St and 20th is Lavender Heights, Midtown's gay and lesbian district, which hosts gay bars, a community center, the **Lavender library**, a September block party and the Saturday **farmers market**.

South of Midtown, at the corner of Broadway and 16th St, the Tower District is dominated by the **Tower Theatre** *(facebook.com/TowerTheatreCA)*, a beautiful 1938 art deco movie palace. From the theater, head east on Broadway to a stretch of the city's most eclectic and affordable eateries.

Parks, Trails & Verdant Paths

Breathe deeply amid urban nature

Snuggled into a curve of the American River, **River Bend Park** *(regionalparks.saccounty.net)*, 14 miles to the east of the city, is a real treat for those looking for some green space. Trails crisscross peaceful riparian landscapes defined by twisted oak trees, grassy meadows and rocky river shorelines.

The verdant **American River Parkway** *(arpf.org)* includes a paved walking, running and cycling path called the Jedediah Smith Memorial Trail that's accessible from Old Sacramento and runs for 32 miles to Folsom. Frustratingly, the closest bike hire option is **Peak Adventures** *(peakadventures.org)* on the Sacramento State University campus. From here you turn right for the long ride to Folsom, or cross the pedestrian/bike bridge and head left to reach Sacramento. Peak Adventures also rents paddle boards for the American River. Bike rental starts at $20 for three hours and paddleboarding is $25 per day.

Sacramento is a fantastic city to cruise around by bike, especially since its highlights are widely scattered. As you pedal from park to park, take the time to admire the city's magnificent trees, including redwoods.

PRIZE PIGS, FUNNEL CAKES AND THRILL RIDES

If you're anywhere near Sacramento during the last two weeks in July, don't miss the enormous **California State Fair** *(castatefair.org; adult/child $16/10)*. Since its inception in 1854, the fair has hosted horse racing, blue-ribbon livestock and agricultural exhibits showcasing California's bounty. It's heaven for kids, many of whom come for the deep-fried Snickers bars and corn-dog eating contests. Other crowd-pleasers include tastings of high-end wines, a huge array of carnival rides and concerts with nostalgic acts whose names often feature in 'dead or alive' trivia contests. Midweek is the best time to come; weekend crowds can be overwhelming. Hotels across the region fill up during the fair weeks.

SINK A DRINK IN SACRAMENTO

Bike Dog Broadway Taproom: Bright and cheery taproom in the Tower District, with a big line-up of house brews. *3-9pm Tue-Fri, noon-9pm Fri & Sat*

Old Soul: A restored horse barn that feels warm and intimate: the perfect spot for a smooth latte and a hot sandwich. *6am-8pm*

Flamingo House Social Club: Evokes bright Florida kitsch; the bar here feels like a tropical fever dream. *5pm-midnight Mon-Thu, 4pm-1.30am Fri, 2pm-2am Sat & Sun*

58 Degrees and Holding Co: Red wine and a refined bistro menu for oenophiles who feel left out in this beer-loving town. *4pm-10pm Mon-Thu & Sun, 10am-midnight Sat*

Beyond Sacramento

The Sacramento Delta's levee-protected towns and reed-covered islands seem stuck in the 1930s and make for ideal back-road exploring.

Places

Sacramento's waterfront on its namesake river is just the start of the sprawling web of waterways that form the Sacramento Delta and eventually flow into the San Francisco Bay. The wetlands cover a huge swath of the state and extend south all the way to Stockton and the edge of the San Joaquin Valley. It's easy to get happily lost here and forget you're surrounded by two of the state's largest metropolitan areas: Sacramento and San Francisco. On weekends, locals gun powerboats on the wandering rivers and cruise winding levee roads beneath twisted oak canopies.

Just to the north, Davis is one of California's most delightful college towns, surrounded by lush vineyards and orchards.

Sacramento Delta

TIME FROM SACRAMENTO: **1HR**

Drive the Delta's back roads

If you have the time to smell the grassy breezes of the **Sacramento Delta** on the slow route between San Francisco and Sacramento, don't miss traveling the region's roads that wind around islands linked by iron bridges. Everything is within one hour's drive of Sacramento. Winding Hwy 160 follows the curvaceous delta levees. Hwy 12 is another good option, as are other two-laners crisscrossing this watery wonderland, such as the evocatively named Grand Island Rd. You will lazily make your way past orderly vineyards, vast orchards, sandy swimming banks, bird-thronged parks and little towns with long histories.

GETTING AROUND

Exploring the scattered delta settlements will require your own vehicle. Davis, though, is well served by the Amtrak regional network – it only takes fifteen minutes to reach the town from Sacramento – while the Yolobus local bus service *(yolobus.com)* also runs routes to Sacramento. Stockton is served by Amtrak regional trains running to the Bay Area, Sacramento and the San Joaquin Valley. Altamont Commuter Express *(acerail.com)* trains serve San Jose.

ALESSANDRARC/SHUTTERSTOCK

Dai Loy Museum

You'll notice signs across the region protesting plans to divert even more fresh water away from the region. Since the 1930s, 75% of the water from the rivers flowing into the delta has been diverted to the Central Valley for agriculture and Southern California.

LOCKE'S RICH CHINESE HERITAGE

Locke was founded by Chinese laborers, who also built the levees that ended perpetual flooding in the Sacramento Delta. This allowed agriculture to flourish and created waterways that helped inland ports grow. After a malicious fire wiped out the settlement in 1912, a group of community leaders approached land baron George Locke for a leasehold; at the time, California didn't allow people of Chinese descent to own property. Locke became the only freestanding town built and managed by Chinese people in the US. These days the weather-beaten buildings are protected on the National Register of Historic Places. Somewhat miraculously, these tightly packed wood structures have avoided the fires that are the bane of California's historic towns.

Locke

TIME FROM SACRAMENTO: **35MIN**

Learn about the railway workers of yore

Locke is the most fascinating of the delta towns. Tucked below a levee, its main street feels like a ghost town. The colorful **Dai Loy Museum** *(locke-foundation.org; free)* recalls the town's Chinese heritage that dates back over 100 years; dusty pai gow tables and an antique safe are among the highlights. Nearby, the **Locke Boarding House Museum State Park** *(locke-foundation.org; free)* preserves the lodging of the hard-working Southern Pacific track workers. Note that these attractions are only open Friday to Sunday. Anchoring Main St is **Al's Place** *(althewops.com)*, a saloon that's been pouring since 1915. Below are creaking floorboards; above, the ceiling is covered in crusty dollar bills and more than one pair of erstwhile undies.

EATING & DRINKING IN THE DELTA: OUR PICKS

Mei Wah Beer Room: Fantastic restored drinking den in Isleton with an opulent Chinese-accented interior and patio. *4-9pm Thu & Fri, noon-8pm Sat & Sun* $

Al's Place: Locke's magnet for amiable Harley crews, where the draw isn't the food so much as the ambience. *10am-10pm* $

Foster's Bighorn: A veritable museum of taxidermy in Rio Vista – with beer. The menu is appropriately carnivorous. *4-8:45pm Tue-Thu, 11am-3pm & 4-8:45pm Fri-Sun* $$

Delta Queen Lodge, Restaurant & Bar: This wooden Isleton lodge dishes up meaty country classics and Mexican mains. *9am-9pm Tue-Thu, to 10pm Fri-Sun* $$

HAVENS FOR BIRDS AND BATS

The Sacramento Delta serves as a rest stop for countless migrating species that arrive in such great numbers they are a spectacle even without binoculars.

October to February Four million waterbirds winter in the warm tules (marshes) on their way along the Great Pacific Flyway. Sacramento National Wildlife Refuge offers tours.

October to January Endangered chinook and steelhead fight their way upstream to spawn. Spot them along Sacramento's American River Parkway.

March to June Cabbage white, painted lady and western tiger swallowtail butterflies come to party. Sacramento National Wildlife Refuge has details.

June to August Hundreds of thousands of Mexican free-tailed bats shelter under the Yolo Causeway in Davis.

Isleton & Around

TIME FROM SACRAMENTO: **45MIN**

Crawdads and campsites

Isleton – aka Crawdad Town, USA – has a long, historic main street with shops, restaurants, bars and buildings that reflect the region's Chinese heritage. The town's **Cajun Festival**, at the end of June, draws folks from across the state, but you can get lively crawdads year-round at **Bob's Bait Shop** *(the masterbaiter.tripod.com)*.

Rio Vista is a humble burg with a nice little waterfront on the Sacramento River. Nearby are good and unpretentious cafes and bars.

Across the delta you'll see signs for the **Delta Loop**, a drive that passes boater bars and marinas where you can rent something to take on the water. At the end is the **Brannan Island State Recreation Area** *(parks.ca.gov)*, which has boat-in, drive-in and walk-in campsites.

Clarksburg Region

TIME FROM SACRAMENTO: **30MIN**

Taste unique Delta vintages

The wines of the Clarksburg region along the Sacramento River have a great reputation, benefiting from blazing sun and cool delta breezes. The **Old Sugar Mill** *(oldsugarmill.com; free)* is the hub of a thriving community of local winemakers. Peruse the tasting rooms and enjoy a bottle on the outdoor patio overlooking vineyards. The region's best-known winery, **Bogle** *(boglewinery.com; free)*, is a few miles southwest of Clarksburg via the winding County Rds 141 and 144. It's set among vineyards on a sixth-generation family farm and is proud of its sustainable practices.

Davis

TIME FROM SACRAMENTO: **25MIN**

Bikes, galleries and tree-lined streets

Much of Davis' energy comes from the free-spirited students who flock to the **University of California, Davis** (UC Davis), which has one of the nation's leading viticulture departments. Bikes outnumber cars two-to-one and students make up half the population. The town makes a good pit stop when traveling in or out of the Bay Area.

EATING IN DAVIS & STOCKTON: OUR PICKS

Mustard Seed: Creative takes on California cuisine using local bounty in downtown Davis. *hours vary* **$$$**

Woodstock's: Friendly Davis pizza joint serving slices at lunch: things get boisterous at happy hour. A fun selection of gourmet pizzas. *11am-midnight* **$**

Sam's Mediterranean Cuisine: Delicious and cheap shawarma makes this little spot a Davis institution. *11.30am-7.30pm Mon-Sat* **$**

Manny's California Fresh Café: A 1950s joint at the edge of Stockton's Miracle Mile, serving flavorful rotisserie meats and fried-chicken sandwiches. *10am-9:45pm* **$**

ALESSANDRARC/SHUTTERSTOCK

UC Davis Arboretum

Strolling the shady downtown, you'll pass family-operated businesses, including some great book and thrift stores, plus public art projects.

The university is all about agriculture and new types of produce that end up in your supermarket are developed here. The 100-acre **UC Davis Arboretum** *(arboretum.ucdavis.edu; free)* is a must-see for its well-marked botanical collections. Afterward, follow the peaceful 3.5-mile loop along one of the state's oldest reservoirs, dug in the 1860s.

The campus has two notable cultural centers. The **Jan Shrem and Maria Manetti Shrem Museum of Art** *(manettishremmuseum.ucdavis.edu; free)* features contemporary artists working across a wide range of mediums in a dreamy modern space. The **John Natsoulas Center for the Arts** *(natsoulas.com; free)* is marked by an outsize mosaic cat on the way into town; the ceramic calico guards one of the state's most vibrant small contemporary art galleries.

The **Davis Farmers Market** *(davisfarmersmarket.org)* is renowned for being one of the best in the country and features over 150 food vendors; on Wednesday evenings bands play in the adjacent park.

THICKER THAN PEA SOUP: TULE FOG

Each year, tule fog causes chain collisions on area roads, sometimes involving hundreds of cars. At its worst, these dense clouds can limit visibility up to a foot. Named after a common marsh grass, tule fog is thickest from November to March, when cold mountain air settles on the warm valley floor and condenses. The fog burns off for a few afternoon hours, just long enough for the ground to warm again and perpetuate the cycle. Interestingly, the amount of fog has decreased in recent years (with the credit going to a drop in pollution and an increase in droughts). If you're driving in fog, turn your low beams on and your brights off, give other cars extra distance and maintain a cautious speed.

DRINKING IN DAVIS: CRAFT BEER & COFFEE

Delta of Venus Cafe & Pub: Converted bungalow with a shaded patio, tons of veggie and vegan options, a bar and live music. *hours vary*

Davis Beer Shoppe: Mellow Davis beer hall with 650 varieties of craft beer, bottled and on tap. *11am-10pm Mon-Sat, to 8pm Sun*

Miskha's Cafe: A quintessential university cafe with a homey twist – the rose and lavender infused lattes are house favorites. *7.30am-6pm*

Three Mile Brewing Company: Microbrewery with a fantastic flight of crisp, hoppy beer made from local ingredients. *3-10pm, from noon Fri-Sun*

JACOB BOOMSMA/SHUTTERSTOCK

Stockton

Stockton

TIME FROM SACRAMENTO: **50MIN**

Stroll a revitalized waterfront

Southwest of Sacramento, **Stockton** is the surprise port city at the east end of the delta. It was once the main supply hub for gold rushers and during WWII it became a major center of American shipbuilding.

The waterfront redevelopment is one of the valley's successful efforts at revitalization and makes for a good stroll, along with the adjoining downtown. Slightly north, you'll find **Miracle Mile**, a second hub of bars and restaurants.

Of all the Central Valley food celebrations, perhaps none pay such creative respect to its main ingredient as Stockton's **San Joaquin Asparagus Festival**, which brings together more than 500 vendors in April to serve the prized green stalks – more than 10 tons! – in every way imaginable.

Sacramento Valley

EXPANSIVE ORCHARDS | PARTY TOWN | CHINESE HERITAGE

The Sacramento River, California's largest, rushes out of the northern mountains from Shasta Lake before hitting the Sacramento Valley basin above Red Bluff. It snakes south across grassy plains and orchards before skirting the state capital, fanning across the delta and draining into San Francisco Bay.

The valley is most beautiful in the bloom of spring, when delicate flowers bejewel the orchards and hillsides. If you're driving through the region to one of California's marquee attractions, swing though Chico for a fun vibe, good eats and famous drinks.

Since so much is grown in the Sacramento Valley, enjoying the fresh, seasonal food in the region is easy. Look for fruit-and-nut stands along the highways, many selling what you can see growing in the surrounding orchards and farmlands. Every city has farmers markets, many open year-round. The vendors are experts and will patiently take you through their vast range of produce.

TOP TIP

The backbone of the Sacramento Valley is I-5, which connects with other major highways like I-80. However, this stretch of the state's north–south spine is no more interesting than the San Joaquin Valley portion. Instead, get close to valley towns and farmlands on Hwys 45, 70 and 99.

GETTING AROUND

The Sacramento Valley is where you will probably opt for your own vehicle. Quiet two-lane roads far from the busy highways are great for cycling, but otherwise you'll need a car to explore the region. Amtrak and Greyhound buses provide service that's barely serviceable.

Party Town & Iconic Brewery

Good times in Chico

With its huge student population, Chico has the wild energy of a college kegger during the school year and a lethargic hangover during summer. The oak-shaded downtown and lively **California State University, Chico** make it one of Sacramento Valley's most attractive hubs. Folks mingle late in the restaurants and bars here, which open onto patios when it's warm.

Though the city – like the rest of the valley – wilts in the summer heat, the swimming holes in impressive **Bidwell Park** *(chico.ca.us)* offer an escape, as does floating down the gentle Sacramento River. The park stretches 10 miles northwest of

HIGHLIGHTS
1 Bidwell Park
2 Sierra Nevada Brewing Company

SIGHTS
3 California State University, Chico
4 Chinese Temple & Museum Complex
5 William B Ide Adobe State Historic Park

SLEEPING
6 Goodman House
7 Hotel Diamond
8 Lake Oroville State Recreation Area Campgrounds
9 Sycamore Grove Camping Area

EATING
10 Shubert's Ice Cream & Candy

DRINKING & NIGHTLIFE
11 Roselle Bar & Lounge
12 Secret Trail Brewing
13 Tender Loving Coffee

ENTERTAINMENT
14 Red Bluff Round-Up

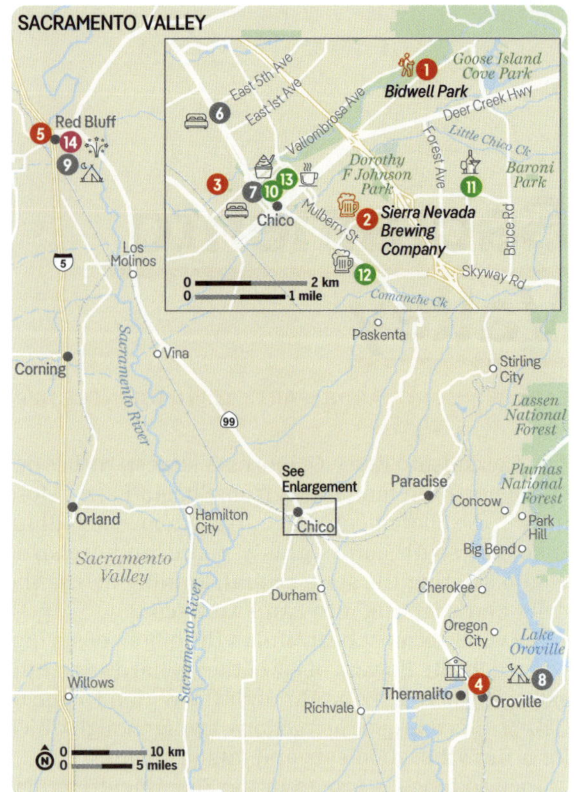

downtown with lush groves and miles of trails.

For many, Chico's top attraction has pilgrimage status: this is the home of the legendary **Sierra Nevada Brewing Company** *(sierranevada.com)*. Founded in 1979, the brewery was one of the pioneers of the craft beer revolution. Today Sierra Nevada continues to try out new styles of beer at the various taprooms at its huge brewery complex near Hwy 99. Take a self-guided tour or go for one of the deep-immersion (not literally) sessions with a brewmaster. Soak up the suds in the excellent restaurant.

DRINKING IN CHICO: OUR PICKS

Secret Trail Brewing: Low-key brewery tucked away from Chico's downtown with live music on Fridays and food trucks outside. *3-7pm Tue-Thu, from noon Fri-Sun*

Roselle Bar & Lounge: Elegant cocktail bar in a nightlife area east of the center. Classy bar food and DJ nights. *4-10pm Wed-Fri, 11am-midnight Sat, 11am-4pm Sun*

Tender Loving Coffee: Craft-roasted coffee and big vegan breakfasts from this community hub near the radical Pageant Theatre. *8am-2pm Tue-Sun*

Sierra Nevada Brewing Company: Hordes of fans gather at the birthplace of Sierra Nevada Pale Ale and Schwarber black ale. *11am-4pm Sun-Thu, to 5.30pm Fri & Sat*

All ages will delight in **Shubert's Ice Cream & Candy** *(shuberts.com)*, a beloved old-time shop where five generations of Shuberts have produced delicious homemade ice cream, chocolates and confections.

Feel the Heat in Red Bluff

Western garb and a historic house

Red Bluff – one of California's hottest towns and the location of the **Round-Up Rodeo** in April – makes a fine pit stop on the way to the famous parks to the northeast. Shop for Western wear downtown, then get a dose of history at **William B Ide Adobe State Historic Park** *(parks.ca.gov; per car $6)*, which preserves an original 1850 one-room adobe house.

The Valley's Chinese Legacy

Wander the wooden homes of Oroville

Quiet **Oroville** has restored 19th-century wooden homes that recall its past as a gold-rush town. The restored 1863 **Chinese Temple & Museum Complex** *(cityoforoville.org; entry $4)* offers a fascinating glimpse into Oroville's Chinese legacy; note that it's only open on Fridays and Saturdays, from 10am to 2pm. Hwy 70 heads northeast to the magnificent Feather River Canyon.

WILD CHICO

It's not just the student parties that are wild in Chico. From the dense trees arching over the streets to the rushing waters of Chico Creek, this city is intertwined with nature. Growing out of downtown, **Bidwell Park** stretches for 10 glorious miles northwest along the creek. Several classic movie scenes have been shot here, from *Gone with the Wind* to *The Adventures of Robin Hood.*

The upper park is an untamed oasis, with miles of trails weaving along creek banks, in between basalt rock formations and across meadows dusted in spring wildflowers. Bidwell is also full of swimming spots for hot Chico days. You'll find pools at One-Mile and Five-Mile recreation areas and swimming holes in Upper Bidwell Park, north of Manzanita Ave.

San Joaquin Valley

COUNTRY MUSIC | AGRICULTURE | WILD RIVER

TOP TIP

To really see the region, skip I-5 and travel on Hwy 99 – a freeway with nearly as long a history as the famous Route 66 to the south. Crank up the twangy country and western or the booming *norteño* (accordion-driven Mexican folk music). Exit for bushels of the freshest produce on earth.

The southern half of California's Central Valley, named after the San Joaquin River, sprawls from Stockton to the Tehachapi Mountains, southeast of Bakersfield. Everything stretches to the horizon in straight lines – railroad tracks, two-lane blacktop and long irrigation channels.

The tiny towns scattering the region meld their Main Street Americana appeal with the cultural influence of the Latinx labor force. This is a place of seismic, often contentious, development. Arrivals priced out of coastal cities have resulted in patches of urban sprawl. What were once ranches and vineyards are now nostalgically named developments and water rights is the issue on everyone's minds.

The valley's cities are not compelling, but each has attractions to lure you off Hwy 99, the spine of the San Joaquin. Distances here are long: it's over 220 miles from Modesto south to Bakersfield. Look to the edges for the improbably scenic Kern River area and Antelope Valley wildflowers.

On the Strip in Modesto

Vintage Central Valley living

Cruising was banned in **Modesto** in 1993, but the town still touts itself as the 'cruising capital of the world.' The pastime's notoriety stems mostly from homegrown George Lucas' 1973

GETTING AROUND

Amtrak's San Joaquin service follows Hwy 99 and links the main valley cities with Sacramento and the Bay Area. There's a connecting bus service onward to the LA Basin from the Bakersfield train station. Other buses connect to Yosemite and Sequoia national parks. Although you'll see plenty of construction – such as the huge new concrete trestles over Hwy 99 north of Fresno – California's much-hyped high-speed rail line linking the Bay Area with LA via the San Joaquin Valley is years away from completion. The main cities have local buses for getting around town.

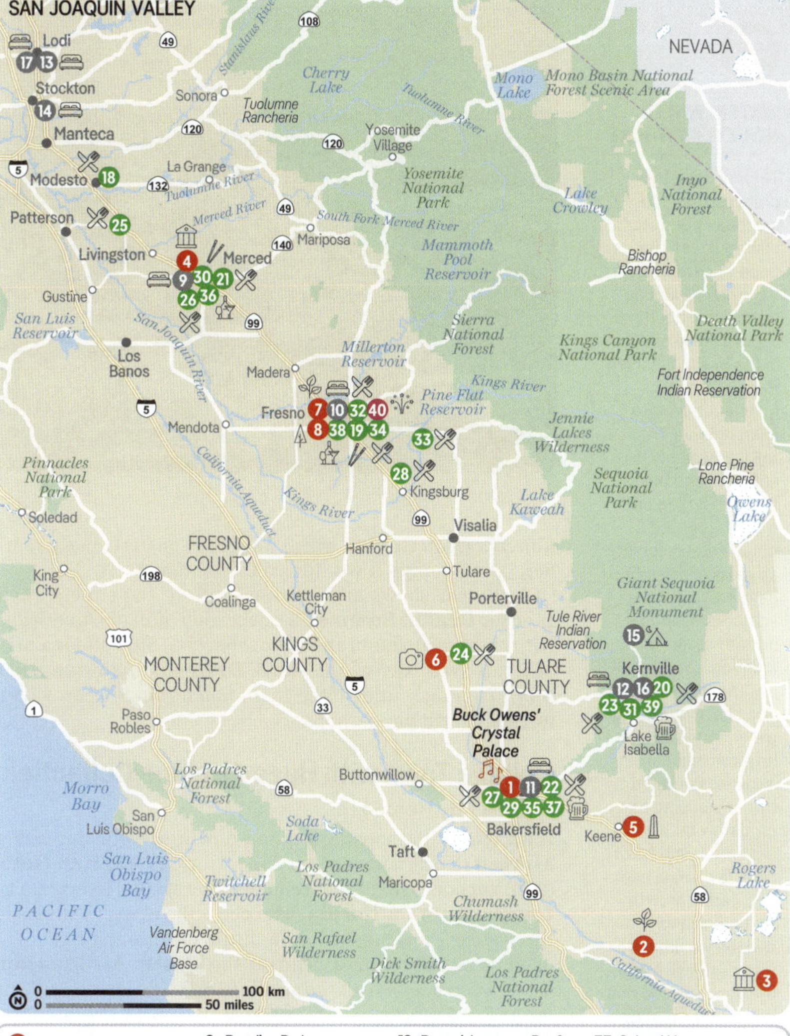

HIGHLIGHTS

1 Buck Owens' Crystal Palace

SIGHTS

2 Antelope Valley California Poppy Reserve
3 Antelope Valley Indian Museum
4 Castle Air Museum
5 César E Chávez National Monument
6 Colonel Allensworth State Historic Park
7 Forestiere Underground Gardens
8 Roeding Park

SLEEPING

9 El Capitan Hotel
10 Hotel Piccadilly
11 Padre Hotel
12 Piazza's Pine Cone Inn
13 Poppy Sister Inn
14 University Plaza Waterfront Hotel
15 USFS Campgrounds
16 Whispering Pines Lodge
17 Wine & Roses

EATING

18 A&W Drive-In
19 Banzai Japanese Bar & Kitchen
20 Big Blue Bear Cafe
21 Branding Iron
22 Cafe Smitten
23 Cheryl's Diner
24 La Pasadita
25 La Taqueria
26 Little Oven Pizza
27 Loncheria Otro Rollo
28 Los Toritos
29 Luigi's
30 New Thai Cuisine
31 Pizza Barn
32 Sam's Italian Deli & Market
33 School House Restaurant
34 Tower Blendz
35 Wool Growers

DRINKING & NIGHTLIFE

36 17th Street Public House
37 Dionysus Brewing Company
38 Goldstein's Mortuary & Delicatessen
39 Kern River Brewing Company

ENTERTAINMENT

40 Tower Porchfest

WATER, WATER, NOT EVERYWHERE

Through the elaborate politics and machinery of water management, the once-arid Central Valley ranks among the most agriculturally productive places in the world, though the profits often go to agribusiness shareholders, not the increasingly disenfranchised family farmer. The region's water issues are a perennial flashpoint, as years of drought have made water a scarce commodity in many areas. In addition, some small towns in the valley don't have drinkable water thanks to high levels of arsenic, an issue exacerbated by the pumping of groundwater. The increasing impact of climate change and population growth isn't going away and the viability of water-intensive crops like almonds and rice is in doubt – realities the powerful agricultural interests would rather ignore.

film *American Graffiti*, which was based on his teenage years here, even though it was filmed in Petaluma.

Classic car shows and rock and roll fill the streets every June for **Graffiti Summer**, a celebration of 1950s Americana with classic car shows and oldies concerts. Stop off for a mug of frosty root beer at the **A&W Drive-In** *(awrestaurants.com)*, a vintage outlet of the chain that began in nearby Lodi in 1919. It still has carhops.

College Town with Huge Airplane Collection

Touring tidy Merced

With one of the most appealing downtowns in the valley, **Merced** makes a good stop. The historic **El Capitan Hotel** (p69) anchors a district of good restaurants and lounges. The **University of California, Merced** – the newest campus in the system – has injected a youthful vibe into the city.

Aviation fans should head to the **Castle Air Museum** *(castleairmuseum.org; adult/child $25/15)*, located on the grounds of a former military base that once saw bombers armed with nuclear weapons. Their huge outdoor collection includes almost every notable US Air Force and Navy plane from WWII and the Cold War. Military mechanics volunteer their time restoring these planes and are often on-site to

MEXICAN FOOD ON HWY 99

La Taqueria: (Exit 213) There's never a line at this sibling of the insanely popular San Francisco icon. Get your burrito 'dorado style' (crispy). *11am-9pm* $

Los Toritos: (Exit 115) Happy patrons fill an array of shaded tables at this food truck known for all things pork. *10am-midnight Mon-Sat, from 8am Sun* $

La Pasadita: (Exit 65) A semi-permanent food truck near Earlimart that cooks up sublime *vampiros* – a sort of cheesy tostada, only better. *10am-10pm* $

Loncheria Otro Rollo: (Exit 21) On the south side of Bakersfield, this red trailer by a gas station dishes up excellent potato tacos and deep-fried tortillas. *11am-7pm* $

JACOB BOOMSMA/SHUTTERSTOCK

Fresno

answer questions. The museum also hosts Open Cockpit Days for you to get an even closer look at these behemoth machines.

Central City with Underground Gardens

Fresno buzzes with history

Smack in the arid center of the state, **Fresno** is the Central Valley's biggest city. It's hardly scenic (the downtown is shabby), but it's beautifully situated, just an hour and a half from four national parks (Yosemite, Sierra, Kings Canyon and Sequoia), making it the ideal last stop for expeditions.

Like many valley cities, Fresno is home to diverse Hmong, Mexican, Chinese and Basque communities, which arrived in successive waves. Don't miss the **Forestiere Underground Gardens** *(undergroundgardens.com; adult/child $24/15)* – it was built by Sicilian immigrant Baldassare Forestiere, who dug out some 70 acres beneath the hardpan soil to plant citrus trees, starting in 1906. With a unique skylight system, Forestiere created a beautiful subterranean space for commercial crops and his own living quarters.

Hidden away in **Roeding Park** *(fresno.gov)* is a moving memorial to the many local Japanese Americans who died serving the United States in WWII. Their sacrifice is bittersweet given that their families were being held in concentration camps

HONORING CÉSAR CHÁVEZ

The **César E Chávez National Monument** is at Nuestra Señora Reina de la Paz, the national headquarters of the United Farmworkers of America and the home of civil rights leader César Chávez from 1971 until his death in 1993. On view are exhibits on Chávez' work, his office and grave. It's in **Keene**, 27 miles southeast of Bakersfield.

Chávez was 11 when his family lost their farm and became migrant farm workers in California. At 14, he left school to labor in the fields. Eventually, he became a champion of nonviolent social change, leading controversial strikes while negotiating for better working conditions in the fields. His 1960s activism led to enormous improvements in the lives of California's farmworkers.

WHERE TO EAT & DRINK IN MERCED: OUR PICKS

Little Oven Pizza: Turning out picture-perfect, New York–style thin crust, this downtown spot has daily specials and a quick, cheap option. *noon-9pm* $

17th Street Public House: Stylish bar right in the heart of Merced's revitalized downtown. *2-10pm Mon-Fri, from noon Sat & Sun* $$

Branding Iron: A roadhouse favorite of Merced ranchers, who order huge platters of steak. *11.30am-2pm Mon-Fri, 5-9pm Sun-Thu, to 9.30pm Fri & Sat* $$

New Thai Cuisine: Downtown Thai restaurant makes an excellent combination pho soup, sweet-and-savory honey-sesame wings and duck curry. *11am-7.30pm* $

GOOD SCENTS ON THE BLOSSOM TRAIL

When the Central Valley fruit and nut trees are in bloom, the winding roads around Fresno and Visalia make for a lovely afternoon drive. The 62-mile **Fresno County Blossom Trail** *(goblossomtrail.com)* is stunning between February and March, with the orchards awash in the pastel petals of apricot, almond, peach, nectarine, apple and citrus. Return in summer to taste the results.

Route maps are available online, though DIY is possible if you don't mind occasional detours on the back roads between Sanger, Reedley, Orange Cove, Selma, Fowler and Kingsburg. Don't miss lunch at **School House Restaurant** in Sanger. Dating from 1921, it serves elevated classic American cuisine in a vintage setting with pulley-powered fans.

ZACK FRANK/SHUTTERSTOCK

Colonel Allensworth State Historic Park

across the Western US at the time. Thousands came from the Central Valley where, more often than not, their farms and homes were seized by their neighbors in their absence.

One of the most interesting parts of town is the **Tower District**, north of downtown. It's an oasis of gay-friendly bars, bookstores, music clubs and interesting restaurants. It's also the location of April's **Porchfest**, which sees free live music on the streets.

Delicious Treats, Nordic Kitsch

Sample Swedish Kingsburg

Around 1873, a rail stop called 'Kings River Switch' was established and two Swedes arrived. Their countrymen soon followed and by 1921, 94% of **Kingsburg's** residents – as it had become known – were of Swedish heritage. Today, the Swedish past mixes with more recent Mexican immigrants who drive the agricultural economy.

Draper St, the main drag, is decked out with swaths of faux half-timbered schtick, all in the shadow of the landmark coffee-pot water tower. Gift shops and little bakeries selling buttery pastries and good coffee abound. Note: everything is closed on Sunday.

Don't miss all things raisin at the **Sun-Maid Market**. Pose next to the giant Sun Maid statue, then wander in for free samples and a selection of snacks.

GATEWAYS TO YOSEMITE

Many San Joaquin Valley cities are excellent launching points for **Yosemite National Park** (p144). Modesto, Merced and Fresno have affordable accommodations and plenty of places to stock up on food and gear for your adventure in the Sierras.

The Valley's Earliest African American Town

The abandoned town of Allensworth

Some 10 miles west of Hwy 99 at Earlimart, **Colonel Allensworth State Historic Park** *(parks.ca.gov)* is an anomaly in the valley: a town built by and for African Americans. Named after its founder, a formerly enslaved person who later became a chaplain in the US Army, Allensworth comprised several dozen houses by 1910. Unfortunately, the same water woes that bedevil the valley today caused the town to go into terminal decline. It was abandoned by the 1930s. Today, it's a state park and buildings are being restored. The land here is table-top flat and except for passing trains, the only sound is the wind whipping across the plain.

Make a Pilgrimage to the Bakersfield Sound

Honky tonk and black gold

Near **Bakersfield**, the landscape bears evidence of California's other gold rush: rusting rigs burrowing into Southern California's vast oil fields. Black gold was discovered here in the late 1800s and Kern County still pumps more oil than some OPEC countries.

This is the setting of Upton Sinclair's *Oil!*, adapted into the 2007 film *There Will Be Blood*. In the 1930s the oil attracted a stream of 'Okies' – farmers who migrated out of the Great Plains – to work the derricks. The children of these tough-as-nails roughnecks put the 'western' in country and western by creating the 'Bakersfield Sound' in the mid-1950s, with heroes Buck Owens and Merle Haggard waving a defiant middle finger at the silky Nashville establishment.

The obvious music choice as you explore the region is Owens' classic 'Streets of Bakersfield,' which combines the gritty local sound with lashings of Mexican *norteño*. Immerse yourself at **Buck Owens' Crystal Palace** *(buckowens.com)*, the north-side music club that's part museum, honky-tonk and steakhouse.

Downtown Bakersfield has been spruced up, which is evident in the upbeat mix of restored buildings and new restaurants, theaters and clubs. Just east, Bakersfield is blessed with Basque culinary traditions brought by shepherds in the 1800s. Restaurants such as **Wool Growers** (p68) serve myriad courses that are meaty, garlicky and good.

KINGS & QUEENS OF THE BAKERSFIELD SOUND

Driving south on Hwy 99 requires getting on a first-name basis with Bakersfield's drawling titans: Merle, Buck and other masters of twanging Telecasters and hayseed heartbreak. The Bakersfield Sound brought honky tonk back home, in an earthy rebuff to orchestrated Nashville country music.

Some of the greatest hits include Merle Haggard's *'Okie from Muskogee,' 'The Bottle Let Me Down'* and *'Swinging Doors.'* Buck Owens, meanwhile, is famous for *'I've Got A Tiger by the Tail,' 'Second Fiddle'* and *'The Streets of Bakersfield.'* Two women who topped the charts are Jean Sheppard and Susan Raye. Jean's songs include *'A Dear John Letter'* and *'Pitty, Pitty, Patter.'* Susan sang *'LA International Airport'* and *'The Great White Horse.'*

WHERE TO EAT & DRINK IN FRESNO: OUR PICKS

Sam's Italian Deli & Market: This market and deli is the real deal, stacking up 'New Yorker' pastrami and some mean prosciutto and mozzarella. *10am-6pm Tue-Sat* $

Banzai Japanese Bar & Kitchen: High-concept Japanese fare in Fresno's Tower District; the spicy garlic edamame is addictive. *5-9.30pm Mon-Thu, from noon Fri-Sun* $$

Tower Blendz: From açaí bowls to bountiful breakfast sandwiches, the food here is freshly prepared and healthy. *8am-4pm Mon-Fri, from 10am Sat & Sun* $

Goldstein's Mortuary & Delicatessen: Sip on a beer from their extensive list, have a seat in a chair made from a shopping cart and listen to live music. *3pm-midnight* $

FORT TEJON MASSACRE

Back toward Bakersfield, **Fort Tejon State Historic Park** is the site of one of the myriad atrocities committed against California tribes in the 1800s. The fort was established in 1854, occupied by the First US Dragoons and then by volunteers and it was an outpost of the US Camel Corps. Its ostensible mission was to prevent stock rustling by the Californios (Californians of Spanish descent), Paiute and Mojave. In 1863, the fort's volunteers launched a murderous onslaught against the Paiute, killing hundreds of people. In July of that year, the remaining 850 who survived the attacks were marched to Fort Tejon; at least 150 people died on the march and the rest faced starvation upon arrival.

White-Water Rafting & Family Floats

Ride the Kern River

A half-century ago, the Kern River originated on the slopes of Mt Whitney and flowed close to 170 miles before finally settling into the Central Valley. Now, after its wild descent from the high country – dropping 60ft per mile – the Kern is dammed in several places and almost entirely tapped out for agricultural use.

Kernville, a cute little town straddling the river, is a hub for water sports. The pristine upper reaches, north of Kernville, have class IV and V rapids during the spring runoff and offer some of the most awe-inspiring white-water trips in the United States. You'll need experience before tackling these sections, but below Lake Isabella, the Kern is tamer and steadier.

Rafting outfitters run trips from May to August, depending on conditions. Excursions include popular one-hour runs, day-long Lower Kern trips and multiday Wild Forks of the Kern experiences. Walk-ins are welcome and experience is not necessary. Prices start at $75 for a 1½hr trip; day trips start at $199.

Kern Valley on Foot

Take to the trails

If you're looking for a more relaxed Kern Canyon experience, there are many hiking trails through the mountainous terrain that are especially lovely in spring when the wildflowers are blooming. Head to the **Kernville USFS Ranger Station** for hiking and camping information, plus maps and wilderness permits.

The areas around Isabella Lake and Kernville offer a number of opportunities for exploring on foot. **Whiskey Flat Trail** (12.4 miles) runs along the river and has two trailheads right outside Kernville. **Cannell Trail** (22.7 miles) is a local favorite for its wildflower meadows and mountain biking opportunities. For something more demanding, the **Powers Peak Trail** (10 miles) takes you through some rugged granite outcrops, with a challenging 3000ft ascent to the summit.

Head further north on winding Mountain Hwy 99 and you'll find numerous trails and campsites in the Sequoia National Forest.

BIG TREES

Some 33 winding miles north of Kernville you come to the 100 Giants Trail, with looping paths taking you through the southernmost grove of the mighty sequoia. For more big trees, head to **Sequoia National Park** (p159).

Old-School Train Station & Cafes

Chugging through Tehachapi

Midway between the San Joaquin Valley and the Mojave Desert, the tidy town of **Tehachapi** is a fine stop for its historic main drag, which has several retro cafes. However, the real star is the **Tehachapi Railroad Depot** – a reconstructed train station with a museum dedicated to the very busy train tracks outside, which link much of California with the rest of the US. Don't miss the little used-book section within.

PARTYONLAUREN/SHUTTERSTOCK

Kern River

The depot is built to a standard design of the Southern Pacific Railroad that dates back to the 1870s. Stations such as this were once a ubiquitous feature of town centers across the state.

The Surprising Antelope Valley

Searching for the golden poppy

A scruffier version of the Mojave Desert, the Antelope Valley is a dry annex to the Central Valley. Somewhat isolated and over the hill from Bakersfield, it has surprises for those willing to look.

The **Antelope Valley California Poppy Reserve** *(parks.ca.gov; per vehicle $10)* explodes in color every spring. The golden poppy is California's state flower and in this park it's given center stage, especially from mid-March through April when the hills are practically aglow in the dainty flower, along with lupine, goldfields and lacy phacelia, all of which provide yellow and purple accents. The reserve is also filled with a wide range of native wildlife and is good for hiking.

Set against the granite outcrops of the Piute Butte, the **Antelope Valley Indian Museum** *(avim.parks.ca.gov; entry*

WHY I LOVE THE KERN VALLEY

Helena Smith, Lonely Planet writer

From the flat plains around Bakersfield, the mountains rise in improbable beauty: boulder-strewn, tree-dotted and astoundingly wild. The Kern River, a dry bed by the time it reaches the city, begins to show in flashes and glints. By the time you reach the little town of Kernville, the Kern is wide and tumultuous, the site of river trips and soul-soothing hikes. The town itself features wooden Wild West buildings and an excellent brewery and is a wonderful place to hole up for some downtime out of season, or to enjoy the rafters' hullabaloo in the summer. From here I often head north for a walk among the giants: the most southerly sequoia grove always shifts my perspective.

WHERE TO EAT & DRINK IN KERNVILLE: OUR PICKS

Kern River Brewing Company: Award-winning seasonal beers, plus a tasty menu with pulled pork tacos. *11am-10pm Sun-Thu, to 11pm Fri & Sat* $

Big Blue Bear Cafe: In the mornings, grab a coffee and breakfast sandwich; at lunch, dive into the sandwiches and salads. Wine and beer, too. *7am-4pm* $

Cheryl's Diner: Classic diner in the heart of Kernville, with a warm welcome, booths and a bar. *6am-9pm* $

Pizza Barn: Come to this wooden saloon for everything from individual slices to whole pies. The cheesy garlic bread is a winner. *1am-9pm* $

ZHUO WEN CHEN/SHUTTERSTOCK

Antelope Valley California Poppy Reserve (p67)

$3) displays thousands of Native American artifacts. Some 4000 years ago, the Antelope Valley was an important trade route linking Native American peoples throughout the Great Basin, California and the Southwest. Today, this out-of-the-way museum presents exhibits related to all three regions in a 1928 Tudor-style structure huddled against the rocks. Some boulders are neatly integrated into the exhibit space, whose highlight is the Hopi kachina collection, carved figurines that depict kachina spirits.

WHERE TO EAT & DRINK IN BAKERSFIELD: OUR PICKS

Luigi's: Best bet for sandwiches in Bakersfield since 1910, with top imported and locally sourced ingredients. *11am-2.30pm Tue-Sat* $

Cafe Smitten: This bright cafe in the heart of downtown serves lighter fare, pastries and drinks. Sunny patio. *6.30am-7pm Mon-Thu, to 9pm Fri, 8am-5pm Sat & Sun* $

Wool Growers: A simple Basque eating hall loaded with character – sit at the mid-century bar and enjoy a drink. Family-style meals. *11.30am-2pm & 6-8pm Mon-Sat* $$

Dionysus Brewing Company: This exceptional brewery specializes in adventurous sours, but has a beer for everyone. *4-9pm Mon-Fri, from noon Sat, 11am-8pm Sun* $

Places We Love to Stay

$ Budget $$ Midrange $$$ Top End

Sacramento

Map p45

HI Sacramento Hostel $ This hostel in a magnificent Victorian mansion offers good trimmings at rock-bottom prices. It's within walking distance of Old Sac and has a piano in the parlor.

Family Laundry & Spa $ Named for their neon sign, this B&B is located in a 1920s Craftsman-style home with three comfortable suites.

Delta King $$ It's a kitschy treat to sleep aboard the *Delta King,* a 1927 paddle wheeler docked on the river in Old Sacramento. It lights up like a Christmas tree at night.

Citizen Hotel $$ This 1924 Beaux Arts tower features luxe linens, an atmospheric reception and an upscale farm-to-fork restaurant on the ground floor.

Davis

University Park Inn & Suites $ Right off the highway, this independent hotel isn't the Ritz, but it's clean, serves breakfast and offers free bikes for guests.

The Vine Inn $$ Located right in the beating heart of Davis, this modern motel has simple, comfortable rooms.

Sacramento Valley

Map p58

Lake Oroville State Recreation Area Campgrounds $ Good campsites if you're willing to hike or even boat: why not sleep on a floating platform?

Sycamore Grove Camping Area $ Beside the river in the Red Bluff Recreation Area you'll find this quiet USFS campground. Shared showers and flush toilets.

Goodman House $$ Delightful B&B in a 1906 home on a tree-lined Chico esplanade. Features include clawfoot baths, French antique beds and a Viennese grand piano.

Hotel Diamond $$$ This 1904 building is the most luxurious place to lay your head in Chico, with a high-thread count, a swanky bar and a top-notch restaurant.

San Joaquin Valley

Map p61

Piazza's Pine Cone Inn $ Originally opened in 1955, the Pine Cone Inn retains its retro feel while offering spotless rooms to rest your head after a long day on the Kern River.

USFS Campgrounds $ Campgrounds line the 10-mile stretch between Lake Isabella and Kernville. Rangers recommend Fairview and Limestone for their seclusion.

Hotel Piccadilly $ Fresno's nicest option, with a lovely pool, big rooms and good amenities.

University Plaza Waterfront Hotel $ If you're spending the night in Stockton, this is the best choice: business travelers mingle with students who live in the lofts on the upper floors.

Poppy Sister Inn $$ This buttercream-yellow Victorian house in Lodi is a welcoming base for vineyard exploring: the home has four cozy rooms.

Padre Hotel $$ A stylish update revived this century-old hotel, adding an upscale restaurant, two bars and a rooftop lounge that instantly became the place for cocktails in Bakersfield.

El Capitan Hotel $$ Adding a good dash of style to Merced, El Capitan features hip guestrooms, a historic theater and a good choice of eating and drinking options.

Whispering Pines Lodge $$ This B&B, blending rustic character with creature comforts, sits on the north edge of Kernville.

Wine & Roses $$$ Surrounded by a vast rose garden, this is one of the more luxurious offerings to spring up amid Lodi's vineyards. There's an acclaimed restaurant and spa.

For places to stay in Gold Country, see p97

CAMPFIRE95666/SHUTTERSTOCK

Above: Folsom Powerhouse Museum and State Park (p81); Right: Placer County Courthouse (p77)

Researched by
Esther Carlstone

Gold Country

LOVELY TOWNS FILLED WITH HISTORY

Discover the hidden towns that put the gold in Golden State. They're rich in heritage, nature and wine tasting.

A visit to Gold Country feels like traveling back in time. Historic buildings in their original glory, clapboard saloons, oak-lined byways and even the clip-clopping of horses all nod to the rich history of the area, famously known as the home of the Gold Rush of 1849.

After a sparkle in the American River caught James Marshall's eye in 1848, more than 300,000 prospectors from around the world streamed into the Sierra foothills and began digging for gold. California soon entered statehood with the official motto 'Eureka,' cementing its place as the land of opportunity.

Though the forty-niners are long gone, their footprints remain. Scenic Highway 49 winds through sleepy towns and state parks alive with traces of the past – historical markers honoring both the thrill of discovery and the toll on Indigenous peoples and nonwhite laborers.

Beneath its relaxed pace, a beguiling culinary renaissance is brewing. Farm-to-table menus, ethnic-fusion cuisine and acclaimed chefs from Sacramento and San Francisco have given the region gastronomic cred. Travelers avoiding the crowds in Napa and Sonoma now head here for low-key wine tastings with equally stunning views.

Stay in a restored vintage hotel with architectural details you won't find elsewhere, modern amenities and maybe even a hidden speakeasy. Take a leisurely road trip through its many beguiling towns and uncover this off-the-beaten-path treasure.

DEVIN POWERS/SHUTTERSTOCK

THE MAIN AREAS

Find Your Way

The Gold Country's core from Nevada City to Sonora can be driven in only a couple hours on the region's spine, Hwy 49, which means most of your time will be spent happily exploring and not driving.

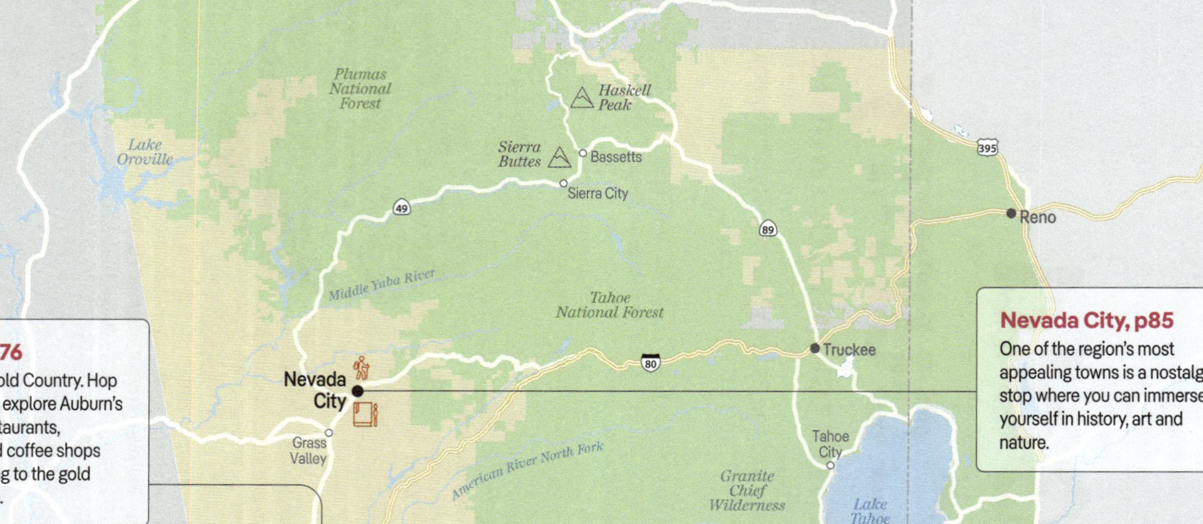

Auburn, p76
The soul of Gold Country. Hop off the I-80 to explore Auburn's Old Town, restaurants, breweries and coffee shops before heading to the gold discovery site.

Nevada City, p85
One of the region's most appealing towns is a nostalgic stop where you can immerse yourself in history, art and nature.

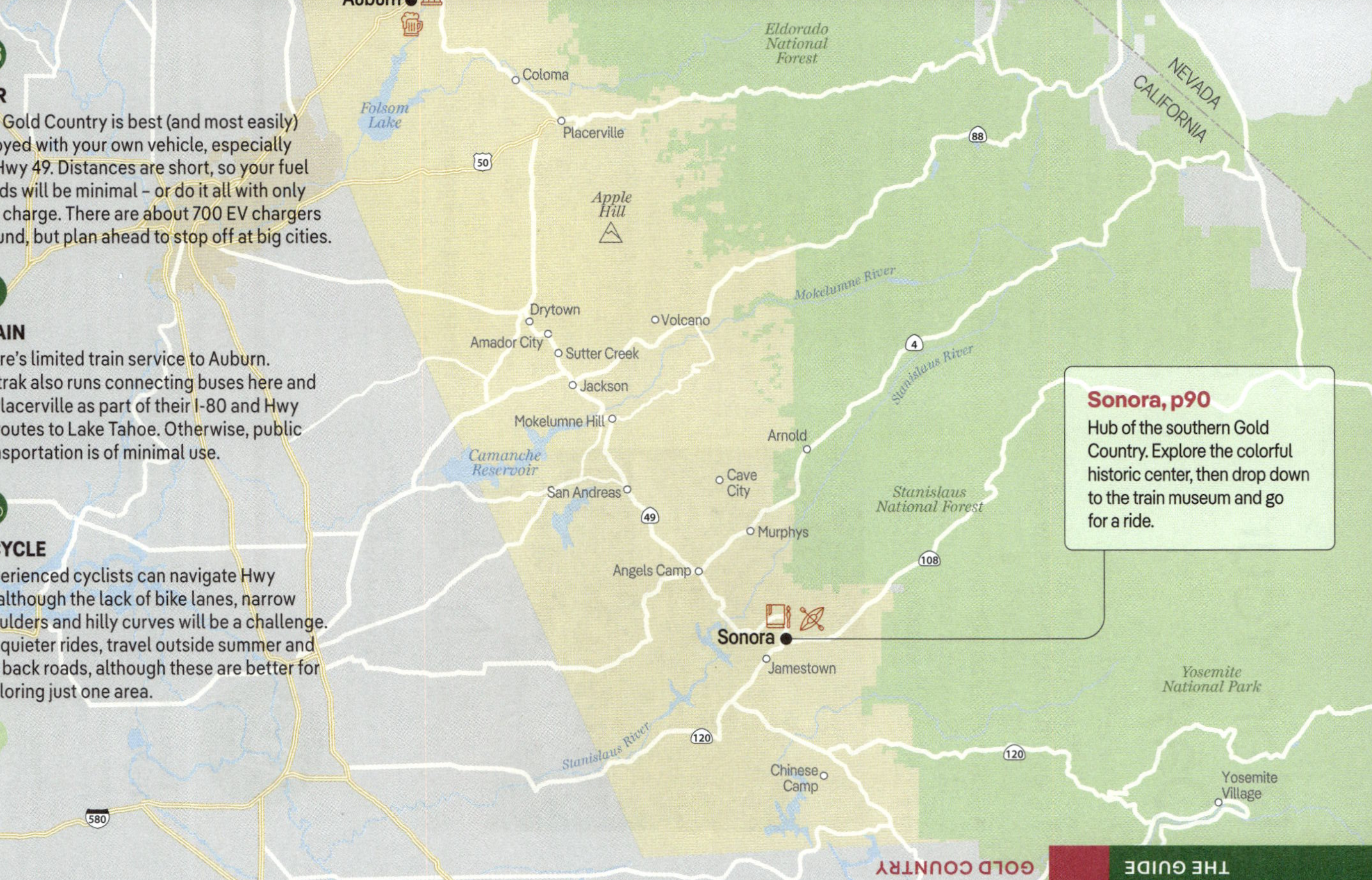

CAR

The Gold Country is best (and most easily) enjoyed with your own vehicle, especially up Hwy 49. Distances are short, so your fuel needs will be minimal – or do it all with only one charge. There are about 700 EV chargers around, but plan ahead to stop off at big cities.

TRAIN

There's limited train service to Auburn. Amtrak also runs connecting buses here and to Placerville as part of their I-80 and Hwy 50 routes to Lake Tahoe. Otherwise, public transportation is of minimal use.

BICYCLE

Experienced cyclists can navigate Hwy 49, although the lack of bike lanes, narrow shoulders and hilly curves will be a challenge. For quieter rides, travel outside summer and use back roads, although these are better for exploring just one area.

Sonora, p90

Hub of the southern Gold Country. Explore the colorful historic center, then drop down to the train museum and go for a ride.

Plan Your Days

Your time in Gold Country won't be spent on the road – it's less than 125 miles between Nevada City and Sonora, which gives you plenty of time to fill with historic sights, hikes, wineries and beguiling towns.

LARA RED/SHUTTERSTOCK

Marshall Gold Discovery State Historic Park (p79)

If You Only Do One Thing

- Drive on Hwy 49 between the compelling towns of **Auburn** (p76) on I-80 and **Placerville** (p80) on Hwy 50. You'll get a taste of the region's awe-inspiring scenery filled with rolling foothills, flowing rivers and lush forests. This route will take you by the **Marshall Gold Discovery State Historic Park** (p79), the origin of Gold Country's name. This multifaceted park can easily occupy half a day if you decide to explore and hike, or just a couple of hours, giving you plenty of time to hit up wine tasting. To really maximize your time, stop at a local shop and pick up some charcuterie or sandwiches to picnic by the American River.

- Meanwhile, the two bookend towns are vintage delights with great eating and drinking. When it's time to wind down, head over to **Restaurant Josephine** (p78) in Auburn for an elegant sit-down meal.

Seasonal Highlights

Whether peak spring and summer months or the quiet of the winter season, there's always something to see, do and eat.

JANUARY

Gold Country towns hold special events and festivals around the January 24 **anniversary of gold's discovery**.

MAY

Angels Camp hops for joy at the **Calaveras County Fair & Jumping Frog Jubilee** (p95) held the third weekend of each May. Look out for the Destruction Derby to close out the weekend.

JUNE

Look for **farm tours and u-pick offers** as you drive Hwy 49 through the prime summer growing season.

Three Days to Travel Around

● Three days is the sweet spot for a visit to Gold Country. You can fully enjoy the essential **Auburn**, **Marshall Gold Discovery State Historic Park** (p79) and **Placerville** with enough leisurely time for detours. You can also venture along the essential portions of Hwy 49 north and south.

● The former includes the can't-miss treasure that is **Nevada City** (p85), where you can stroll the wonderful town center and hike into the countryside. The latter gives you a rapid-fire succession of charmers, including **Sutter Creek** (p83), **Angels Camp** (p95), **Columbia** (p94), **Sonora** (p90) and **Jamestown** (p93). Cozy **Murphys** (p93) is the briefest of worthy detours. Fill your days with wine-tasting and frolic.

With More Time

● Take the many fascinating detours off Hwy 49. Tiny **Volcano** (p84) and the meaningful **Indian Grinding Rock State Historic Park** (p84) are on one of the best back roads into the Sierras.

● Venture north to remote **Downieville** (p88) and **Sierra City** (p89) for alpine action. Stop off at **Columbia State Historic Park** (p94), filled with nostalgia and gold mining history. Go white-water rafting on the **American River** (p91). Wander curvy country roads to taste wine in **Amador County** (p82) and **pick apples** (p80) east of Placerville. Take a haunted ghost tour in **Placerville** (p80). Check out local breweries in **Auburn** (p76). Spend a night in the historic small towns of **Nevada City** (p85), **Grass Valley** (p87), **Sutter Creek** (p83), **Murphys** (p93) and **Columbia** (p94) and soak up the timeless vibe.

JULY

No 4th of July in Gold Country is complete without the **Folsom Pro Rodeo** (p82), culminating in a patriotic fireworks show. Amador County stages its huge **county fair** in Plymouth near the end of the month.

AUGUST

The Sierra foothills are hot and you'll find **music festivals** across Gold Country, most with a country-and-western or rock theme.

OCTOBER

Amador County vineyards host the three-day **Big Crush Harvest Festival** (p82), featuring special wines, food and music.

DECEMBER

Postcard-perfect **Nevada City** becomes a Christmas card of joyous events each Sunday before December 25.

Auburn

ENDURANCE SPORTS | LOCAL BEER | SCENIC NATURE

TOP TIP

Wander the brick-paved sidewalks of Historic Downtown while you browse among antique shops, boutiques, cafes and popular local restaurants. Grab a locally-brewed pint at the always lively **Auburn Alehouse** (p78).

Often considered the heart of Gold Country and the 'Endurance Sport Capital of the World,' Auburn is the region's largest town and steeped in gold-rush charm. A towering 45-ton statue of French gold panner Claude Chana greets visitors, while ice-cream shops, antique stores and historic districts add to its appeal. Once a key stop on the Central Pacific's transcontinental route, Auburn remains lively thanks to the Union Pacific line, a growing wine- and ale-tasting trail and a scenic landscape known for cycling, trail running and other heartpounding activities.

At its center, the domed 1898 Placer County Courthouse bridges the gap between the Old Town's kitschy, restored streets and the more polished Historic Downtown. Auburn thrived as the Placer County seat while other gold-rush towns faded and today it's a favorite stop for I-80 travelers heading between the Bay Area and the Sierras – an ideal base for your Gold Country adventure.

Touring Gold Country History

History-filled museums

Stroll the Old Town for buildings dating to the 1850s – all with free admission. For online information, go to *placer.ca.gov* and navigate to each museum via the Experience Placer tab. On the south side, the **Bernhard Museum Complex**, built

GETTING AROUND

Downtown and Old Town Auburn are compact enough to get around on foot or scooter. To explore other parts, you'll be better off in a car or renting a bike or e-bike. As the public transit gateway to Gold Country, Amtrak's Capital Corridor runs one train daily to Sacramento and Bay Area, with Thruway buses extending to Sacramento and Reno. Auburn Transit and Placer County Transit have buses that operate daily routes within town and to connect you to Nevada City and Grass Valley on weekdays, but it'll be slow-going.

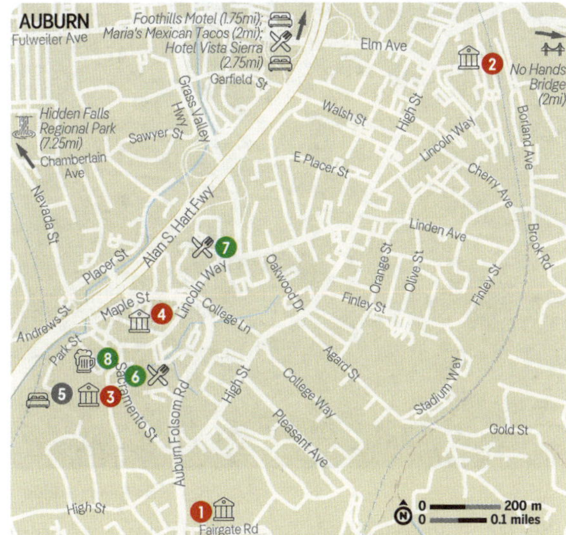

- **SIGHTS**
  1 Bernhard Museum Complex
  2 Gold Rush Museum
  3 Joss House
  4 Placer County Museum
- **SLEEPING**
  5 Park Victorian
- **EATING**
  6 Restaurant Josephine
  7 The Pour Choice
- **DRINKING & NIGHTLIFE**
  8 Auburn Alehouse

in 1851 as the Traveler's Rest Hotel and later serving as the home of the Bernhard family, exhibits depictions of typical 19th-century farm life. Volunteers in period garb show you around. Open 11am to 4pm Tuesday to Sunday.

Rebuilt by the Yue family in the 1920s after a mysterious fire, the clapboard **Joss House** *(auburnjosshouse.org)* stands on 'Chinese Hill,' one of many Chinese communities established during the gold rush and gives an intimate look at what life was like for Chinese laborers back then. Tours run every Saturday between 10.30am and 2.30pm.

The 1st floor of the historic **courthouse** is home to the **Placer County Museum**. It has Native American artifacts, a 1877 stage coach and a gold collection featuring huge chunks of unrefined gold. Open 10am to 4pm.

Up in the Historic Downtown in the old Auburn train station, the kid-friendly interactive **Gold Rush Museum** includes a reconstructed mine and gold panning. Open Thursday to Sunday from 10.30am to 4pm.

Venture just a short distance south along Hwy 49 for a deeper taste of Gold Country, including the site where gold was discovered.

Nature's Bounty

Hike in the hills

Auburn is home to many scenic trails with some real not-so-hidden gems. A moderate 4.9-mile round-trip hike through oak-studded hills leads you to **Hidden Falls**, a secluded 30-foot waterfall that feels like a secret garden, especially stunning when spring blooms are at their full glory.

AUBURN'S HIDDEN GEMS

Tammy Cleek, local educator and mom of three

Auburn is known for its gold-rush roots and endurance sports, but its hidden gems shine just as bright. Local shops, galleries, markets and festivals reflect a strong community spirit. Favorites include **Old Town Gallery**, the Saturday **Foothill Farmers' Market**, coffee stops and hikes to **Hidden Falls** (p77) or **No Hands Bridge**. Don't miss the **Placer Artists Tour** in November and Old Town Christmas in December. From microbreweries with food trucks to foothill vineyard picnics, Auburn is full of charm and family-friendly adventures.

BOB REYNOLDS/SHUTTERSTOCK

No Hands Bridge

Not far off, the **No Hands Bridge** trail delivers gold-rush vibes with a thrill. Built in 1912 without railings (hence the name), this lofty stone bridge once carried trains and mules over the American River. Don't worry, there are safety rails across the whole bridge now and it's a favorite for hikers and trail runners chasing epic views and fresh canyon air. The relatively easy two-mile walk from the Western States Trail is suitable for all experience levels and families.

EATING & DRINKING IN AUBURN: OUR PICKS

Pour Choice: Downtown coffee shop that serves top-notch pastries, sandwiches and even cocktails. *7am-7pm Sun-Wed, to 9pm Thu & Sat* $$

Restaurant Josephine: Local go-to for a special occasion; dine on seasonal French cuisine in a handsome brick building. *5-9pm Tue-Thu, 4-10 pm Fri & Sat* $$$

Auburn Alehouse: Popular craft brewery with an expansive patio and local beers paired with gastropub fare. *11am-10pm Fri-Sat, to 9pm Sun, 11.30am-9pm Mon-Thu* $$

Maria's Mexican Tacos: Indulge in Maria's authentic tacos, burritos, tortas and fajitas right off the 80 at this local favorite. *10am-8pm Tue-Sat* $$

Beyond Auburn

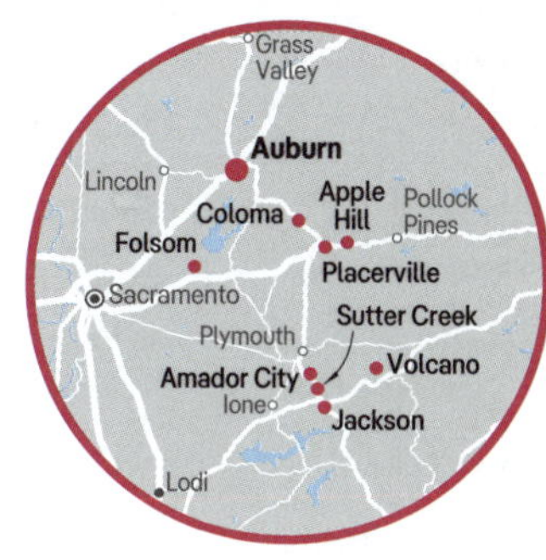

The spine of Gold Country, Hwy 49, winds through the hills, linking towns brimming with 1850s appeal.

In the heart of the pine-and oak-covered Sierra foothills, this is where gold was first discovered – Spanish-speaking settlers named it El Dorado County after the mythical city of riches. Today, visitors discover evocative hillsides dotted with historic towns, sun-soaked terraces and the fertile soil of one of California's burgeoning wine-growing regions. This central part of Gold Country comprises some of its most compelling sights – and that's after you've spent a few engrossing hours in the very place where a glint of gold caught James Marshall's eye in 1948. Surprises abound, including an amazing Native American site that's thousands of years old. This is the most visited portion of Gold Country. Travel here midweek if possible to avoid weekend crowds and prices.

Places

Coloma

TIME FROM AUBURN: **30MIN**

Where the gold rush began

The **Marshall Gold Discovery State Historic Park** *(parks.ca.gov; $10 per car)* comprises a fascinating collection of buildings in a lovely riverside setting at the site of James Marshall's discovery. A half-hour drive southeast of Auburn, the park is a tranquil setting where many bring picnics and spend the day exploring and relaxing by the water. The museum provides easily digested background on the discovery, including stories of some of the forgotten early settlers, such as a group of African Americans.

There's a fascinating replica of Sutter's Mill, which (figuratively) put the wheels in motion that led to finding gold. Follow a short path along the south fork of the American River to the place where James Marshall made his fateful discovery and started the revolutionary birth of the 'Golden State,' with its horrific consequences for the state's Indigenous people.

Check out the displays on panning and hydraulic mining, along with the 1860 Wah Hop Chinese Store. Try your hand at gold panning or head off the beaten path on a hike bathed in wildflowers in the spring (just beware the poison ivy).

GETTING AROUND

Amtrak runs Thruway buses that stop in Placerville on their route between Sacramento and Lake Tahoe via Hwy 50. Otherwise, the only way to easily travel through the region is with your own wheels. There are chargers for EV vehicles in most of the towns, but it'd be smart to charge up in Auburn or Placerville where they're plentiful.

ALL THAT GLITTERS IS TRAGIC

John Sutter, who had a fort in Sacramento (p44), partnered with James Marshall to build a sawmill on the swift stretch of the American River at Coloma in 1847. It was Marshall who discovered gold here on January 24, 1848 and though the men tried to keep their findings secret, prospectors from around the world stampeded into town. In one of the ironies of the gold rush, the men who made this discovery died nearly penniless. Many of the new immigrants who arrived seeking fortune were indentured, taxed and bamboozled out of anything they found. Meanwhile, the world of the local Native American Nisenan people was collapsing due to disease and displacement.

Monumental hikes

The **James Marshall Monument** marks the spot where the man was buried in 1885, a penniless ward of the state. You can drive a short road here, but it's much better to meander on foot up to the monument, which overlooks the discovery site.

A three-mile **hike** follows a steep route up from Coloma. Take High St from the town center, then Marshall Park Way, winding through oak woodland to the monument, via James Marshall's barebones cabin and an 1865 Catholic church and pioneer cemetery. You then join the **Monroe Ridge Trail**, which leads along the ridge, looping back down into Coloma.

For a hike that honors the legacy of the many Chinese miners and laborers, hit the 2.5-mile **Gam Saan Trail** that links the discovery site with **Hennigsen Lotus Park**, a small riverfront park built on the site of Chinese mining camps.

Placerville

TIME FROM AUBURN: **1HR**

The Old West comes alive

Pronounced PLASS-er-ville, locals cherish its wild reputation as 'Hangtown' – a name earned when a handful of men swung from the gallows in the mid-1800s after stealing from other miners. It's a character-filled hideaway to explore while traveling on Hwys 49 and 50.

Busy Main St may look like a movie set, but it's lined with stores catering to local needs, which save Placerville from sugary artificiality. Most of the buildings date to the 1850s, including the spindly **Bell Tower**, a relic that once rallied volunteer firefighters. About a mile north of town, **Hangtown's Gold Bug Park & Mine** *(goldbugpark.org; free, tour adult/youth $12/8)* stands on the site of four mining claims that yielded gold from 1849 to 1888. You can pan for gold and visit the working blacksmith's shop or descend into a mine for a self-guided audio tour.

Save your sweet tooth for **Annabelle's Chocolate Lounge**, a fantastic chocolate shop (with wine tasting!) in El Dorado, 5 miles southwest of Placerville. It's open 11am to 6pm daily except Sunday.

Apple Hill

TIME FROM AUBURN: **1HR**

Bounties of farms and vineyards

Bountiful Apple Hill, a 20-sq-mile area east of Placerville and north of Hwy 50, has more than 50 orchards, farms and wineries. Growers sell directly to the public, usually from August

EATING & DRINKING BEYOND AUBURN: OUR PICKS

Argonaut: Coffee and Provisions: Local beer, breakfast, sandwiches and gelato in the heart of Coloma. *7.30am-2.30pm* $

Savory Pies of the World: Tiny spot on Placerville's Main St, serving delicious and savory pies. A top lunch stop. *noon-7.30pm Mon-Thu* $

Taste: List of top regional wines paired with creative California cuisine in Plymouth. *hours vary, closed Tue* $$

Element: Serving breakfast, dinner and great cocktails in Sutter Creek. *8am-noon Sat & Sun, 5-8pm Wed-Sat* $$$

PAUL BRADY PHOTOGRAPHY/SHUTTERSTOCK

Placerville

to December and some let you pick your own; bakeries offer all manner of apple treats. Plan on 90 minutes driving to get here from Auburn. One Saturday a month, **Wakamatsu Farm** *(arconservancy.org/wakamatsu; $10 per car)* opens its gates to the public to learn more about the site of the first Japanese settlement in America and the Wakamatsu Tea and Silk Farm Colony.

Folsom

TIME FROM AUBURN: **30MIN**

Follow in the footsteps of Johnny Cash

The town that became Folsom began – like so many others – during the early days of the gold rush. Its position on the American River proved fortuitous as early dams spurred developments like the state's first commercial electrical generation, an accomplishment preserved at the **Powerhouse Museum and State Park** *(parks.ca.gov)*. The 19th-century downtown is a walkable delight. Just upstream, **Folsom State Prison** is the place Johnny Cash immortalized in 'Folsom Prison Blues.' It's an easy 30-minute drive southwest from Auburn.

BEST TOURS TO RAFT THE AMERICAN RIVER

Wet River Trips *(raftwet.com)* Family-run outfitter running tours on South, North and Middle Forks; around since 1978.

Raft America *(raftcalifornia.com)* Operates on South, North, Middle and Lower Middle Forks. Some tours can be combined with wine tasting.

Mother Lode River Center *(malode.com)* In business since 1947, has tours on the South, Middle and North Forks. Each boat accommodates six or eight guests.

All-Outdoors *(aorafting.com)* Family-owned company that's been around over 60 years. They run a 'Tom Sawyer Float Trip' for young kids.

OARS *(oars.com)* One of the world's biggest whitewater rafting operators. Offers a variety of itineraries and combo trips.

EATING BEYOND AUBURN: OUR PICKS

Gold Dust Pizza: Loaded crisp pizzas in a location surrounded by wine tasting-rooms in Sutter Creek. *11am-8pm* $$

Mel & Faye's Diner: Retro Jackson diner with a modern verve. Great versions of all the classics from breakfast to dinner. *5am-10pm Mon-Fri, to 11pm Sat & Sun* $

Timmy's Brown Bag: Creative sandwich shop in Placerville serving spam and kimchi and smoked oyster sammies, tacos and more. *11am-3pm Sun-Thu, to 5pm Fri & Sat* $

Volcano Union Pub: Vintage hotel-saloon with the best restaurant in the Volcano area. Creative, seasonal food. *4.30-8pm Mon & Fri, noon-8pm Sun & Sat* $$

PLACER WINE & ALE TRAIL

Mt Vernon Winery *(mtvernonwinery.com)* Escape to this countryside retreat with rolling vineyards and a cozy patio perfect for lazy afternoons.

Casque Wines *(casquewines.com)* A sweet unassuming tasting room. Summer concerts on the patio make for an ambiance-filled afternoon.

Miraflores Winery *(mirafloreswinery.com)* Sip award-winning wines on the patio, at the bar, or in the barrel room – plus build-your-own charcuterie.

Knee Deep Brewing Co. *(kneedeepbrewing.com)* Family-run microbrewery pouring hoppy IPAs just steps from where they're brewed.

PaZa Winery *(pazawines.com)* Relax in Adirondack chairs, soak up the scenery and sip a refreshing glass of ice-cold rosé.

Wild West thrills

Every year around the 4th of July, the **Folsom Pro Rodeo** rides into town for a quintessential small-town patriotic celebration. A tradition since 1960, you can expect to find all the rodeo classics: barrel racing, bull riding, ropers, cowboy entertainers, livestock and more. Each night of the rodeo culminates with a dazzling fireworks show.

Amador City

TIME FROM AUBURN: **70MIN**

Vintage shops and back door walks

Right off Hwy 49, Amador City was once home to the Keystone Mine – one of the most prolific gold producers in California. It's now known as the smallest city in the state with a population of 200 as of the 2020 census. It's sweet and quaint: antique shops, wine tasting rooms and cafes line the main drag. Grab a drink or a fresh meal at the recently remodeled Imperial Hotel. Getting here from Auburn is a one-hour drive south.

From cowboy boots to wine festivals

Amador County may be home to lots of small towns, but it's also home to several annual events that are big on charm. The Amador County Fair, touted as 'The Happiest Place on Dirt,' is packed with carnival games, livestock showings, rodeo-style events, live music and so much more. The fairground in Plymouth hosts the fair every late July or early August and sees over 20,000 visitors each year.

For wine lovers, the **Big Crush Harvest Festival** runs over a weekend in October in over 45 family-run wineries across the county and is a two-day celebration of the grape and the robust harvest it provides. Visitors get a behind-the-scenes

CAMPFIRE95666/SHUTTERSTOCK

Mokelumne Hill

peek at the harvesting process while they enjoy sampling wine among picturesque vineyards and blue skies. Think wine stompings, barrel tastings and live music.

Sutter Creek

TIME FROM AUBURN: **75MIN**

Iconic gold-rush town

Perch on the balcony of one of the gracefully restored buildings on this particularly scenic Main St and view Sutter Creek, a gem of a Gold Country town with raised arcade sidewalks and high-balconied buildings with false fronts.

With a town walking-tour map from the **Sutter Creek Visitor Center** explore the 1860s buildings, many bearing traces of the homelands of the Cornish, Yugoslavian and Italian immigrants who built them. **Miners Bend Park** at the town's south end offers history in the open air. There are many good food and lodging options and a dozen wine tasting-rooms.

Jackson

TIME FROM AUBURN: **80MIN**

Get off the beaten path

Jackson has historic buildings and a small downtown, but it feels more functional than alluring. The main attraction is the **Kennedy Gold Mine** *(kennedygoldmine.com; adult/child $7/3)*. The ominous steel headframe is 125ft high and the shafts date to 1860. Guided tours take you around the site.

The somewhat undiscovered settlement of **Mokelumne Hill** is 7 miles south of Jackson. Settled by French trappers in the early 1840s, it's a good place to see historic buildings without a glut of antique stores and gift shops. Driving here from Auburn takes about 90 minutes, but plan on many stops along the way.

HAUNTED HISTORY

Given its rich gold-rush history, it's no surprise that Amador County is also filled with supernatural lore. Towns like Jackson and Ione have long been rumored to be haunted. About 14 miles southwest of Amador City in Ione, **Preston Castle** in particular –a former reform school – is considered a hotspot for ghost hunters. A housekeeper was reportedly murdered there in the 1950s and is said to still roam the halls. Spooky fans can take tours of the castle around Halloween for the ultimate scare. The iconic **National Hotel** (p97) in Jackson is also said to be haunted, with visitors reporting flickering lights that some believe are caused by long-gone miners and gamblers who never checked out. Room 215 is particularly notorious.

DANITA DELIMONT/SHUTTERSTOCK

Miwok roundhouse

Volcano

TIME FROM AUBURN: 1½HR

Nostalgic sleepy town

One of the fading plaques in Volcano, 12 miles upstream from the town of Sutter Creek, calls it a place of 'quiet history.' Even though the little L-shaped village on the bank of Sutter Creek yielded tons of gold and a Civil War battle, today it slumbers away in remote solitude. It exudes an end-of-the-road vibe, even if the road eventually joins Hwy 88 in the Sierras. Winding your way here from Auburn is a commitment. Little Sutter Creek is lined with large sandstone rocks that were blasted from surrounding hills by hydraulic mining before being scraped clean of their gold.

In continuous use since 1852, the fantastically atmospheric **Sizemore Country Store** has creaky floorboards and a long wooden counter. You can get a simple burger and a beer from the cooler.

Native heritage

Indian Grinding Rock State Historic Park (*parks.ca.gov, $8 per car*) is a sacred area for the local Miwok. The awe-inspiring centerpiece is a limestone outcrop covered with 360 faint petroglyphs – some over 2000 years old – and more than 1100 ancient mortar holes called *chaw'se*, used for grinding acorns and seeds into meal.

There's a small museum, a traditional wooden roundhouse and a village site. The Miwok continue to hold ceremonies here featuring crafts, dances and games. Look for the display of elaborate feathered dance capes. Trails weave through the park with signs describing the plants and animals and their significance to the Miwok. The park is in a lonely patch of forest on the road to the equally lonely town of Volcano.

Nevada City

QUAINT BUILDINGS | NATURE HIKES | LIVE MUSIC

A real-life *Gilmore Girls'* Stars Hollow exists in California – Nevada City. The main draw is the town itself: a perfect blend of restored brick buildings, wrought-iron trims and deep gold-rush history. Its walkable streets are lively in summer and transform into a snow-dusted Victorian wonderland in December, earning national praise as one of the best Christmas towns in the US. Signs in shop windows reflect the residents' progressive spirit.

Cultural life is central here. The 1856 Miners Foundry, once a site for manufacturing Pelton water wheels, now serves as a vibrant arts center, hosting music, theater, dance and festivals. The brick Nevada Theatre, dating to 1865, has welcomed legends like Jack London and Mark Twain and now hosts independent films and live performances. The Onyx Theatre adds to the town's creative charm with unusual film series and community events. Nevada City's warm, bohemian heart makes it a town worth returning to.

TOP TIP

Nevada City is quickly becoming a hotspot for live music in the Sierra Nevada Foothills, so be sure to check out the calendar of events at local watering holes like Crazy Horse Saloon & Grill, Golden Era and Stone House to catch a rousing show while you're in town.

Gold Country's Star Town

Walking Nevada City

You can stroll around this charming town in just an hour if you're in a hurry, but it's best to take a leisurely stroll stopping to eat, drink and shop along the way. Begin at **Firehouse No 1 Museum** *(nevadacountyhistory.org)*, a stately 1861 building and home to a small exhibit featuring curated items that tell the story of the local people, from stunning Nisenan baskets to preserved Victorian bridal wear. The prize exhibits are relics from the Chinese settlers who often built but seldom profited from the mines. It's open Wednesday to Sunday from May to October.

GETTING AROUND

The heart of Nevada City is extremely strollable and can be seen on foot in just a couple hours. Even many of the popular hiking trails can be accessed via walking or bikes. Local buses provide limited service. A few weekday buses serve Auburn and Colfax, where you can connect to Amtrak buses and trains.

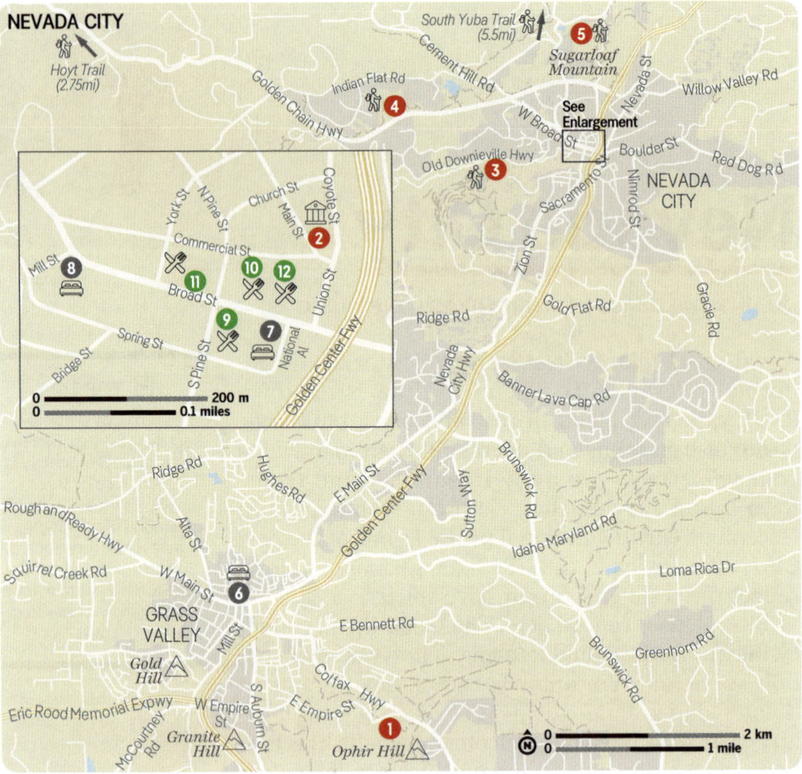

SIGHTS
1 Empire Mine State Historic Park
2 Firehouse No 1 Museum

ACTIVITIES
3 Deer Creek Tribute Trail
4 Hirshman Trail
5 Sugarloaf Mountain

SLEEPING
6 Holbrooke Hotel
7 National Exchange Hotel
8 Two Room Inn

EATING
9 Communal Cafe
10 Heartwood Eatery
11 Java Johns
12 Three Forks Bakery & Brewing Co

DRINKING IN NEVADA CITY: COZY COFFEE SPOTS

Three Forks Bakery & Brewing Co: Come for the organic and fair trade coffee, stay for fresh pastries. *8am-8pm Mon-Thu, to 9pm Fri & Sat* **$$**

Communal Cafe: Hipster menu items like mushroom coffee and a vibrant butterfly pea matcha pair well with their farm-to-table fare. *7am-6pm* **$**

Heartwood Eatery: Signature lattes, like their fragrant rose cardamom latte, nourishing bowls and farm fresh salads make this a local go-to. *10am-4pm* **$$**

Java Johns: Homey family joint with extensive coffee and tea menu. Prepare to wait during the weekends. *7am-2pm Mon-Fri, to 4pm Sat & Sun* **$**

Follow Commercial St to numbers 309 to 316. These are the tiny survivors of the 19th-century Chinese Quarter. The South Yuba Canal Building (1855) is among the town's oldest. The renovated **National Exchange Hotel** (p97) *(thenationalexchangehotel.com)* welcomed its first guest in 1854 and is still the best place to stay in town and to sample a craft cocktail. Take a break at **Three Forks Bakery & Brewing Co** (p86), which has something for everyone: great beers and coffee, luscious baked goods and artisanal pizzas.

Grass Valley

Tiny town with rich history

Only four miles southwest, Grass Valley is the smaller and quieter stepsister of Nevada City. But dig into the attractive downtown and you'll find a dense cluster of Victorian and art deco buildings and great independent boutiques and cafes. Head to **Empire Mine State Historic Park** *(entry $5)* to awe at some of the state's oldest shaft mines. Rest your head or grab a four-star dinner at the gorgeously redone **Holbrooke Hotel** (p97) *(holbrooke.com)* - and don't miss the hidden speakeasy in the basement.

NEVADA CITY'S BEST HIKES

Deer Creek Tribute Trail: Popular hike that starts downtown and leads to the woods. Follow signs to the Angkula Seo Suspension Bridge or the Chinese Tribute Bridge.

Hirshman Trail: Tranquil, 4.1-mile round-trip walk through wooded scenery leading to Hirschman's Pond. Especially stunning in the fall.

Sugarloaf Mountain: Short 1.8-mile round-trip trail that offers fantastic views of the town and surrounding landscape.

Hoyt Trail: Moderate 1.6-mile scenic river walk that leads to swimming holes along the South Yuba River and Hoyt Crossing.

South Yuba Trail: For the adventurous hiker or mountain biker, a portion of this quiet 20-mile trail takes you along the South Yuba River.

Beyond Nevada City

Civilization disappears as you ascend Hwy 49 into the Sierras. The drama of the gold rush is replaced by pure wilderness awe.

Places

GETTING AROUND

The towns outside of Nevada City are best reached with your own vehicle, especially if you plan on hitting up a few in one day. If you're driving an EV, charge up at one of the over 20 chargers in Grass Valley. Parking in most places is plentiful, especially during non-peak seasons. Public transportation is limited and infrequent.

The forty-niners hit it big in Nevada County – the richest score in the region known as the Mother Lode. Beyond the resulting wealth you can see written on the facades of Nevada City, you'll find lovely, remote wilderness areas, a clutch of historic parks and fascinating remnants of the long-gone miners, including a ghost town. The northernmost segment of Hwy 49 follows the North Yuba River through some stunning, isolated parts of the Sierra Nevada, known for great wilderness adventure. An entire lifetime outdoors could hardly cover the trail network that hikers, mountain bikers and skiers blaze every season. In summer, snow remains at the highest elevations and many places have roaring fireplaces year-round.

Downieville

TIME FROM NEVADA CITY: **70MIN**

Mountain biking, monster hiking

The biggest town in remote Sierra County (though that's not saying much), Downieville is located at the confluence of the North Yuba and Downie rivers. With a reputation that quietly rivals Moab (Utah), this is one of the premier places for mountain-biking in the US and a staging area for true wilderness adventures. By car, it's a winding one-hour drive from Nevada City. The **Downieville Downhill**, a world-class mountain biking trail, shoots riders over the Sierra Buttes and a molar-rattling 5000ft down into town. There are plenty of other scenic biking trails to explore, including Chimney Rock, Empire Creek and Rattlesnake Creek. Operators like **Downieville Outfitters** and **Yuba Expeditions** will take care of all the logistics for you, including mountain bike rentals, guided tours and shuttles to popular trails. June to September are peak biking season, although the fall months through November offer cooler temperatures and lovely foliage. As with most gold-rush towns, it wasn't always fun and games: the first justice of the peace was the local barkeep and a placard tells the story of the racist mob that hanged a Chicana woman named Josefa on the town bridge in 1851, the only recorded lynching of a woman in California.

Sierra City

TIME FROM NEVADA CITY: **1½HR**

Rugged mountains, fantastic fishing

Sierra City is the primary supply station for people headed to the **Sierra Buttes**, a rugged, rocky shock of mountains that are probably the closest thing to the Alps you'll find in California without hoisting a backpack. It's also the last supply point for people headed into the fishing paradise of the Lakes Basin. There's just one main drag in town and all commerce happens here. The hotels have the best restaurants – when they're open, that is. Wintertime is quiet.

Hiking for views

The area is rife with beautiful hikes for all experience levels, all with Instagram-worthy views. For families or those who want a more leisurely stroll, **Loves Falls** is just a short walk from the intersection of Hwy 49 and the Pacific Crest Trail. The easily walkable half-mile path takes you to a cascading waterfall nestled under an arched stone bridge, where taking a photo is a must. Those seeking a more challenging hike won't be disappointed by the **Sierra Buttes Fire Lookout**, which on clear days offers panoramic views all the way to Mt Shasta and Lake Tahoe. It's five miles each way and a vigorous climb through a forest, followed by a steep set of stairs to end up at the old fire lookout perched on a rocky bluff – be sure to pack plenty of fluids.

Malakoff Diggins State Historic Park

TIME FROM NEVADA CITY: **40MIN**

Digging into the past

An otherworldly testament to the mechanical determination of the gold hunt, **Malakoff Diggins State Historic Park** *(parks.ca.gov, $10 per car)* is a place to get lost on fern-lined trails and take in the raw beauty of a landscape recovering from brutal hydraulic mining. There is a mesmerizing ghost town here. California's largest hydraulic mine left behind massive gold and crimson cliffs and small mountains of tailings. The forestland has recovered since the legal battles between mine owners and downstream farmers shut down the mine in 1884. Tours of the town provide the chance to see some impressive gold nuggets. The 1-mile **Diggins Loop Trail** is the quickest way to get a glimpse of the scarred moonscape.

WHY I LOVE SIERRA COUNTY

Esther Carlstone, Lonely Planet writer

There's something magical about Sierra County – and it definitely feels like one of California's best-kept secrets. I love how small towns like Downieville and Sierra City feel frozen in time. Having traveled the state extensively, I've yet to encounter any place quite like it. I've hiked wildflower-covered ridges, marveled at roaring waterfalls, panned for gold and eaten pie at mom-and-pop diners. It feels timeless and untouched – in a good way. There are no crowds or long lines for popular attractions: just miles and miles of nature-filled quiet where you can hear yourself think and remember why the great outdoors is so good for the soul.

EATING & DRINKING BEYOND NEVADA CITY: OUR PICKS

Two Rivers Cafe: Riverside gem with craft beer, wood-fired pizza, hearty burgers and a laid-back mountain vibe overlooking the river. *11am-9pm* $$

Red Moose: Cozy, welcoming cafe serving breakfast burritos, sandwiches and pastries in Sierra City. Perfect for post-hiking. *8am-3pm Wed-Sun* $

Sierra Pines Resort: Rustic lodge along the Yuba River serving hearty American fare with mountain views, cozy vibes and local charm. *8-11am & 5-8pm Mon-Sun* $$

La Cocina de Oro Taqueria: Homestyle Mexican food in Downieville with farm-to-table ingredients in a laid-back riverside setting. *11am-8pm Thu-Sat, to 5pm Sun* $

Sonora

MOUNTAIN GETAWAY | ARTISANAL SHOPS | VINTAGE CHARM

TOP TIP

Only 10 minutes southeast of Sonora but off-the-beaten-path, head to **Llamas of Circle Home** *(experiencellamas.com; $60)*, where you can meet, greet and help tend to the llamas. Reservations are required and can be made through an AirBnB link on their website.

Settled in 1848 by miners from Sonora, Mexico, this portion of the goldfields was once a cosmopolitan center of commerce and culture with parks, elaborate saloons and the Southern Mines' largest concentration of gamblers and gold. Racial unrest drove the Mexican settlers out and the American immigrant usurpers got rich on the Big Bonanza Mine, where Sonora High School now stands. That single mine yielded 12 tons of gold in two years (including a 28lb nugget).

Today, people en route to Yosemite National Park or starting the Hwy 49 Gold Country tour from the south use Sonora as a staging post. The historic center is so well preserved that it's a frequent backdrop in films. Washington St is the vintage main drag. Don't miss the 1885 Sonora Opera Hall, which was built on the bones of a flour mill. Local civic boosters built the grand courthouse with its landmark clock tower in 1898.

Untold Stories

Historic nuggets

In the former 1857 Tuolumne County Jail, you'll find the great little **Tuolumne County Museum** *(tchistory.org; free)*, with a fortune's worth of gold displayed in the form of nuggets and gold-bearing quartz. Each of the former jail cells spotlights a different theme, one of which is the little-told story of African

GETTING AROUND

Public transit is limited in the area, so the best way to see the highlights is really by car. While there's no direct Amtrak service, **YARTS** (Yosemite Area Regional Transportation System) offers limited seasonal bus routes, but they don't cover Sonora's main attractions. Top off your EV in nearby Modesto or Stockton, as there are few charging stations in town.

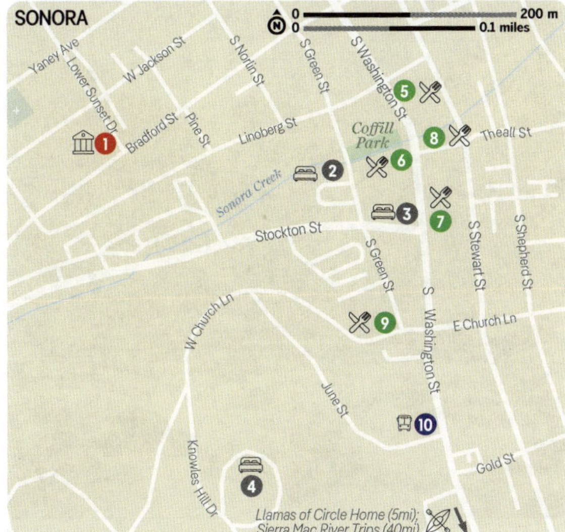

SIGHTS
1 Tuolumne County Museum

SLEEPING
2 Hotel Lumberjack
3 Sonora Inn
4 The Inn on Knowles Hill

EATING
5 Diamondback Grill
6 El Arroyo
7 Emberz Wood-Fired Foodz
8 Legends Books, Antiques & Old-Fashioned Soda Fountain
9 The Armory

TRANSPORTATION
10 YARTS

Americans during the gold rush. You can learn about former enslaved man William Suggs, who set up a leather harness business, built a mansion in the town and successfully campaigned to overturn segregation in local schools.

Running the Rapids

Ready, set, paddle!

Sonora is a popular white-water rafting base. The **Upper Tuolumne River** is known for exciting class IV and V rapids and beloved by adrenaline junkies, while the **Stanislaus River** is more accessible with class I to III rapids, making it more suited for first-timers and families. Both locally-owned and family-run **All-Outdoors California Whitewater Rafting** and **Sierra Mac River Trips** run tours of all the local rivers, including, ahem, fully immersive ones lasting several days. The best time of year to go rafting in the area is between April to June, after the snowmelt but before it gets blazing hot.

EATING & DRINKING IN SONORA: OUR PICKS

Emberz Wood-Fired Foodz: Popular local eatery with American fare and hand-crafted cocktails. *11.30am-9pm Sun-Thu, to 10pm Fri & Sat* $$

Diamondback Grill: Hearty American fare like grilled steaks and pasta with local wines. *11am-9pm Mon-Thu, to 9.30pm Fri & Sat, to 8pm Sun* $$

El Arroyo: Rejuvenate with a fresh juice (or margarita) and tender tacos, sizzling fajitas and filling burritos. *Thu-Sat 11am-9pm, to 8pm Sun-Tue* $$

The Armory: Lovely patio dining and beer garden with eclectic menu featuring salads, tacos, pasta, burgers and more. *11am-10pm Fri & Sat, to 9pm Sun, 4-9pm Tue-Thu* $$

THE BEST PLACES TO PAN FOR GOLD

For the casual gold-panner, it's easier (and more efficient) to go with a local outfitter or historic site that provides everything for you.

California Gold Panning *(gold-panning-california.com)* Jamestown outfitter provides all needed equipment at Woods Creek and beyond.

Marshall Gold Discovery State Historic Park The site where gold was first discovered offers gold panning lessons.

Roaring Camp Mining Co *(roaringcampgold.com)* Fish, hike, swim and pan for gold during an all-day tour in the Mokelumne River Canyon.

Columbia State Historic Park Take part in gold panning at Matelot Gulch then stroll historic Main St afterward.

SARAH CEBRYNSKI/SHUTTERSTOCK

Upper Tuolumne River (p91)

Sodas Above, Books Below

Browse vintage finds

Sonora has cafes and restaurants to rival those across Gold Country, but none compare to **Legends Books, Antiques & Old-Fashioned Soda Fountain**. This former bank is the place to sip sarsaparilla, snack on a Polish dog, quaff a beer or share a scoop of huckleberry ice cream at a 26ft-long mahogany bar that's been here since 1850. Then browse antiques and books downstairs in what was once a mine shaft – many of them lining the old tunnel that miners used to deposit their stash directly into the former bank.

Beyond Sonora

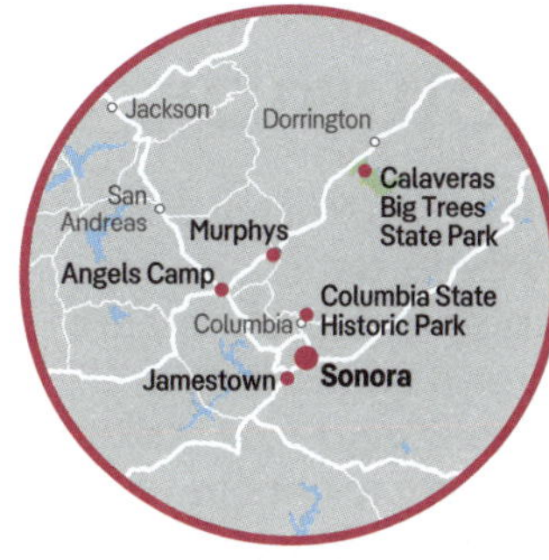

Wine, water and steam are just a few of the highlights in this region, which has some of Gold Country's most authentic sights.

The southern region of Gold Country is hot as blazes in the summer, so cruising through its historic gold-rush hubs will demand more than one stop for ice cream. The tall tales of yesteryear come alive through one of the region's most famous former residents: author Mark Twain got his start writing about a jumping frog contest in Calaveras County.

Adorable Murphys is a popular wine-tasting destination. Tasting-rooms line Main St Columbia preserves – and re-creates – an authentic gold-rush town in a noncommercial setting. Tiny Jamestown, in the shadow of Sonora, is home to one of the region's most popular sights, which is a dream destination for train fans. The historic towns in the region feature several old hotels that have been restored; they're the perfect antidote to the national chains.

Places

GETTING AROUND

A local transit system with five routes can get you around the county, from Sierra Village to Columbia and the Jamestown area, but it's much faster to drive. YARTS offers seasonal service along Hwy 120 and a stop at Chicken Ranch Casino Resort for those that want to head out to the national park area.

Jamestown

TIME FROM SONORA: **10MIN**

Scrappy Jamestown

Diminutive Jamestown is just 3 miles south of Sonora. Founded around the time of Tuolumne County's first gold strike in 1848, it has more authenticity than traffic- and tourist-thronged Sonora. Busy Hwy 49 bypasses Jamestown to the west. The usual antique stores fill dusty storefronts in the small center. **Railtown 1897 State Historic Park** (*railtown1897.org; adult/child $23/18*) is a short walk east; taking the 45-minute excursion ride on a historic train through the Gold Country from April to October is a must for train enthusiasts.

Murphys

TIME FROM SONORA: **30MIN**

Idyllic wine-tasting stop

Murphys is one of the more scenic communities along the southern stretch of Gold Country, befitting its nickname as 'Queen of the Sierra.' Its location 8 miles east of Hwy 49 gives it an appealing end-of-the-road quality. Wine bars and upscale pubs good for a pint abound – many, predictably,

TOP EXPERIENCE

Columbia State Historic Park

Step onto Main St and feel instantly transported to a bygone era. The state's largest concentration of historic gold-rush structures is a sight to behold – horse-drawn stagecoach and all – filled with storefronts original from the 19th-century, cafes and activities. In 1850, Columbia was founded as the 'Gem of the Southern Mines,' and as much as $150 million in gold was found here. It's only 10 minutes by car from Sonora.

MICHAEL VI/SHUTTERSTOCK

TOP TIPS

- If you come on a weekday, you may get stuck in the gridlock of multiple school field trips.
- Summer can get very hot so come first thing in the morning.
- Don't approach the feral cats – they're known to be inhospitable.

Experience Gold-Rush Life Firsthand

Steep yourself in period-appropriate activities to truly get a sense of the history. Pan for gold early in the day before the temperature rises. Stop at **Quartz Mountain Stage Line** *(qmcarriage.com; adult/child $11/10)* at the start of Main St and book a stagecoach ride. Head across the street to commemorate your day with vintage costumes and sepia-toned photographs at **Kamice's Photographic Establishment** *(10.30am-5pm)*. Pop into the bookshop and the emporium for souvenirs and spend some time in the bowling saloon.

Immerse Yourself in Gold-Rush History

Meet at the museum at 11am for a free guided tour or take a self-guided walking tour past the Calverie-Chinese store ruins, the old firehouse, Masonic lodge and the oldest two-story brick schoolhouse in the state.

Eat Lunch at an Old-Timey Saloon

Locals say the **St Charles Saloon** *(11am-8pm Sun-Thu, to 9pm Fri & Sat)* has some of the best pizza in the area. Don't forget to order sarsaparilla to wash it all down. Grab a pick-me-up at **Brown's Coffeehouse & Sweets Saloon** *(9am-5pm)*, home of locally loved brownies.

PRACTICALITIES

Scan the QR code for information on the park and tours.

with Murphys in the name and shamrocks on the wall. In a solid 1856 brick storefront, **Pop the Bubbly** has a name that says all you need to know. Strolling the postcard-size Main Street is a must. Drive out to idyllic **Ironstone Vineyards** *(ironstonevineyards.com)* and **Locke Vineyards** *(thebarnatlockevineyards.com)* for an even more picture-perfect day.

For kids and adults who like a sense of adventure with their cave tour, **Mercer Caverns** obliges. You'll walk a quarter of a mile on 440 twisting steps through the spectacular caverns. Think of it as a self-propelled thrill ride.

Angels Camp

TIME FROM SONORA: **20MIN**

Mark Twain's inspiration

On the southern stretch of Hwy 49, one figure looms over all others: literary giant Mark Twain, who got his first big break with the short story 'The Celebrated Jumping Frog of Calaveras County' (1865). It was written and set in Angels Camp and they make the most of it. There are gentlemanly Twain impersonators and statues and bronze frogs on Main St honoring jumping contest champions of the past. Today the town is an attractive mix of buildings, but does suffer from traffic on Hwys 4 and 49.

Calaveras County Fair and Jumping Frog Jubilee

If you're traveling through the area in May, check out one of California's quirkiest small-town traditions. The **Calaveras County Fair & Jumping Frog Jubilee** is a mash-up of a traditional quaint county fair filled with Americana, classic carnival rides, livestock, rodeo, fried foods and games with an actual competitive frog jumping content as inspired by Mark Twain's famous aforementioned tale. Set among majestic oak trees and rolling green hills, this four-day fair culminates with contestants encouraging their amphibian friends to leap as far as they can across a lily pad-covered stage. The current record belongs to Rosie the Ribetor who jumped over 21ft back in 1986. Anyone who can break her record will win $20,000.

Calaveras Big Trees State Park

TIME FROM SONORA: **45MIN**

Gold Country's biggest trees

In the forests above the foothills of Gold Country, few big trees survived the widespread logging that occurred during the gold rush. One place you can still see old-growth magnificence,

BELOVED MURPHYS

Kirsten Locke, local vintner

As someone lucky enough to live and work here, I can say Murphys has rightfully earned its place as one of California's most beloved small towns. Nestled in the Sierra foothills, it has a vibrant wine and food scene that draws visitors year-round. Main St is always buzzing with tasting rooms, local shops and delightful restaurants offering casual and fine dining experiences.

Just beyond town, you'll find caverns, alpine lakes, the awe-inspiring Calaveras big trees and – my favorite – local family vineyard estates. There's something magical here: the pace slows, conversations linger and community still matters. Whether you're here for a day or a weekend, Murphys is easy to fall in love with and hard to leave.

EATING BEYOND SONORA: OUR PICKS

Alchemy Cafe: Elevated modern American dishes with an extensive wine list. *hours vary* $$

JoMa's Artisan Ice Cream: Makes small batches of creamy hand-crafted treats, many with seasonal fruit. In Murphys. *noon-6pm* $

Grounds: This casually elegant Murphys cafe serves superb breakfasts, good lunches and weekend dinners. *hours vary* $$

Woods Creek Cafe: Cow decor reigns supreme at this unique Jamestown spot that's popular for their hearty brunch and breakfast. *6am-2pm* $$

RAILTOWN GOES TO HOLLYWOOD

Railtown 1897's history goes far beyond just being a historical park beloved by locomotive enthusiasts. Known as 'The Movie Railroad,' the vintage trains and tracks you see at the park today have a glamorous history and have starred in over 200 film and TV productions, including iconic titles such as *Back to the Future Part III*, *Lone Ranger*, *East of Eden*, *Little House on the Prairie* and *Bonanza*. The first noted filming was back in 1919 for a silent series, *The Red Glove*. One particular train, the Sierra No 3, earned its nickname 'The Movie Star Locomotive' for appearing in more productions than any other railcar.

SAM SPICER/SHUTTERSTOCK

Calaveras Big Trees State Park

however, is at **Calaveras Big Trees State Park** *(parks.ca.gov, $10 per car)*.

Home to giant sequoia trees that reach as high as 250ft with trunks that are over 25ft in diameter, these leftovers from the Mesozoic era are thought to weigh upwards of 2000 tons. The giants are distributed in two large groves, one easily seen on the North Grove Trail, a 1.5-mile self-guided loop, near the park entrance. On the more remote South Grove Trail, it's a 5-mile round-trip hike to Agassiz Tree, the park's largest specimen.

Places We Love to Stay

$ Budget $$ Midrange $$$ Top End

Auburn

Map p77

Foothills Motel $ Good value retro-modern motel with an on-site bowling alley with 24 lanes, a bar and a diner. Five minute drive to Old Town.

Hotel Vista Sierra $$ Newly reopened in 2025; features family suites and poolside cabanas for the ultimate getaway.

Park Victorian $$$ Beautifully renovated historic house with six suites overlooking Old Town. Note you have to rent the entire home. Walk across to the popular Auburn Alehouse.

Amador City

Imperial Hotel $$ Newly renovated hip-meets-vintage historic brick building from the 1850s. Book one of the three off-site cottages for extra privacy. They're also pet friendly.

Coloma

Coloma Resort $ Family-friendly cabins, yurts, tents and activities across from the Marshall Gold Discovery State Historic Park and the American River. Major summer camp vibes.

American River Resort $ Spacious RV hookup area, campground, fishing pond, pool and playground along the South Fork of the American River.

Grass Valley

Map p86

Holbrooke Hotel $$ A renovated 1852 California Historic Building in the heart of Grass Valley filled with charm, a stellar restaurant and bar and even a hidden speakeasy downstairs.

Jackson

National Hotel $$ Revamped historic hotel with luxe amenities. Walkable to many restaurants and shops. Kennedy Gold Mine is just a couple of miles away.

Murphys

Victoria Inn $$ On Main St surrounded by tasting rooms and restaurants, the claw-foot bathtubs add to the historic appeal. Don't miss the homemade breakfast.

Dunbar House $$ Six-room bed and breakfast in a historic Victorian home with a wraparound porch and lovely gardens to enjoy coffee in.

Nevada City

Map p86

The National Exchange Hotel $$ Built in 1865 and restored and reopened in 2021 filled with lush furnishings, vintage wallpaper and one of the town's best restaurants and cocktail bars.

Two Room Inn $$ Sweet two-room Victorian cottage with stained glass lattice windows and a prime spot on Broad St, just steps away from all the action.

Placerville

Historic Cary House Hotel $$ Step back in time where Mark Twain, Elvis and Bette Davis once stayed – right on Main St, with free parking to boot.

Eden Vale Inn $$ Romantic off-the-beaten-path bed and breakfast with an on-site spa catering to couples. Farm-to-table breakfast delivered each morning. Approximately 20-min drive to Main St.

Sonora & Jamestown

Map p91

Hotel Lumberjack $ Good value, modern motel within walking distance to wineries and breweries. Limited parking in the lot shared with sister hotel Sonora Inn.

Sonora Inn $$ Historic 1896 hotel redone for modern times. Rooms and suites are pet-friendly for an added fee. The rooftop pool is a beloved respite on hot days.

Chicken Ranch Casino Resort $$ Ultra modern 197-room hotel with a 100,000 sq ft casino in Jamestown. All guests must be 21 or over.

The Inn on Knowles Hill $$ Perched above Sonora two blocks from the historic downtown area. Nosh on a handmade two-course breakfast in the dining room each morning.

Sutter Creek

Hotel Sutter $$ Charming 21-room saloon-esque hotel with a hidden cellar bar on historic Main St steps away from wineries and shopping.

Hanford House $$ Spacious bungalow and cottages with fireplaces and modern amenities. Daily hot scones delivered to your door. Kids will love the on-site chicken coop.

Researched by
Suzie Dundas

Lake Tahoe

BEACHES, SKIING, MOUNTAINS AND CASINOS

The largest alpine lake in the US is surrounded by ski resorts, hiking and cycling trails and some of the country's best lake beaches, all with amazing views.

Lake Tahoe sits more than 6000ft above sea level, straddling the California–Nevada border. The lake's almost unreal shades of blue and turquoise aren't found anywhere else in California and the surrounding Sierra Nevada mountains frame the lake with dramatic peaks and dense pine forests. The lake was formed about two million years ago, with nearby volcanic eruptions creating a natural dam that filled the basin with water and Ice Age glaciers forming features like Emerald Bay and Fallen Leaf Lake.

Lake Tahoe was home to the Washoe people, who spent summers fishing and hunting nearby. The modern-day word 'Tahoe' was derived from a mispronunciation of their phrase 'Da ow a ga,' meaning 'edge of the lake.' The area's modern history took off in the 19th century with the silver and logging booms, leaving behind a patchwork of glamorous estates and historical hiking trails. It quickly became a tourism hot spot after Palisades Tahoe hosted the 1960 Winter Olympics, the first to be televised.

Today, Tahoe is a year-round destination, with slow seasons a thing of the past. Winter brings deep snow and a flurry of activity at ski resorts like Heavenly Mountain and Northstar California and in summer, visitors flock to the boulder-covered beaches of Sand Harbor State Park and the lush hiking and cycling trails encircling the lake's 72 miles of forested shoreline.

CSNAFZGER/SHUTTERSTOCK

THE MAIN AREAS

THE SOUTH SHORE
Lively late nights and happening casinos.
p106

THE WEST SHORE
Laid-back towns and primo state parks.
p112

THE NORTH SHORE
Big-mountain skiing and outdoor adventures abound.
p120

THE EAST SHORE
A protected, undeveloped paradise.
p131

For places to stay in Lake Tahoe, see p137

MICHAEL HIDDIE/SHUTTERSTOCK

Left: Skiing, Lake Tahoe (p108); Above: Hidden Beach (p136)

Find Your Way

'Lake Tahoe' is the catch-all name for the many towns around Tahoe's sun-kissed shoreline. Driving around the lake is a must-do for first-time visitors. Most major towns are on the north or south shores; east and west also offer plenty to see and do.

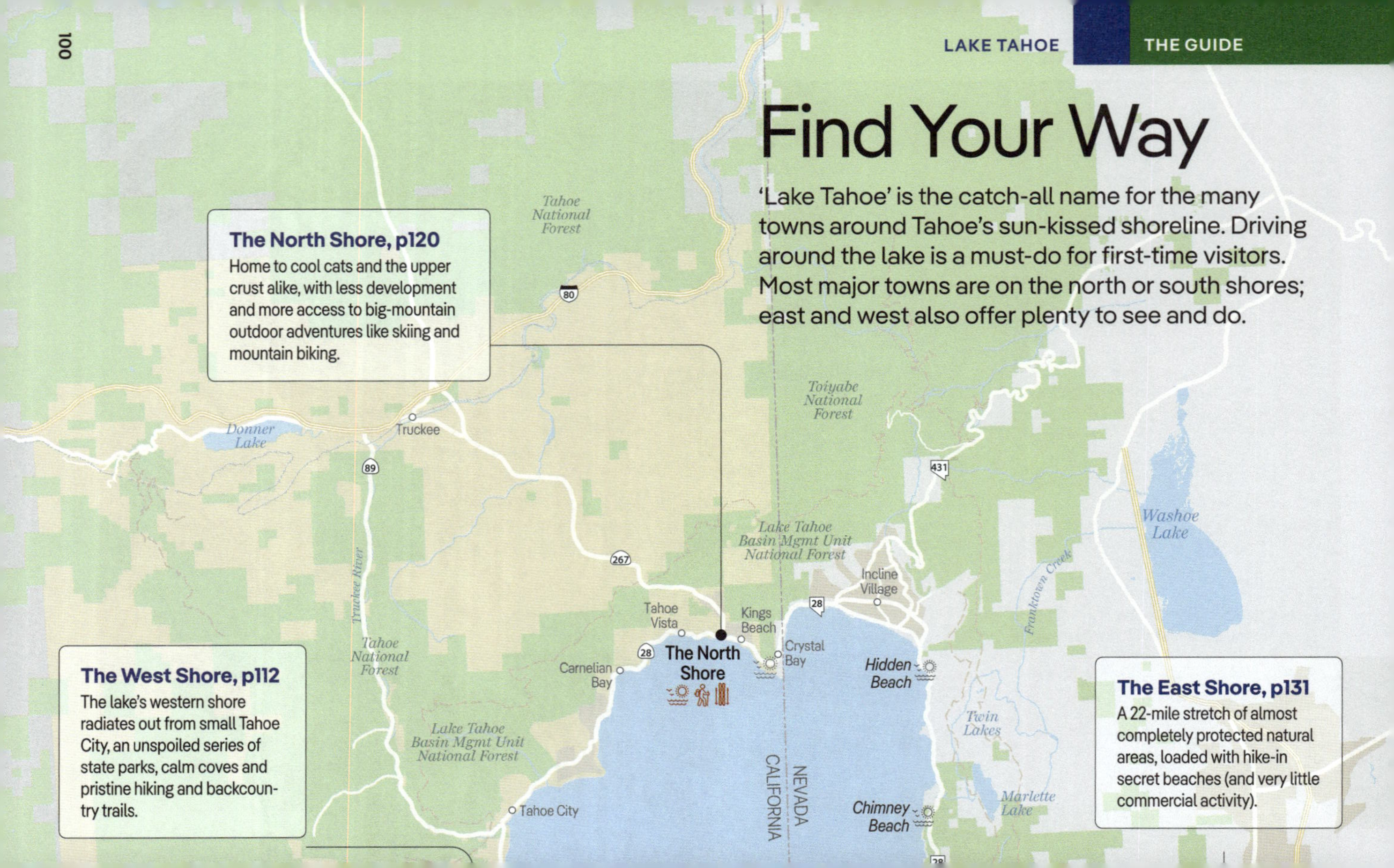

The North Shore, p120

Home to cool cats and the upper crust alike, with less development and more access to big-mountain outdoor adventures like skiing and mountain biking.

The West Shore, p112

The lake's western shore radiates out from small Tahoe City, an unspoiled series of state parks, calm coves and pristine hiking and backcountry trails.

The East Shore, p131

A 22-mile stretch of almost completely protected natural areas, loaded with hike-in secret beaches (and very little commercial activity).

CAR

Driving is the easiest way to access all that Tahoe offers – and the only way, as many public transportation options don't connect between towns. In winter, you'll need a 4WD and snow tires; most non-paved roads close. Stay up to date on chain requirements with **Caltrans** *(quickmap.dot.ca.gov)*.

BUS

Tahoe Transportation District *(tahoetransportation.org)* serves the south shore and bike-rack-equipped Tahoe Area Regional Transit (TART) serves Truckee, the north shore and the Tahoe City area. Many ski resorts require parking reservations on weekends. Without one, you'll have to take public transit.

WALKING

Sections of Tahoe are explorable on foot, such as Tahoe City, Truckee and Stateline. However, heavy winter snow can mean icy and covered sidewalks. Visitors who prefer dirt under their shoes will find Tahoe to be a dream destination, from flat historical trails to multiday circuits.

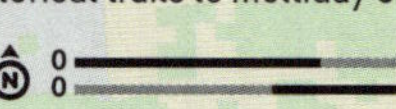

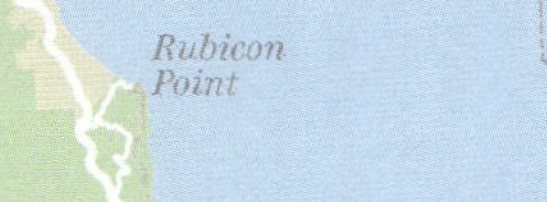
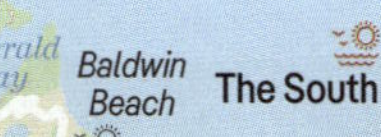

The South Shore, p106
Dive deep into casino life and the busy epicenter of Tahoe's most developed shore where marinas, ski resorts and slot machines vie for your attention.

Plan Your Days

Generally, the south shore is lively with more attractions, the north is quieter and more outdoorsy, the east shore is beach central and the west shore is homey and quaint. Pick your poison.

NICK FOX/SHUTTERSTOCK

Eagle Falls, Emerald Bay State Park (p114)

Pressed for Time

- In Tahoe, if it's not snowing, it's sunny. Summer visitors with just one day will want to get an early start to drive around the lake. Park early at **Emerald Bay State Park** (p114) for a morning hike, then drive to **Tahoe City** (p134) for a lakeside lunch. Stop and kayak in **Kings Beach** (p122) or **Sand Harbor** (p131) before catching sunset at **Nevada Beach** (p133). End your day with dinner at a south shore brewery or live music at a **casino** (p110).

- Winter trip? Spend the day at your resort of choice, then stick around for après-ski (roughly 4pm to 6pm) before soaking in your hotel hot tub and heading out for a late dinner in downtown **Truckee** (p127) or the **Heavenly Village** (p106).

Seasonal Highlights

Summer in Lake Tahoe is beach time, but nights still demand insulated jackets. Winter sees months of snow (ski season can run into June), while fall and spring have moderate temperatures and fewer tourists.

FEBRUARY

The **ski season** is in full swing and towns around the lake are packed, with hotels, restaurants and winter guiding companies operating at full capacity.

MAY

Most **trails** are starting to melt, with days frequently warm enough for **beach time**. Most ski resorts close in May, though Palisades Tahoe occasionally runs into late June.

JUNE

Beach season kicks off – as does events season, with hits like **Truckee Thursdays** (p127) in Truckee and concerts at **Commons Beach** (p119) in Tahoe City. Ski resorts host summer events and nearly all trails are hikable.

Three Days to Play

- With three days, more time gives you a chance to explore Tahoe on foot. Near South Lake, you can hike into **Desolation Wilderness** (p112) or hike the entire **Rubicon Trail** (p115) from Emerald Bay. In the summer, spend at least one day at a beach on the **east shore** (p131), especially if you can score a parking pass to kayak or paddleboard between boulders at **Sand Harbor State Park** (p131). For an adrenaline rush, try mountain biking at **Northstar California** (p129) near Truckee or **rent a Jet Ski** (p109) from a south shore marina. Night owl? Plan an evening's bar hopping in Stateline or downtown **Truckee** (p127).

- In winter, replace hiking and mountain biking with skiing at resorts like enormous **Kirkwood** (p124) or a smaller, family-friendly resort like **Diamond Peak** (p124).

A Week to Explore

- With even more time, slow your roll and stay longer at each spot you visit around the lake. See a show at the outdoor **Lake Tahoe Shakespeare Festival** (p133), book a tour on the **MS Dixie II paddle-wheel boat** (p104), dive into history at the **Tallac Historic Site** (p110) or ride the alpine coaster from the **Heavenly Gondola** (p106).

- During winter, you'll have time to visit a few resorts. Kirkwood, Heavenly and Northstar are all on the **Epic Pass** (p124), while Palisades Tahoe and Alpine Meadows are on the **Ikon Pass** (p124).

- You'll also want to take a day or two to try cross-country skiing or snowshoeing at places like **Granlibakken Resort** (p117) or **Hope Valley** (p111), or rev up a snowmobile on the **south shore** (p106).

JULY

The lake is as busy as it gets, with perennial favorites including the **Lake Tahoe Shakespeare Festival** (p133) and various music, beer and golfing events.

AUGUST

Nearly every day in summer is dry and sunny, which means **wildfire risk** can be high by August. Be conscious of following all wildfire regulations and consider replanning trips if there are fires near Lake Tahoe.

SEPTEMBER

Still-warm temps and fewer tourists make September 'local's summer,' with notable events like **Oktoberfest** (p125) at Palisades. Hiking and camping are still in full swing; beach days are also not out of the question.

DECEMBER

Lifts are spinning for the **ski season** come late November and early December, but snowstorms can bring closed and icy roads – not to mention extreme traffic delays – for the next four months.

Getting on the Water

Lake Tahoe has 72 miles of shoreline and many places to access its clear, cool waters. Deciding where to go can be tricky, especially as it's easy to circle the lake in a day – visitors can simply stay on one shore and explore beaches on the other. While swimming and paddling are how most people see the lake, they're hardly the only ways. If you want to do something a little unexpected, your options go far beyond just kayak rentals.

Where to go if you love...

Soaking Up the Sun

On summer weekends, the Truckee River between Tahoe City and Alpine Meadows becomes an unofficial floating party, with hundreds of swimsuit-clad locals on the calm, roughly 6-mile stretch. Nearby grocers sell tubes for around $30 and the float takes anywhere from two to four hours, depending on water levels. Families may prefer booking a four-person raft with paddles (and round-trip transport) with **Truckee River Raft Co** *(truckeeriverraft.com; adult/child $70/40)*. Check the website in advance as the start date changes each year. If you're doing it yourself, arrive early at the Tahoe Transit Center for free parking next to the river put-in.

High-Energy Adventures

In the spring when water levels are at their highest, novice and experienced paddlers alike can try white-water rafting with **Tahoe Whitewater Tours** *(gowhitewater.com; adult/child from $110/100)* on the Truckee River, Lake Tahoe's only outlet. Trips usually start in Truckee, with guests paddling through the Sierra Nevada in the Truckee River canyon. Wildlife sightings aren't uncommon.

Fishing

You can fish for salmon and trout on the lake, or try fly-fishing in the Truckee River. **Mile High Fishing** *(fishtahoe.com; from $150)* runs charters on Lake Tahoe, while **Trout Creek Outfitters** *(troutcreekoutfitters.com; 2 people from $425)* leads guided fly-fishing tours.

Epic Sunsets

The MS *Dixie II* paddle-wheel boat with **Zephyr Cove** *(zephyrcove.com; adult/child $150/75)* has multiple cruises, but for the best Tahoe photos, take the sunset cruise during golden hour. Boarding starts 30 minutes before departure; being among the first to board is the best way to score a window seat.

Multisport Days

From South Lake Tahoe, make the 25-minute drive to the summer-only **Echo Chalet** *(echochalet.com)*. Catch the $20 water taxi across Echo Lakes and you'll be at a trailhead for **Desolation Wilderness** (p112). From here, you'll be a 3-mile hike (with a 600ft gain) from swimmable and stunning Lake Aloha. Be sure to ask about timing with the last boat back, or you'll have to walk an extra 4 miles back to the chalet. To make the hike a little longer, circle to the other end of Lake Aloha and add on out-and-back extensions to Susie Lake (an additional 2.6 miles) or Dick's Peak (an additional 6 miles).

ZEROBLACK/SHUTTERSTOCK

Sand Harbor (p131)

HOW TO

Stay warm Tahoe's surface temps are tolerable in summer, but bring a rash guard or ask about wetsuit rentals if you're prone to getting cold.

Park Demand usually exceeds availability. Get to beaches early or take public transit. Shoulder parking is usually OK, but may be further away than you'd like.

Play with pups Most beaches aren't dog friendly, but it's a rule often overlooked. Keep your dog under your command at all times.

Stay safe Personal flotation devices (PFDs) are required by law. Tour organizers will provide them, but have one handy if you're on your own kayak or paddleboard.

Choose the perfect beach

If you'd rather just have an old-fashioned beach day, you have plenty of stunning options. Around the lake, free public beaches like **Commons Beach** (p119), **Kings Beach State Recreation Area** (p122) and **Baldwin Beach** are family-friendly picks. On the East Shore, hike-in-only beaches like **Skunk Harbor** (p136) and **Secret Harbor** (p136) provide a more undeveloped experience, while state park beaches like those at **DL Bliss** (p116) and **Sand Harbor** (p131) have full amenities and prime locations on the prettiest shoreline, but parking can be tough if you don't arrive by 7.30am to 8am. Truckee's public **West End Beach** and **Donner Memorial State Park** (p128) have sandy stretches, otherwise beat the crowds by heading just north of Truckee to **Boca Reservoir** (p129). Nearly all of Tahoe's alpine lakes are swimmable unless otherwise posted, including Lake Aloha, Lake Genevieve in Meeks Bay and Spooner and Marlette Lakes on the east shore.

Beach recreators leaving trash and plastic behind is a problem in Tahoe. Remember to take out everything you carry in and never leave anything outside a trash can. Using natural and reef-safe sunscreen can help keep Tahoe blue; remember to reapply often and drink more water to account for elevation impacts.

The South Shore

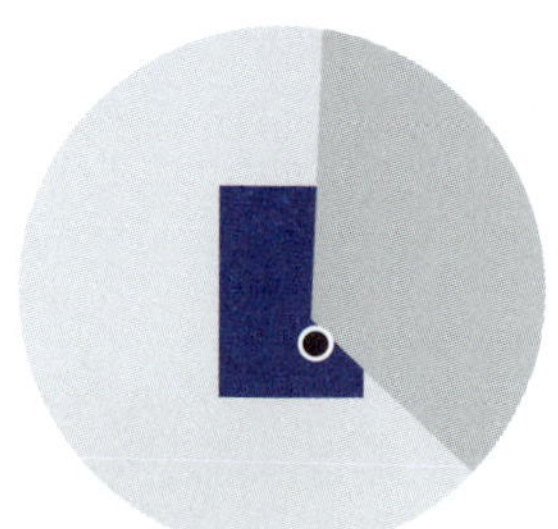

NIGHTLIFE | FAMILY ACTIVITIES | EASY BEACH ACCESS

TOP TIP

Hotels, resorts and vacation apartments abound and casinos offer basic, affordable lodging. Stay as close to the lake as possible to allow for car-free outings. Almost everywhere in Stateline is walkable to the main attractions, though staying on the California side offers better access to Emerald Bay and Desolation Wilderness.

South Lake Tahoe (on the California side) is the largest city on the lake, with casinos, restaurants and souvenir shops framed by picture-perfect ridgelines. It abuts Stateline (on the Nevada side), though the whole area is referred to as 'South Lake' or the south shore. It has the most visitor-focused activities and thanks to the sprawling and walkable Heavenly Mountain Village, plenty to do year-round.

After a day spent outdoors, SLT's nightlife, casino and dining scene heats up, making it the lake's go-to region for late-night action. It also has the most to do for families, friend groups and non-skiers, plus a lineup of fun summer festivals and events.

The main drag is a 5-mile stretch of Lake Tahoe Blvd (Rte 50), connecting most hotels, shops and restaurants and making the area highly walkable. It has more budget tourist options than the north shore, though congestion can be frustrating on busy weekends.

High-Elevation Family Fun

Heavenly isn't just for winter

The **Heavenly Gondola** *(skiheavenly.com; adult/child from $79/39)* soars guests from the **Heavenly Village** in Stateline to Tamarack Lodge at more than 10,000ft above sea level. There's an observation deck at the halfway point with panoramic

GETTING AROUND

The south shore is the easiest part of Tahoe to visit without having your own vehicle, though having one will give you more flexibility. Reno-Tahoe International Airport is the closest major airport, with one bus company, **South Tahoe Airporter** *(southtahoeairporter.com)*, offering daily shuttle service. Local public transportation comes from the **Tahoe Transportation District** *(tahoetransportation.org)*, but it has a limited route and can be impacted by weather and staffing challenges.

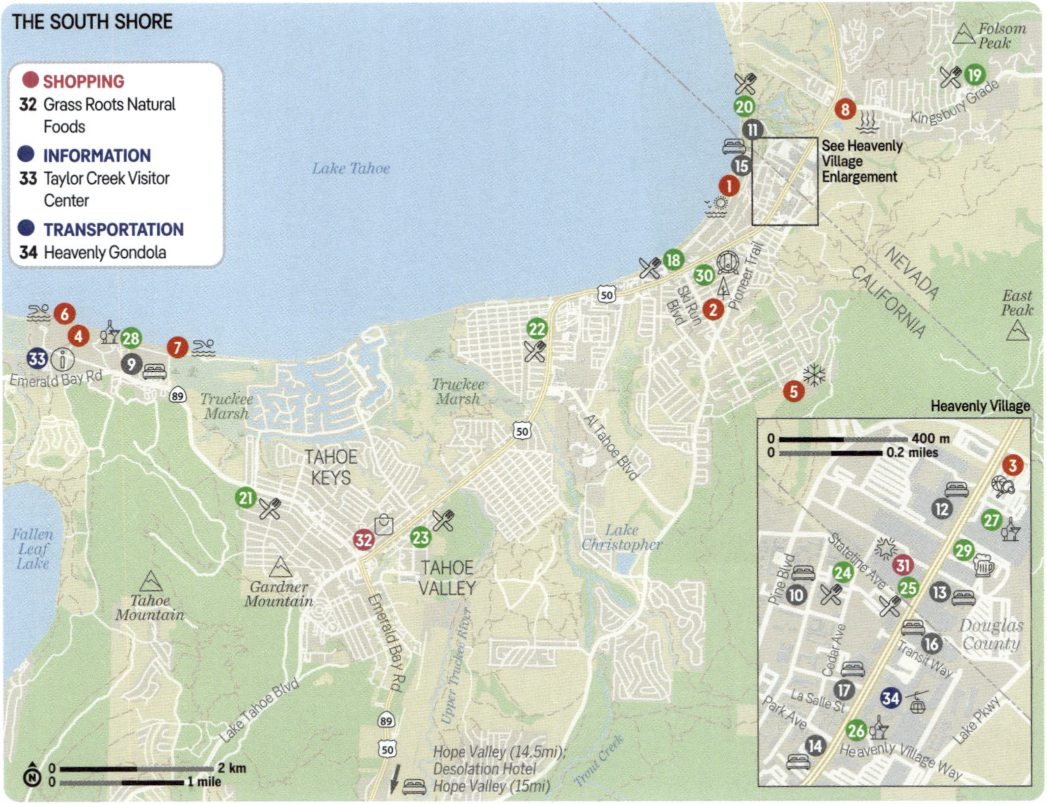

THE SOUTH SHORE

SIGHTS
1 Lakeside Beach
2 Ski Run Community Park
3 Tahoe Blue Event Center
4 Tallac Historic Site

ACTIVITIES
5 Heavenly Mountain Resort
6 Kiva Beach
7 Pope Beach
8 Tahoe Forest Baths

SLEEPING
9 Camp Richardson
10 Coachman Hotel
11 Edgewood Tahoe Resort
12 Golden Nugget Lake Tahoe
13 Harrah's Lake Tahoe
14 Hotel Becket
15 Landing Tahoe Resort & Spa
16 Margaritaville Resort Lake Tahoe
17 Stardust Lodge

EATING
18 Artemis Lakefront Cafe
see 34 Base Camp Pizza Co
19 Chart House
20 Edge Restaurant & Lounge
21 Evans American Gourmet Café
22 Gastromaniac Homemade Pizza & Pasta
23 Primo's Pizzeria
see 22 Sprouts Cafe
24 Trailfolk Coffee & Juice
25 Wolf by Vanderpump

DRINKING & NIGHTLIFE
26 Azul Latin Kitchen
27 Blu Nightclub
28 Grove Beach Bar
29 Lake Tahoe AleWorx
see 29 Noel's Coffee & Apothecary
30 Shedcat Distillery & Kitchen

ENTERTAINMENT
31 Caesars Republic Lake Tahoe
see 34 Loft Theatre

SHOPPING
32 Grass Roots Natural Foods

INFORMATION
33 Taylor Creek Visitor Center

TRANSPORTATION
34 Heavenly Gondola

HEADING NORTH?

The east shore is one of the few stretches around the lake with minimal tourist infrastructure, including a total absence of restaurants or concessions for most of the 22-mile drive. From the south, the final cluster of restaurants before the shoreline turns *au natural* is in Zephyr Cove, just north of Stateline. Beyond that, you'll need to drive all the way to Incline Village for everything from snacks to sunscreen. Remember that glass containers are banned on nearly all of Tahoe's shoreline and you'll need to pack out all your trash and empty cans. Never leave waste or styrofoam containers outside dumpsters or trash cans.

ALISA_CH/SHUTTERSTOCK

Heavenly Mountain Resort

views of the entire Tahoe Basin, with summer activities like a zipline, a mountain coaster, tubing and hiking trails at the top. The gondola runs year-round for sightseeing, though the mountain may limit capacity for non-skiers on busy weekends.

'Soak' in a Cedar Bath

Lounge at Tahoe Forest Baths

At **Tahoe Forest Baths** *(tahoeforestbaths.com; from $155)* in Stateline, visitors can try a different kind of soak: spending about 20 minutes relaxing in a heated tub of cedar shavings imported from Hokkaido, Japan. It's said to help with everything from detoxification to stress reduction to boosting immunity, but whether or not those are true, it's at least relaxing. It's a dry experience, though you'll want to wear a swimsuit as it's followed by a post-bath rinse and cooldown period. It's popular with couples, though up to four people can 'soak' at the same time.

Ski Between Two States

Hit the slopes

Heavenly Mountain Resort *(epicpass.com; Epic Pass single-day ticket adult/child from $94/48)* is perhaps the most well-known in California (we've given the non-peak

EATING ON THE SOUTH SHORE: BEST PIZZA

Base Camp Pizza Co: An extensive pizza menu and happening outdoor patio with live music. *hours vary* $$

Gastromaniac Homemade Pizza & Pasta: No-frills pizza and pasta in an unassuming strip mall that belies the tastiness inside. *hours vary* $$

Lake Tahoe AleWorx: BYO pizza place by day, late-night bar crowd by night. *4pm-midnight Mon-Thu, to 2am Fri & Sat* $$

Primo's Pizzeria: A spin-off of a beloved Italian restaurant with the same hand-made pies and pasta. *hours vary* $$

pre-purchase rates here, but peak walk-up window rates can easily be $280 or more for a single day). Heavenly sits steps from the shoreline with some of the most flabbergasting views you'll find in North America, plus trails that look like you're about to ski into the lake. With a base area at 6200ft above sea level and a summit above 10,000ft, it has the most skiable vert (vertical feet top-to-bottom) in Tahoe.

Follow the sun by skiing on the Nevada side in the morning for desert views, then moving to the California side in the afternoon. Snowboarders will want to carry speed on some flats to avoid hopping between states. Buy an Epic Pass single-day ticket, rather than buying day-of at the ticket window, to save some dough. (For more on the Epic and Ikon ski passes, see p124.)

See Nature in Action

Catch the annual salmon run at Taylor Creek

Taylor Creek is a pleasant place for a stroll year-round, but it's especially popular in September and October when it hosts the annual kokanee salmon run – and the salmon's top predator: black bears. There are four self-guided trails, including the Forest Tree Trail past towering Jeffrey pine trees and the wheelchair-accessible Rainbow Trail through an underwater salmon-viewing tunnel, complete with information signage.

The grounds are open year-round but the **visitor center** *(taylortallac.org/taylor-creek; 8am-4pm Wed-Sun)* is open from Memorial Day to Labor Day. Stop in to grab a map and make sure you're aware of bear safety practices before starting a walk.

Find the Best Lakefront Real Estate

Hit the south shore beaches

The south shore may be more developed than the rest of the lake, but that hasn't compromised the shoreline.

Visitors near Stateline can walk to **Lakeside Beach** *(lakesideparkassociation.org; adult/child $30/20)*. Unlike others in the area, it's private, with paid entry, but that means it comes with amenities like a grill, optional beach-gear rentals and a free summer shuttle. A few miles west are two other perennial favorites: **Kiva Beach** and **Pope Beach** *(tahoepublic beaches.org)*, each with picnic tables and barbecue grills, accessible from the **Tallac Historic Site** (p110).

EXCITING WAYS TO GET AROUND

Helicopter & balloon: Get a bird's-eye view of the lake with **Lake Tahoe Helicopters** *(tahoehelicopters.us; from $180)* or **Lake Tahoe Balloons** *(laketahoeballoons.com; $399)*.

Slingshot: Rent an open-air, four-person slingshot with **Lake Tahoe Slingshots** *(rolltahoe.com; 4 people from $350)* to smell the pine-scented air.

Jet Ski: Rent Jet Skis from Lakeside Marina with **Action Watersports** *(action-watersports.com; from $179)*. The Tahoe Keys Marina is better for visitors on the California side, with rentals via **Tahoe Sports** *(tahoesports.com; from $179)*.

Surrey bike: Rent two- or four-person covered, four-wheel surrey bikes with **Tahoe Bike Company** *(tahoebikeandski company.com; from $35)*.

Snowmobile: Try snowmobiling on a groomed track perfect for first-timers with **Tahoe Snowmobiles** *(tahoesnowmobiles.com; from $95)*.

DRINKING ON THE SOUTH SHORE: BEST COCKTAILS

Azul Latin Kitchen: An impressive tequila list and a lengthy cocktail menu heavy on ingredients like jalapeño and mescal. *hours vary*

Noel's Coffee & Apothecary: Creative cocktails with unique ingredients in old-school speakeasy surrounds. Reservations generally required. *hours vary*

Shedcat Distillery & Kitchen: Complex cocktails with house-made gin, bourbon, vodka and grappa. *noon-10pm Thu-Mon, to 11pm Fri & Sat*

Grove Beach Bar: Lakefront cocktails served steps from the sand on the deck of one of Tahoe's earliest resorts. *hours vary*

ENVIRONMENTAL PROTECTION

Caroline Waldman, local expert and South Lake Tahoe resident, works for the Tahoe Fund, a nonprofit working to improve and protect Tahoe's environmental resources. *tahoefund.org*

Start your sustainability success tour at Taylor Creek. Enjoy the interpretive trail to the viewing platforms and try to spot wildlife in action: kokanee salmon swimming, black bears napping or bald eagles soaring. Next, head to Ski Run Blvd, where you'll find an empty lot transformed into the new **Ski Run Community Park**, complete with a climbing boulder. Head to Stateline and in front of the **Tahoe Blue Event Center** you'll see a sculpture of a bald eagle holding a Lahontan cutthroat trout, crafted entirely from litter removed from Lake Tahoe by scuba divers.

Beat the Winter Weather

Family-friendly indoor fun

Rain isn't common in Lake Tahoe, but when it happens, there's not a lot to do – unless you're on the south shore. The 'Magic Fusion' show at the **Loft Theatre** *(thelofttahoe.com; adult/child $57/45)* has been running for more than a decade (the 9pm shows are adults-only), while **Harrah's** (p137) has a huge, non-smoking arcade ideal for indoor fun when the ski lifts stop spinning. And sports fans may want to snag budget-friendly tickets for a **Tahoe Knight Monsters** *(knightmonstershockey.com; from $17)* hockey game. It's Tahoe's only minor league sports team, with games between October and April at the **Tahoe Blue Events Center** in Stateline.

Try Your Luck

Gambling hot spot

On the Nevada side, multiple large casino and hotel complexes loom over the lake. All have vast spaces dedicated to slots and table games, with glitzy decor to make you forget the lake is steps away. **Harrah's Lake Tahoe** *(caesars.com)* is the most luxurious, **Caesars Republic Lake Tahoe** *(caesars.com)*, formerly Harvey's,runs an A-list summer concert series at its outdoor amphitheater and was Tahoe's first high-rise, Bally's draws late-night partiers to **Blu Nightclub** *(casinos.ballys.com)* and **Golden Nugget Lake Tahoe** *(goldennugget.com)* is generally the most affordable. All offer discounted rooms throughout the year, though being within walking distance of Heavenly means the deals aren't as low as you'd find in cities like Las Vegas or Reno.

See How Tahoe's Elite Lived

Walk through history at the Tallac Historic Site

The **Tallac Historic Site** *(taylortallac.org)* is a sprawling park preserving three historic homes dating between 1894 and 1923 (the Pope, Baldwin and Valhalla estates). It sits on the archaeologically excavated grounds of the former Tallac Resort, a posh vacation retreat for San Francisco's high society in the early 1900s.

There's a self-guided walking tour that leans into the site's glamorous (and seedy) history as well as a free on-site museum, but tours of the homes require payment. If you're into plant life, don't miss the Pope estate garden, home to the only

EATING ON THE SOUTH SHORE: ROMANTIC RESTAURANTS

Chart House: White-tablecloth dining a few miles from the tourist strip; lake views and wildlife sightings aren't uncommon. *4-9.30pm Mon-Sat, to 9pm Sun* $$$

Edge Restaurant & Lounge: The tables are next to floor-to-ceiling windows. Check what time sunset is and make your res for 30 minutes beforehand. *hours vary* $$$

Wolf by Vanderpump: Arguably the most chichi casino restaurant in the area, with over-the-top decor and cocktails. *5-10pm Sun-Thu, from 4pm Fri & Sat* $$$

Evans American Gourmet Café: Reliably delicious and non-pretentious, with creative daily specials. *5-9pm Tue-Sat* $$$

KIT LEONG/SHUTTERSTOCK

Hope Valley

giant sequoia trees in Lake Tahoe. Plan to spend three to four hours here if you want to walk the complete loop and tour all the buildings (or more if you plan to hit the beaches, too). The site is open year-round, but the visitor center is staffed from roughly Memorial Day to Labor Day.

Seek Spring Wildflowers & Fall Foliage

Explore Tahoe's less-busy valley

Despite being only 20 minutes from South Lake Tahoe, **Hope Valley** sees just a fraction of its crowds. If Tahoe has dramatic peaks and steep ridgelines, Hope Valley is its more mellow little sister. The massive valley is a wide expanse more reminiscent of Montana or Wyoming, complete with narrow, snaking rivers and thickets of aspens. Hikers and cyclists can trace the old Emigrant Trail or climb a hillside overlooking foliage on the way to Scott's Lake, while winter calls for snowshoeing and cross-country skiing, with gear rentals at nearby **Desolation Hotel Hope Valley**. The Hope Valley Wildlife area is extremely popular with birders, but be sure to BYO binoculars – there aren't a lot of nearby tourist amenities in Hope Valley aside from the accommodations.

LAKE TAHOE'S WILDFIRE RESILIENCY

Wildfires are part of the natural cycle of growth for any forest, but South Lake Tahoe's dense development, increased traffic and unpredictable cycles of snow and drought have made fires worse. In August 2021, the Caldor Fire raced through South Lake Tahoe, causing a city-wide evacuation. Despite the use of snowmaking cannons to fight the flames, the blaze destroyed tiny Sierra-at-Tahoe resort (it reopened in 2022). You can see the remains of burned trees while driving on Rtes 50 or 89 just south of South Lake Tahoe. If visiting in summer, be sure to check for any wildfire reports that could impact your trip *(fire.ca.gov/incidents)*. Consider reducing your outdoor activity when the air quality is poor.

EATING ON THE SOUTH SHORE: HEALTHY BITES

Sprouts Cafe: Budget-friendly and mostly vegetarian bowls, wraps and sandwiches, with a few add-on options for meat eaters. *9am-7pm* $

Grass Roots Natural Foods: A small-but-packed grocery store with tons of organic picnic (and premade grab-and-go) snacks. *9am-8pm Mon-Sat, 10am-7pm Sun* $

Trailfolk Coffee & Juice: A coffee shop, sure, but more known for its excellent selection of juices, smoothies and fruit bowls, going beyond just açai. *7am-2pm* $

Artemis Lakefront Cafe: Mediterranean classics like dolmas, pitas and gyros, plus mainstream basics like burgers and salads. *11am-9pm Mon-Fri, from 9am Sat & Sun* $$

The West Shore

HIKING | PADDLING | CYCLING

TOP TIP

Most lodging options on the west shore are campgrounds (Emerald Bay State Park offers tiered sites overlooking the famous bay), vacation rentals or smaller, locally owned resorts. Hwy 89 around Emerald Bay closes frequently during winter storms and can be extremely backed up on summer weekends with tourist traffic. Plan accordingly.

Most of the west shore is residential, giving it a quieter and more nostalgic vibe than the busier north or south shores. Rather than casinos and resorts, you'll find rugged state parks, bicycle and kayak rentals, hiking trails and lakeside restaurants with decks overlooking the water and plenty of long-time locals.

History fans will find lots to explore on the west shore, including the historic Hellman-Ehrman Mansion and Emerald Bay State Park, home to a Viking-inspired chalet and some unique stories from Tahoe's early days of tourism. Desolation Wilderness beckons hikers willing to work for uninterrupted Sierra views and west shore state parks have some of the most lush and convenient campsites you'll find in Tahoe. The west shore's sole established town, Tahoe City, is a walkable, lakeshore town with great access to sprawling Commons Beach and a plethora of high-end dining options.

Explore Tahoe's Backcountry

Venture into Desolation Wilderness

Sculpted by powerful glaciers eons ago, **Desolation Wilderness** *(fs.usda.gov)* covers 100 sq miles of high-elevation forest spread between the south and west shores. With no roads, the only way to visit is on foot, with dozens of hiking trails passing polished granite peaks and leading to deep-blue

continues on p116

GETTING AROUND

You'll need a car to travel the length of Tahoe's west shore. On the north side, TART buses only run as far south as Homewood, with no public transportation options covering the remaining distance between Homewood and South Lake Tahoe. In the winter, check road closures around Emerald Bay in advance *(quickmap.dot.ca.gov)* and expect bumper-to-bumper traffic trying to travel from Tahoe City to Truckee on Sundays when skiers are leaving at the end of the weekend.

THE WEST SHORE

See Enlargement
Tahoe City
River Rd
Truckee River
Sunnyside
W Lake Blvd
Ward Creek
Lake Tahoe Basin Management Unit National Forest
Homewood
Tahoma
Ellis Peak
Tahoe National Forest
Miller Lake
General Creek
Meeks Creek
Meeks Bay
Eldorado National Forest
Lake Tahoe
Emerald Bay Rd
Lake Genevieve
DL Bliss State Park
Emerald Bay State Park
Bayview Trailhead
Cascade Falls
Mt Tallac (0.8mi)
Desolation Wilderness (11mi)

Bunker Dr
Fairway Dr
Red Cedar St
Pioneer Way
Grove St
Tahoe St
North Lake Blvd
Tahoe City Golf Course
Tahoe City Public Beach
Lake Tahoe
Mackinaw Rd
West Lake Blvd
William B Layton Park
0 400 m
0 0.2 miles

HIGHLIGHTS
1 Emerald Bay State Park

SIGHTS
2 Commons Beach
3 DL Bliss State Park
4 Ed Z'berg Sugar Pine Point State Park
5 Fanny Bridge
6 Gatekeeper's Museum
7 Inspiration Point
see 1 Vikingsholm Castle

ACTIVITIES
8 Eagle Falls Trailhead
see 1 Kayak Tahoe
see 1 Rubicon Trail
9 West Shore Sports (Homewood/Obexer's)

SLEEPING
10 Basecamp Tahoe City
11 evo Tahoe City Hotel
12 Granlibakken Resort
13 Inn at Boatworks

EATING
14 Christy Hill
see 9 Dockside Trading Co
15 Fire Sign Cafe
16 Sunnyside Restaurant
17 Tahoe House Bakery
see 16 West Shore Market
18 Za's Lakefront

DRINKING & NIGHTLIFE
19 Chamber's Landing

DDUB3429/SHUTTERSTOCK

Rubicon Trail

TOP EXPERIENCE

Emerald Bay State Park

If you only see one Tahoe sight, make it Emerald Bay State Park, where the lake's only island sits surrounded by sheer granite cliffs and sparkling waters that change shades, depending on the lighting. The park protects the teardrop-shaped cove and a historic, Viking-inspired mansion within, as well as the thundering waterfalls and rocky bluffs sitting 700ft above the sandy shoreline.

DON'T MISS

- Vikingsholm tours
- Rubicon Trail
- Eagle Falls
- Emerald Bay State Park Lookout
- Kayaking with Kayak Tahoe

Tour an Unexpected Historic Home

Vikingsholm Castle *(sierrastateparks.org; adult/child $18/15)* is an unexpected architectural treat. Its original owner, Lora Knight, purchased 240 acres around Emerald Bay, including Fannette Island, for a mere $250,000 in 1928. Knight, a wealthy widow, designed it with heavy guidance from her architect nephew. The two traveled across Scandinavia to find inspiration for what would become her dream home, much of which is still visible today. Inside, dragon-carved beams

PRACTICALITIES

Scan the QR code for more information on Emerald Bay State Park access and tours.

welcome visitors and most of the home's furniture was custom-made based on discoveries during their trip. Even without going inside the home, visitors can see Scandi-inspired features on the home's exterior, including a grass-covered roof on the north side, intricately carved braiding motifs on the triangular eaves and a cantilevered room made entirely of timber above the stone facade. All pay homage to popular design trends in 19th-century Norwegian and Swedish architecture. Tours are run between 10.30am and 4pm daily from Memorial Day to Labor Day.

Walk the Prettiest Trail in Tahoe

A brilliantly scenic trail on Lake Tahoe's western shore, the **Rubicon Trail** (500ft gain) ribbons along the lake for 4.5 mostly gentle miles, starting at the north end of Vikingsholm Beach. Heading north, you'll pass small, private coves perfect for taking a cooling dip and relaxing in the shade of towering pines. The trail ends at Calawee Cove in DL Bliss State Park, but is often done as an out-and-back. When planning, be sure to account for the 1-mile walk into Emerald Bay along the steep paved path.

Get a Bird's-Eye View

The Upper Eagle Falls hike packs a punch, gaining 150ft of elevation over a 0.5 mile loop. But it's worth the effort to see the waterfall cascading down granite cliffs toward Emerald Bay. One of the best views is from the footbridge, with the surrounding Sierra Nevada landscape in the background. The **Eagle Falls Trail** begins from a parking area across Rte 89 about 0.2 miles south of the Emerald Bay parking lot, but given how busy the area gets, it's best to just walk if you've already found a spot. You can get a view of the smaller but still impressive Lower Eagle Falls on the lake side, directly across from the Upper Eagle Falls parking area.

Paddle to Tahoe's Only Island

Kayaking around Emerald Bay takes a bit more effort than other at rental locations, considering the hike in and the fact that you may have to wait your turn with the first-come, first-served system. But when you get a chance to rent a sit-on-top kayak from **Kayak Tahoe** *(kayaktahoe.com; from $38)*, you'll know it was worth the wait. Get a close-up view of Fannette Island, paddle along the shoreline of the former Emerald Bay Resort, or just paddle out to relax in the sun on the calm, color-changing water. Rentals are available from roughly Memorial Day to Labor Day, with guided tours available once or twice a week.

TAKE THE PERFECT PHOTO

Emerald Bay is best viewed from above. **Inspiration Point** gets less crowded than the Emerald Bay parking area, but has partially blocked views thanks to fast-growing pines. The best views are from the path between Inspiration Point and the Emerald Bay parking lot, from the granite slabs in the parking lot (marked on maps as 'Emerald Bay State Park Lookout') and from the top of the footpath into Emerald Bay.

TOP TIPS

- The park gets extremely crowded. Parking often fills by 8am in the summer and shoulder parking on Rte 89 may mean a long walk to the park.
- The path into the park is 1 mile and drops 500ft. There are no shuttles (though visitors with disabilities may be able to arrange a ride in advance through the park website).
- The park is accessible year-round, but the walking path isn't plowed in the winter.
- Vikingsholm tickets are sold on-site; no reservations required.
- Bring a picnic, as there are no concessions in the park (potable water is available in summer).

YOU'RE IN THEIR HOME: BE BEAR AWARE

Black bears are cute from a distance, but leaving food and other items out brings them close to people – and when bears get too close to people, they face severe penalties. Help keep bears alive by following basic bear safety rules: never leave scented items unattended (or in your car), close kitchen doors and windows at night and never leave trash outside next to a full dumpster. Bear canisters are mandatory for all overnight camping in the Tahoe basin. You can rent them from the Taylor Creek Visitor Center in South Lake Tahoe between June and October. If you see a bear in need of help, inform the **Tahoe Bear League** *(savebears.org)*.

continued from p112

alpine lakes, glacier-carved valleys and resplendent pine forests that thin quickly at higher elevations. It has exceptional wildflower hiking well into July. Six major trailheads provide access from the Lake Tahoe side. Tallac and Eagle Falls get the most traffic, but solitude comes quickly once you've scampered past the day hikers.

Permits are required year-round for both day and overnight explorations, though day hikers can get them from self-issue stations at trailheads. For backpacking permits, you'll need to get one in advance online. Quotas are in effect from late May through the end of September; 70% of permits are made available six months in advance on recreation.gov, while the other 30% are available as same-day walk-ups from the Tahoe Basin Management Unit Supervisor's Office at 35 College Dr, South Lake Tahoe. Be prepared to face hefty fines if you're not fire and bear aware.

The West Shore's Best Beaches

Spend the day in Bliss

Just a few miles north of Emerald Bay State Park is **DL Bliss State Park** *(parks.ca.gov; parking $10)* and while it's named for an early Tahoe tourism magnet, it could also be in honor of

EATING ON THE WEST SHORE: CHEAPER PICKS

Tahoe House Bakery: A Swiss-style bakery and deli plus to-go breads, cheese and chocolate. *6am-3pm* $

West Shore Market: Fresh sandwiches and gelatos scooped lakeside at the deli. *7am-8pm, deli 10am-3pm or 3.30pm* $$

Fire Sign Cafe: A west-shore institution with constant crowds and wildly fluffy pancake stacks. *7.30am-2.30pm* $$

Dockside Trading Co: Grilled items, plus grab-and-go sandwiches and cheese-tastic burritos. *7am-7pm* $$

SUSANNE POMMER/SHUTTERSTOCK

DL Bliss State Park

how you'll feel when you relax on its picture-perfect beaches. The park's Lester Beach and Calawee Cove are walk-in-only beaches tucked into small coves that somehow never seem too crowded. The park's Balancing Rock Trail goes past an oddity of nature that time seems to ignore, while the Lighthouse Trail heads to a historic lighthouse built by the Coast Guard in 1916. At 8600ft above sea level, it's the country's highest-elevation public lighthouse.

Find a West Shore Winter Wonderland

Old-timey sports at Granlibakken

Granlibakken Resort *(granlibakken.com; from $26)* is as old-timey as it gets when it comes to winter sports, making it a low-key place for beginners or families to try winter sports without the crowds (or cost) of the larger ski resorts. The area around Granlibakken has been a winter play area since the late 1920s, making it the oldest still-operating resort in the basin. Sledding hills, ski rope tows and cross-country trails await visitors. It's one of the few places in Tahoe where you won't need reservations and can snag an all-day weekend lift ticket for under $50.

THE BEST HIKES IN DESOLATION WILDERNESS

Desolation WIlderness has more trails than you could ever fit into one visit. While the snow-covered peaks may look intimidating, the sheer volume of hikes means everyone from beginners to experienced backcountry trekkers have good options.

Easier: Skirt the edge of Desolation with a gentle hike to flowing Cascade Falls (1.5 miles round trip; 200ft gain), starting from the Bayview Trailhead near Emerald Bay.

Moderate: Lake Genevieve from Meeks Bay (10 miles round trip; 1220ft gain) packs on the miles, but spreads the elevation out into a manageable wooded hike to a swimmable alpine lake.

Difficult: Ascending Mt Tallac (10 miles round trip; 3700ft gain) is a bucket-list Tahoe hike, with panoramic views over Lake Tahoe and Fallen Leaf Lake.

EATING & DRINKING ON THE WEST SHORE: LAKEFRONT DINING

Chambers Landing: A lively boat-up bar without a bad seat in the house. *hours vary seasonally mid-May-Sep* $$

Za's Lakefront: A Tahoe City staple for pizza and pasta with outdoor tables next to the marina. Popular on summer Sundays after Commons Beach concerts. *11.30am-9pm* $$

Sunnyside Restaurant: Upscale American fare with outdoor tables on a wide wooden pier. *from 4pm* $$$

Christy Hill: Panoramic lake views from indoors and out, plus the summer-only, shoes-optional Sandbar out back. *5-9pm Tue-Sun* $$$

BILLY MCDONALD/SHUTTERSTOCK

Ed Z'berg Sugar Pine Point State Park

See the West Shore by Water

Kayak and paddleboard past mansions

With no waves, gorgeous shoreline and plenty of no-wake zones, Lake Tahoe is a fantastic place to try kayaking, paddleboarding and other water sports. **West Shore Sports** *(westshoresports.com; from $25)* has three west shore locations – Obexer's Boat Company, Sunnyside Marina and Sugar Pine Point State Park – with rentals, basic instruction and directional guidance included. All have access to pretty shoreline, but of the three, Obexer's may be the most scenic launch point. Paddle south to grab an on-the-water beer from popular Chambers Landing, or paddle north to pass the lakeside mansions, including the famous Fleur de Lac estate from *The Godfather: Part II* fame.

See Tahoe's Natural & Human History

A day in Ed Z'berg Sugar Pine Point State Park

While Vikingsholm Castle is the crown jewel of historic mansions, it's not the only one. The Hellman-Ehrman Estate at **Ed Z'berg Sugar Pine Point State Park** *(sierrastateparks.org; parking $10)* was built in 1903, predating Vikingsholm by more than 20 years. At the time, the mansion was one of the most luxurious in California, with rarities like indoor plumbing and steam-powered lighting. Tours run daily between 10.30am and 2pm from late May to late September, with options like private breakfasts or chef's-table dinners for deep-pocketed visitors.

NATURE INSPIRING ARTISTS

Lake Tahoe' shoreline has long inspired artists, including landscape photographer Ansel Adams (1902–84). While he's most famous for shooting in **Yosemite National Park** (p144), he also photographed **Sequoia & Kings Canyon National Parks** (p159), Mt Shasta and even Tahoe's **Emerald Bay** (p114).

This is the largest state park in the basin and draws guests year-round with winter camping, groomed cross-country skiing trails and a public pier (rare on the west shore). Just south of the mansion is a set of old train tracks leading into the lake that's popular with photographers and to the north along the shoreline are the park's namesake sugar pine trees. You can recognize them by their downward-curving branches, pulled toward the ground by the weight of their massive cones (which can grow up to 22in long).

Tahoe History & Basket Artistry

Celebrate arts and artifacts

In a reconstructed log cabin close to town, the **Gatekeeper's Museum** *(gatekeepersmuseum.org; adult/child $10/free)* has a small but fascinating collection of Tahoe memorabilia, including relics from the early steamboat era and tourism explosion around the lake. The don't-miss exhibit is the exquisite array of Native American baskets collected from more than 85 indigenous California tribes.

Wander Through Downtown Tahoe City

Hit the beach and go for a stroll

Words like 'charming' and 'quaint' are often tossed around when discussing Tahoe City – and both are accurate. The entire downtown area is found along one 0.7-mile stretch, with a flat, paved walking path on the lake side and a sidewalk on the other. You can take in downtown's top sights on a 1-mile walking loop from the North Lake Tahoe Visitor Center.

Take the lakeside walking path to **Commons Beach** (home to free Sunday night outdoor concerts from June to September), then continue to the Tahoe City pier. From here, cross Rte 28 and walk back through downtown, stopping to check out artisan shops and galleries, outdoor stores and thrift stores. From here, walk back toward **Fanny Bridge** to explore the Gatekeeper's Museum and adjacent park.

TAHOE'S BEST BACKCOUNTRY LINES

Jeremy Jones is a local expert, professional snowboarder and founder of Protect Our Winters, an organization leading the outdoor movement for climate action. *protectourwinters.org*

My favorite winter spot is **Mt Tallac**. It's in Desolation Wilderness with amazing terrain on all sides of it, so no matter the conditions, you'll find a smooth, soft surface there to ski or ride. It's incredible. You have to hike it, but it's a Tahoe gem and a really special place to experience. It's amazing that it's not just protected land, but completely open to the public. Be sure to go with a buddy if it's your first time exploring the terrain.

The North Shore

BEACHSIDE TOWNS | BIG-MOUNTAIN RECREATION | HISTORICAL DRAWS

TOP TIP

The north shore is the less-crowded, more outdoorsy solution to the south shore. It tends to be pricier than the rest of the lake and Incline Village's multi-million-dollar homes have given it a not-inaccurate nickname: Income Village. Note that it's probably the priciest town around the lake for visitors.

Tahoe's north shore is often called North Lake Tahoe, though it's not an official town like South Lake Tahoe. Instead, it's a collection of cute, low-key towns – many fronting superb sandy beaches – with unbeatable access to some of California's best hiking and skiing, especially at Palisades Tahoe.

Oozing old-fashioned charm, the north shore is a blissful escape from the teeming crowds of the south shore. It's more outdoorsy, with less development and fewer budget accommodations and dining. The north shore stretches from roughly Carnelian Bay, just east of Tahoe City, to Incline Village, Nevada. The state divide runs through Crystal Bay, where you'll find a few old-school casinos with smaller crowds.

Recreation reigns supreme on the north shore. It's also home to the notorious Cal-Neva Lodge, famously owned by Frank Sinatra and sitting atop Prohibition-era bootlegging tunnels later used to smuggle the Rat Pack's famous friends, including Marilyn Monroe.

Hit the Beach, 1960s-Style

Romping around vintage Kings Beach

Few places in Tahoe have been as untouched by recent development as **Kings Beach**, a once-modest beachside town equidistant from both Truckee and Tahoe City. The humble

GETTING AROUND

The north shore is about 45 minutes' drive via Hwy 80 from Reno-Tahoe International Airport, or two hours from Sacramento International Airport. High-elevation Donner Pass and Mt Rose Hwy frequently close during snowstorms and you can count on needing a 4WD all winter long. On Friday evenings and Sunday afternoons, ski traffic can bring area roads to a standstill. Have patience and use public transportation options like **TART** *(tahoetruckeetransit.com)*.

SIGHTS
1 Kings Beach State Recreation Area
2 Moon Dunes Beach

ACTIVITIES
3 Diamond Peak
4 Kings Beach Mini Golf
5 Monkey Rock
6 North Tahoe Lions Club Disc Golf Course
7 Old Brockway Golf Course
8 Tahoe Backyard
9 Tahoe Rim Trail
10 Tunnel Creek Trail
11 Waterman's Landing

SLEEPING
12 Cedar Glen Lodge
13 Hyatt Regency Lake Tahoe
14 Mourelatos Resort

EATING
15 Big Water Grille
see 16 Char-Pit
16 Log Cabin Ice Cream
17 Sage Leaf Tahoe
see 10 Tunnel Creek Cafe

DRINKING & NIGHTLIFE
18 Crystal Bay Casino
see 17 Drink Coffee, Do Stuff
see 1 Grid Bar & Grill
19 Incline Public House
20 Village Pub

THE IMPRESSIVE TAHOE RIM TRAIL

The 165-mile-long **Tahoe Rim Trail** *(tahoerimtrail.org)*, or TRT, was first envisioned in the early 1980s, but wasn't completed until 2001. It encircles the lake, traversing its summits with an elevation gain/loss of about 24,000ft. In one go, it'll take an experienced hiker about 12 days to finish. Fortunately, there are 12 official trailheads throughout the basin, allowing hikers to explore select segments as day hikes or overnight trips.

Mountain bikers are also allowed, but with caveats. Bikes are banned in designated wilderness areas and on sections that overlap with the Pacific Crest Trail. Bike-friendly segments include Brockway Summit to Watson Lake, Kingsbury Grade to Armstrong Pass and Tahoe Meadows to Spooner Summit. Be aware of wildlife and altitude risks while on the trail.

and walkable town has a smattering of modest retro motels and a host of old-school dining establishments, from the vintage **Char-Pit** *(charpit.shop)* for burgers to family-owned **Log Cabin Ice Cream** *(logcabinicecream.squarespace.com)*.

In summer, all eyes are on **Kings Beach State Recreation Area**, a seductive 700ft-long beach that often gets deluged with sunseekers (if it's too crowded, drive just down the road to slightly-less-busy **Moon Dunes Beach**). The nostalgic 1920s **Old Brockway Golf Course** *(oldbrockway.com; green fees adult/child from $60/50)* will please golfers with its peekaboo lake views and a popular lakeview bar, complete with bocce ball courts. Less serious golfers can enjoy **Kings Beach Mini Golf** *(kingsbeachminiaturegolf.com; $15)*, usually running from Memorial Day to Labor Day.

Paddleboard Yoga

There's no prettier place for it

With easy access, blue skies nearly all summer and virtually no waves, paddleboard yoga on the north shore is as beginner-friendly as it gets – though that doesn't mean you'll stay dry. **Waterman's Landing** *(tahoewaterman.com; from $32)* is the hub for outdoor activities in Carnelian Bay, with near-daily paddleboard yoga (also called 'SUP yoga') classes straight from the beach. Classes take yogis through basic poses, all while balanced on a paddleboard against the backdrop of the sandy private beach. It's a serious core workout, but beach yoga classes are also available if you'd rather stay dry.

Hang Out in the Backyard

A communal space for visitors and locals alike

In Kings Beach, **Tahoe Backyard** *(tahoebackyard.com)*, aka the Backyard, may be next to a microbrewery, but it's as family-friendly as it gets. The large outdoor space is surrounded by said brewery and craft stores, with a big green area loaded with picnic tables, lawn games and an outdoor stage. It plays host to a swath of activities, including trivia nights, poetry slams, makers markets, live music and more. It's in central Kings Beach and walkable from anywhere in town. Hours vary seasonally.

An Easy Hike to Gorgeous Tahoe Views

Hiking Monkey Rock and the Flume Trail

The north shore is loaded with great lookout points. But one of the most popular is the quick trail to **Monkey Rock**, which

DRINKING ON THE NORTH SHORE: BEST APRÈS-SKI

Big Water Grille: This lake-view restaurant near Diamond Peak is popular for sunset happy hours for deep-pocketed locals. *hours vary*

Incline Public House: Alibi Brewing's large location in Incline Village is a year-round favorite, with about a dozen local beers. *hours vary*

Slot (The): An institution for cheap beer, loud music and '80s ski movies on repeat. *hours vary*

Le Chamois: Ski-in bar at Palisades Tahoe with Adirondack chairs, pizzas, an outdoor bar and plenty of post-ski sun in spring. *hours vary*

SKURZEI3/SHUTTERSTOCK

Monkey Rock

shares a parking area with the longer **Tunnel Creek Trail**. The trail starts behind Tunnel Creek Cafe, climbing about 480ft over 1.3 miles. At 0.9 miles, you face a choice: choose the steeper left shortcut to Monkey Rock, or continue on the main trail for 0.3 miles before turning left at the next split; they both end at Monkey Rock. From the rocky outcropping overlooking the lake, face north and you'll see Monkey Rock sitting about 15ft down the hill. Double back, or stay on the trail for another mile to intersect with the historic Flume Trail.

Go for a Hole-in-One

Give disc golf a try

If you've never played disc golf, Incline Village is a great place to try it, with an 18-hole wooded course behind the town's recreation center. It's an excellent way to spend some time out in pretty Tahoe forests without the need for a long hike. The **North Tahoe Lions Club Disc Golf Course** *(yourtahoeplace .com/parks-rec)* usually has a good mix of serious players along with families and groups of friends just out for afternoon fun. The course is free to play and discs are available to rent for $5 from the Incline Village Recreation Center, though many stores in town sell them, too.

DRINKING ON THE NORTH SHORE: BEST NIGHTLIFE

Auld Dubliner: The closest thing Tahoe has to an Irish pub, with a huge wooden bar and packed crowds on winter weekends. *hours vary*

Village Pub: Old-school digs and affordable drinks, plus pool and shuffleboard tables. Open some nights until 4am. *hours vary*

Crystal Bay Casino: A nearly 100-year-old casino with modern updates that offers frequent concerts and late-night drinking and gambling. *24hr*

Grid Bar & Grill: Catch games at one of the few late-night places in Kings Beach, with reliably good burgers. *11am-midnight*

EPIC VS IKON

Independent ski resorts are few and far between these days and two season passes cover Tahoe's major resorts: the **Epic Pass** (Northstar, Heavenly and Kirkwood) and the **Ikon Pass** (Palisades and Alpine Meadows). The rivalry has reshaped the ski industry, igniting controversy as both companies aggressively acquired independent ski resorts over the last two decades. It makes skiing more affordable, with both season passes priced at up to $1000, but critics say the corporatization of skiing is driving up ski-town prices, crowding slopes and making resorts lose their local character. Tahoe still has a few locally owned resorts, including **Diamond Peak**, **Homewood Resort** and **Sugar Bowl Resort**, a Truckee locals' favorite for tree skiing and pow stashes that limits pass sales to keep crowds down.

A Hub for Big-Mountain Winter Sports

Winter at Palisades Tahoe

Combined, **Palisades Tahoe** *(palisadestahoe.com)* and Alpine Meadows (connected by lift and sharing one lift ticket) have 6000 skiable acres, making it the biggest ski resort in California. Though it's known for its expert runs and chutes (including KT-22 and the Slot), it has an expansive beginner area with a unique feature: it's near the top. That means beginners get expert-level views, even on their first day. Lift tickets are expensive, pushing $300 per day on winter weekends, so an all-season Epic Pass may be a better deal for repeat skiers. Parking reservations are required on winter weekends and holidays *(parkpalisadestahoe.com)*. Parking reservations have helped with congestion, but it's still best to leave Truckee before 7am on powder days. If skiing isn't your thing, other winter draws include an all-ages snowtubing area, a year-round sightseeing gondola and the 'Cushing Crossing' pond skim each May.

EATING & DRINKING ON THE NORTH SHORE: BREAKFAST PICKS

Tunnel Creek Cafe: Indoor/outdoor seating and a huge coffee menu at the base of the Flume Trail. *hours vary* $

Crest Cafe: House-made breakfasts and piping-hot coffee drinks on the river at the base of Alpine Meadows. *8am-3pm Wed-Mon* $

Drink Coffee, Do Stuff: High-elevation coffees owned by a former pro snowboarder; locations in Truckee and Incline Village. *7am-5pm* $

Sage Leaf Tahoe: Locally owned and a locals' favorite for leisurely brunches from the former chef at Incline's priciest restaurant. *hours vary* $$

DANIEL51003/SHUTTERSTOCK

Palisades Tahoe

Warm-Weather Days in Olympic Valley

Palisades is poppin' in the summer, too

Winter sports put Palisades on the map, but summer and fall are every bit as lively, with popular festivals like **Tuesday Bluesdays**, **Oktoberfest** and 'Guitar Strings and Chicken Wings.' A relatively new draw is the **Tahoe Via Ferrata** *(tahoe via.com; from $160)*, offering cable-assisted climbing up the resort's famously unskiable 'Tram Face' wall, though hiking along a roaring waterfall to Shirley Canyon (4 miles round trip; 1400ft gain) is where most locals head on weekends.

High Camp, at 8200ft above sea level, is home to an **Olympic Museum** and the starting point for lakeview hikes and rental shops in the valley make it easy to cycle the flat, 7-mile riverfront path to Tahoe City and back. Hikers that reach High Camp from the Granite Chief Trail (3.7 miles; 1900ft gain) can take the gondola back down for free (dogs are OK!). **Heavenly** (p106) offers the same deal.

RAILROADS IN LAKE TAHOE

The modern history of the north shore of Lake Tahoe wasn't shaped by gold, like much of Northern California, but by the railroads. The transcontinental railroad ran north of Tahoe through Truckee. There, Tahoe's earliest tourists switched to a smaller train to reach Tahoe City, then took steamboats from the Tahoe City pier to luxury lakeside resorts. In Incline Village, the Sierra Nevada Wood & Lumber Company operated its own railway that carried logs 1500ft up the hillside. The wood was then dropped into a 12-mile-long flume system connecting to Virginia and Carson Cities, where it was used to build mines and saloons. This is how Incline Village's Flume Trail, now beloved by both hikers and mountain bikers, got its name.

Beyond The North Shore

Places

GETTING AROUND

You'll need a car to explore anything beyond the Tahoe basin. While Reno is accessible from the north shore all year via Hwy 80 through Truckee, roads to other destinations outside the basin (including Virginia City, everything north of Truckee and the mountain passes around Carson Pass) frequently close during heavy snow. It's extremely important to have snow tires and/or tire chains for winter exploration, especially as cellphone service can be spotty outside the basin.

Just beyond the North Shore lie historic railroad towns, old-timey Western boomtowns and the biggest little city in the world.

The lake and Sierra Nevada peaks are why most people come to Tahoe, but a quick drive over one of the mountain passes will lead to so much more to explore. North of the lake is Truckee, a historic railroad town that's grown into a trendy outdoor hub without losing its gold rush–era charms. To the east is Reno, a former gambling stop now in the midst of an artistic and culinary renaissance. Further afield is Virginia City, where saloon trapdoors still lead to former silver mines, as well as Hope Valley, a peaceful escape when Tahoe feels too crowded. Venture even further and you'll find riverfront towns like Downieville, hot springs near Sierraville and trail crossings like Carson Pass.

Reno, Nevada

TIME FROM THE N SHORE (INCLINE VILLAGE): **45MIN**

Detour to underrated Reno

With a clutch of big casinos in the dusty shadow of the Sierra Nevada, Reno has a reputation for being a lesser Vegas. That's somewhat accurate, but these, days Reno is much more. Beyond the garish downtown, with its mid-century modern architecture, neon signs and alpine-fed Truckee River, sprawls a city of workaday neighborhoods. In the last decade, Reno has become host to server farms supporting familiar Silicon Valley names and the formerly gritty Midtown District offers funky bars, top-notch restaurants and vibrant arts spaces. Sights around town include the **National Automobile Museum** *(automuseum.org)*, the **Nevada Museum of Art** *(nevadaart.org)* and the **Nevada Historical Society Museum** *(nvhistoricalsociety.org)*, packed with vintage casino memorabilia. It's a fun urban adventure only an hour from Lake Tahoe.

Truckee

Truckee

TIME FROM THE N SHORE (KINGS BEACH): **15MIN**

A lively town hundreds of years in the making

Truckee is a steeped in Old West history. It was put on the map by the railroad, grew rich on logging and ice harvesting and is now one of the trendiest ski towns in the US. Today, tourism fills much of the city's coffers, thanks to a well-preserved historic downtown and its proximity to Lake Tahoe, Hwy 80 and nearly a dozen winter resorts. The aura of the Old West still lingers over Truckee's teensy one-horse downtown, where railroad workers and lumberjacks once milled about in raucous saloons, bawdy brothels and shady gambling halls.

With a recent influx of families and entrepreneurs from the Bay Area, most of the late-19th-century buildings now contain creative restaurants and upscale boutiques. Strolling through Truckee's **downtown** *(downtowntruckee.com)* is one of the best ways to spend an afternoon after a morning hike or ski sesh. Downtown becomes pedestrian-only on summer Thursdays for the **Truckee Thursdays** weekly evening street festivals.

WHY I LOVE TRUCKEE

Suzie Dundas, Lonely Planet writer

I love Truckee because it's where big-mountain adventures meet gold-rush lore. You can hike along trails used hundreds of years ago by settlers, then fit in a quick afternoon mountain-bike ride on some of the best trails in California. Downtown Truckee has a unique blend of hipster artisans tucked into former saloons and there's no better way to spend a summer afternoon than floating in the Truckee River. It's more of a year-round community than most towns around the lake, but we still have access to Lake Tahoe just 15 minutes away. Better yet, we also have Donner Lake, a gorgeous alpine gem that would be a resort destination unto itself were it not in the shadow of Big Blue.

EATING IN TRUCKEE: WHERE THE LOCALS GO

Burger Me: A Truckee institution specializing in locally sourced burgers with veggie options. *11am-9pm* $

Donner Lake Kitchen: Hearty breakfasts and brunch just across from Donner Lake. Expect a wait. *7am-2pm* $$

Stella: An open-air kitchen and cozy courtyard are the backdrop for a menu of internationally inspired dishes with a Cali twist. *hours vary* $$$

Great Gold: Housemade pizza and pasta just far enough off the usual tourist track. *hours vary* $$$

TOP EXPERIENCE

Donner Summit & Donner Memorial State Park

Truckee's western end is home to Donner Lake (site of the Donner Party tragedy), now a popular state park with a fascinating museum. Just past it is Donner Summit, with hiking opportunities and a wealth of history, including ancient petroglyphs, remains of America's first long-distance highway, the first transcontinental railroad's tracks and sites where California trail pioneers hoisted their wagons through the mountains.

JUAN CARLOS MARTINEZ/SHUTTERSTOCK

Donner Lake

TOP TIPS

- Hit the **Donner Lake Overlook** for stunning sunset photos.
- Donner Lake has 37 free public piers; expect to share space on busy weekends.
- Donner Pass Rd can close in heavy snow. Carry chains from December to April and BYO snowshoes/skis for the park's groomed winter trails.

PRACTICALITIES

- *parks.ca.gov*
- Parking $10
- Visitor center 10am-5pm; camping Memorial Day to Labor Day
- Kayak rentals from $25 *(donnerlakemarina.com)*

Hike, Paddle or Snowshoe All Day

A poignant tribute to one of the West's most harrowing pioneer stories, **Donner Memorial State Park** sits at the edge of Donner Lake where the ill-fated Donner Party spent the brutal winter of 1846–47. The park's striking **Pioneer Monument**, topped with a statue at the height of that season's snow, honors all early emigrants. In summer, visitors can hike forested trails, swim, fish or paddle on the lake. In winter it transforms into a snowy escape for cross-country skiing and snowshoeing, with interpretive displays at the **Emigrant Trail Museum** open year-round.

Hike Through Centuries of History

High above the lake, Donner Summit blends natural beauty with fascinating relics of westward expansion. Here you'll find **petroglyphs** carved by the ancient Martis people and abandoned railroad tunnels from the 1860s, blasted by Chinese laborers to complete the Transcontinental Railroad. On the 3.6-mile **Donner Summit Canyon Trail**, visitors can walk along segments of the old Lincoln Hwy – the nation's first coast-to-coast highway – still visible in places beside dramatic cliffs and alpine views. The 5.2-mile **Judah Loop hike** passes by signage marking notable sites along the California Emigrant Trail, which crossed these rugged summits.

Spend an Afternoon at Relaxing Boca Reservoir

Truckee can get quite crowded and traffic to Donner Lake can be slow and frustrating. If it feels crowded in town, consider spreading out just to the northeast with a visit to **Boca Reservoir**. It's rarely crowded, with easy access for putting in paddleboards or kayaks, plus small beaches and numerous walking trails. Nearby, you can walk the quick interpretive loop through the **Boca Townsite**, where Truckee's ice (and beer) industries once flourished. Note that Boca Reservoir has no amenities, save for a pit toilet in the summer and is about 15 minutes' drive past Truckee.

Northstar California

TIME FROM THE N SHORE (KINGS BEACH): **10MIN**

Ski or Hike in Style

Among Tahoe ski resorts, **Northstar California** *(northstarcalifornia.com)* has a reputation for being the most luxurious, as well as one of the best for families. But hey, this is Tahoe and even a luxury resort has plenty of gnarly terrain. That's true in both winter and also summer, when the resort turns into Tahoe's only lift-serviced bike park. The village's central ice-skating rink switches to roller-skate central come June and hiking is also popular, with options for connecting to the Tahoe Rim Trail. Scenic lift rides are more affordable than gondola rides at other resorts and on winter weekends the resort hosts 'S'more O' Clock (4pm) around the firepits (first-come, first-served).

DRINKING BEYOND THE BASIN: OUR PICKS

Good Wolf Brewing Company: A book-laden brewery with moody art. Expect local craft beers and unexpected, locally sourced experimentals. *hours vary*

Pigeon Head Brewery: Starting with German lager, it now brews multiple variations and seasonal beers. *2-8pm Mon-Thu, noon-8pm Fri & Sat, noon-6pm Sun*

Truckee Brewing Company: A big beer menu, with two public locations in Truckee: a beer-only brewery and a full restaurant closer to Northstar. *hours vary*

Great Basin Brewing Co: One of Reno's biggest beer-scene successes, makers of the popular Ichthyosaurus IPA and winners of international beer accolades. *hours vary*

Washoe Club: Virginia City's oldest saloon, opened in the 1960s, has cheap drinks and daily tours of the supposedly haunted building. *hours vary*

Cottonwood Restaurant & Bar: Epic Truckee views from the outdoor deck, housed in one of the first ski lodges in California. *hours vary*

Bar of America: BoA, in a building dating to 1891, is now a popular restaurant with a large wooden bar and live music on weekends. *hours vary*

Pastime Club: This dive bar slinging cheap drinks is Truckee's oldest saloon, dating to 1896. *2pm-2am*

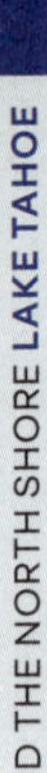

SEE HISTORIC TRUCKEE ON FOOT

Walk the same streets as early pioneers, gold prospectors and (maybe) Wild West gangsters.

START	END	LENGTH
Old Truckee Jail Museum	Old Truckee Jail Museum	0.5 mile; 15 mins

Start at the 1 **Truckee Old Jail Museum**, from 1875. Records are spotty, but depending on the docent, you might hear stories of it housing everyone from 'Baby Face' Nelson to 'Machine Gun' Kelly. Near the jail is one of the town's original coffee joints: 2 **Coffeebar**. With a sunny outdoor patio, it's a great place to relax before your stroll. Next, walk to the main street (Donner Pass Rd). Hanging a left puts you at the start of what was the original downtown Truckee. Today the block has specialty stores, restaurants and bars. Stop at 3 **Sweet's Handmade Candies**, where bakers often dip caramel apples during the day. Across the street is the town's original railroad depot, now a gallery with rotating local artists and the 4 **Truckee Railroad Museum** inside a vintage train caboose. Nearby are shops like 5 **Bespoke**, an eco-minded jewelry and homegoods store and 6 **Word After Word**, an old-school bookstore with ceiling-high shelves and sliding ladders. The basement holds a vinyl shop and a discount rack with books as low as $2. Historic buildings line the row, once home to newspaper offices, brothels and shoot-outs. At the end is 7 **Bar of America** (p129), named for its former use as a bank. Turning left on Bridge St will eventually loop you back to the 8 **Truckee Old Jail Museum**.

The **'Welcome to Truckee' mural** on the side of the post office is a great place for a cheesy vacation photo.

If there's one thing Truckee doesn't lack (other than snow), it's coffee shops. While at **Coffeebar** get the lavender tea latte.

Walk down Church St to see **Gray's Cabin.** Built in 1858 and used as an early hotel, it's Truckee's oldest still-standing structure.

High St
Jiboom St
Bridge St
Church St
Spring St
Donner Pass Rd
West River St
START/END
0 100 m
0 0.05 miles

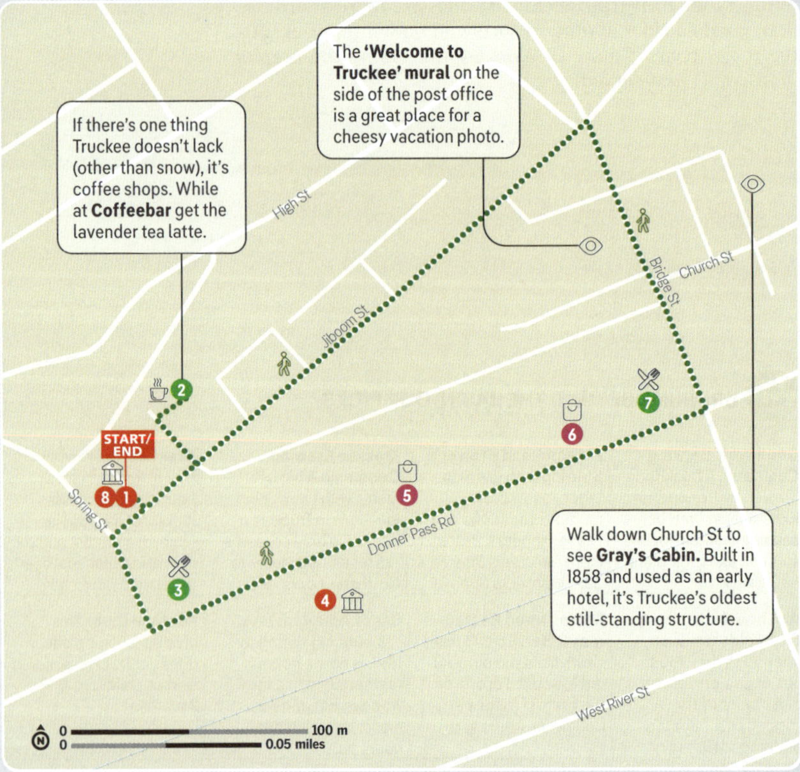

The East Shore

UNDEVELOPED BEACHES | EPIC SUNSETS | LAKEVIEW HIKING

Though Tahoe is usually associated with California, the entire east shore is in Nevada. The sole road through is Rte 28/Rte 50, stretching from south of Incline Village to Stateline, with undeveloped shoreline on one side and Sierra Nevada peaks on the other. Much of the east shore is protected as Lake Tahoe–Nevada State Park, making almost the entire shoreline north of Glenbrook open to the public via a series of beaches. While beaches are the main draw, hiking will attract visitors keen on Tahoe's most epic views. Despite having few homes and fewer amenities, the east shore gets extremely busy in summer. Fortunately, a new walking/cycling path from Incline Village makes it easier to access most of the state park's draws. East shore visitors will have a better time if they treat it not as a box to check off the to-do list, but as a place to spend time outdoors without a set schedule.

TOP TIP

The east shore's Sand Harbor State Park is probably the most popular in Tahoe, especially when it's hosting the Lake Tahoe Shakespeare Festival. Between mid-April and mid-October, day-use reservations *(reservenevada.com)* are required to park on-site. If you don't arrive by 10.30am you'll lose your spot. Arrive on bicycle or on foot and you can skip the reservation step.

Take the Perfect Family Photo

Pull over at Memorial Point Scenic Overlook

If you're deterred by Sand Harbor's crowds and aren't keen on hiking to a beach, stop at the **Memorial Point Scenic Overlook** just north of Sand Harbor. Walk around the public bathrooms to the lake to find dozens of coves and boulder piles ideal for a photo session. Parking is free but limited to 30 minutes.

A Must-Do Tahoe Experience

Lounging at Sand Harbor State Park

If you've seen photos of kayakers and paddleboarders on crystal-clear water floating between giant boulders, it was probably from crowd-pleasing **Sand Harbor State Park** *(parks.nv.gov)*, just 3 miles south of Incline Village. Here, two sand spits form a shallow bay with brilliant, warm turquoise water and white, boulder-strewn beaches easily explored by kayak.

GETTING AROUND

There's no public transportation that connects between Incline Village to the north and Stateline to the south. Visitors will need to have a car, or limit themselves to areas accessible via bicycle and walking paths, like the Tahoe East Shore Trail to Sand Harbor State Park or the footpaths linking Nevada Beach and South Lake Tahoe.

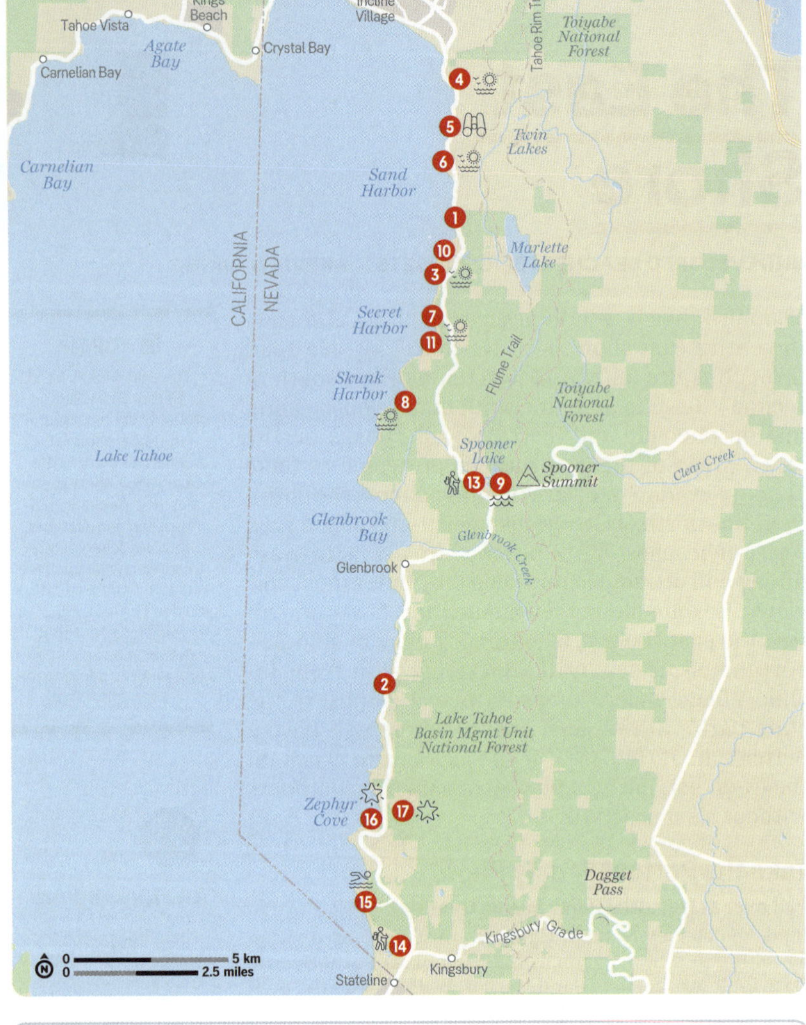

SIGHTS
1 Bonsai Rock
2 Cave Rock
3 Chimney Beach
4 Hidden Beach
5 Memorial Point Scenic Overlook
6 Sand Harbor State Park
see 7 Secret Cove
7 Secret Harbor Beach
8 Skunk Harbor
9 Spooner Lake
10 Thunderbird Lodge
11 Whale Beach

ACTIVITIES
12 Clearly Tahoe
13 Flume Trail
14 Lam Watah Nature Trail
15 Nevada Beach
see 16 Zephyr Cove
16 Zephyr Cove Marina
17 Zephyr Cove Stables

ENTERTAINMENT
see 6 Lake Tahoe Shakespeare Festival

The views west across the water are of snow-capped peaks and sublime sunsets. It gets busy here, especially during July and August, when the **Lake Tahoe Shakespeare Festival** *(laketahoeshakespeare.com; adult/child tickets from $32/17)* is underway. It mixes works by the Bard and contemporary pieces, performed outdoors by the lake. Buy your tickets early and note Sand Harbor's parking rules.

Hit the Water (or Trails)

Play tourist in Zephyr Cove

Zephyr Cove is the gem of Hwy 50, found as you approach Stateline. It's a mile-long stretch of sandy beach that's rarely uncrowded, but it doesn't get quite as many visitors as the south shore. **Zephyr Cove Marina** has everything from Jet Ski to party boat rentals and is the departure point for the **MS Dixie II** (p104).

Inland, you'll want to make advance reservations for the mellow horseback rides through the forest at **Zephyr Cove Stables**. A special-use permit allows the company to operate on national forest land. Both the one-hour and 1½-hour tours traverse scenic trails; the longer route reaches the most impressive Tahoe viewpoint.

Learn about Tahoe's Earliest Residents

Stroll the interpretive nature trail

The mostly flat, stroller-friendly **Lam Watah Nature Trail** traverses Rabe Meadows, a summer home for the local Washoe tribe for more than 1000 years. Along the path, interpretive signs provide insights into Washoe life in the area, as well as later 20th-century uses for the meadow. The trail passes through land once slated for casino development, but preserved through efforts by the Nature Conservancy and now managed by the US Forest Service (USFS). The out-and-back route is roughly 2 miles, though a 3-mile loop takes you to **Nevada Beach**, one of the best places to catch a Tahoe sunset. Winter sunsets can bring an alpenglow effect that paints the mountains in rosy shades of pink and orange as visitors look toward the west.

Look Down on a Floating Lake

Visit Spooner Lake

Just north of the Rte 50 and Hwy 28 junction is **Spooner Lake** *(parks.nv.gov; parking $10-15)*, popular for catch-and-release fishing, picnicking and cross-country skiing, as well as the starting point for the Spooner to Marlette Hike (10 miles return; 1700ft gain). At Marlette there's a historic homesite and dam and the opportunity to hike to **Snow Valley Peak**, where you'll look down on an amazing sight: vivid blue Marlette Lake seemingly hovering 1000ft above Tahoe, separated by just a small stretch of pines. Spooner Lake is also the start of the famous 14-mile **Flume Trail**, a holy grail for experienced

continues on p136

CAVE ROCK'S CONTROVERSIAL HISTORY

Cave Rock is hard to miss if you drive the east shore: Rte 50 runs directly through the volcanic formation. It holds deep spiritual significance for the Washoe tribe, for whom the site is sacred to creation stories, with only a select group of learned Washoe elders allowed to visit it. But in the 20th century, non-indigenous visitation surged, with the highway tunnel blasted through its base in 1931 and rock climbers bolting routes into its walls. Years of conflict followed and in 2003 the Washoe and allies were able to advocate for a ban on climbing. Today, hiking to the summit is extremely popular, though many Washoe still see that as an affront to its cultural significance.

ROAD TRIP

The History of Tahoe in 72 Miles

See the sights that not only define Tahoe, but explain how it came to be a tourism and outdoor adventure hot spot. Driving around the lake is a must-do activity for first-time visitors, both to get a sense of just how vast the lake is, but to also marvel at its beauty. Going clockwise is recommended so you're always driving on the lake side.

1 Tahoe City

Start in Tahoe City, where the **Gatekeeper's Museum** (p119) chronicles the cultural history of Lake Tahoe, with exhibits on the Washoe people and others who shaped what Tahoe would become. When it's open, **Watson Cabin**, Tahoe's oldest remaining building, is a can't-miss stop.

The Drive: It's 30 minutes to Incline Village, passing by 1950s-era motels in vintage Kings Beach.

2 Incline Village

Visit the **UC Davis Tahoe Environmental Research Center** for exhibits on the lake's clarity, climate science and humans' impact. Consider making the quick hike up to scenic **Monkey Rock** (p122).

The Drive: As you drive, imagine owning everything you see. That was the reality for eccentric millionaire George Whittell, Jr, who owned most of the east shore in the 1940s.

3 Lake Tahoe–Nevada State Park

Lake Tahoe–Nevada State Park stretches from south of Incline Village to about halfway down the east shore. Within it, **Sand Harbor State Park** (p131) is the most popular recreation area, but other great places to stop include **Bonsai Rock** (p136), **Chimney Beach** (p136) and **Spooner Lake**.

CRAIG COOPER/SHUTTERSTOCK

Old railroad tracks, Ed Z'berg Sugar Pine Point State Park

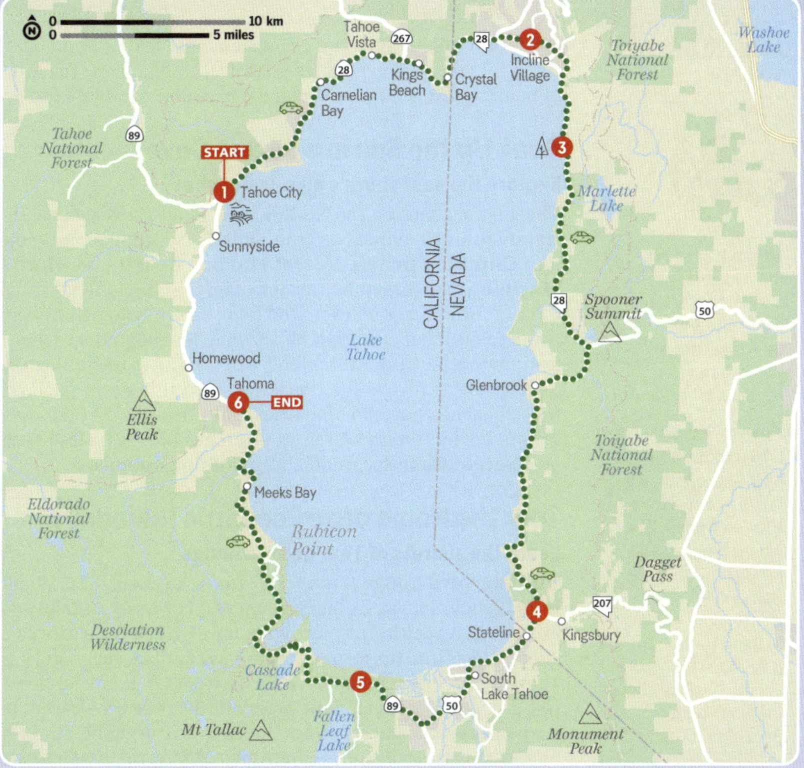

The Drive: Keep cruising down the east shore, which gets progressively more developed as you head south.

❹ Rabe Meadows

Rabe Meadows was home to the Sky Harbor Airport and Casino, plagued by numerous crashes in its poorly planned attempts to bring tourists to Tahoe in the 1940s. The meadows' **Lam Watah Nature Trail** (p133) is packed with info on Tahoe's first residents.

The Drive: The drive should only take about 20 minutes, but can be double that with traffic (or if you want beach breaks).

❺ Tahoe's Southwestern Corner

Loop through South Lake Tahoe to visit the **Tallac Historic Site** (p110) and **Camp Richardson** (p137). The latter was developed as Tahoe's earliest motor lodge and now has exhibits on Tahoe's tourism history. Off the tourist track, hike to the ruins of **Glen Alpine Springs**, a once-thriving wellness resort.

The Drive: Expect heavy weekend traffic on the winding roads north of Camp Richardson en route to Tahoma.

❻ Tahoma

Tahoe views abound on the west shore, though it can be hard to find places to stop for more than a few seconds along the narrow road hugging the shore. Fortunately, destinations near Tahoma like **Ed Z'berg Sugar Pine Point State Park** (p118) and **Chambers Landing** (p117) sit in primo places to spend a few hours. For a cool photo op, stop at the **old railroad tracks**, which seem to disappear straight into the lake. Then return to Tahoe City for a lakeview dinner, or continue north to Truckee.

FAMILY OUTINGS AROUND INCLINE VILLAGE

Shane Hammett, local expert and chef-owner at Sage Leaf Tahoe, on the best place for a family outing. *sageleaftahoe.com*

I love taking my family to the new East Shore Trail and heading down to **Hidden Beach**. It's a beautiful, paved biking and walking trail that takes you from Incline Village to Sand Harbor, with places to stop and access the lake along the way. Hidden Beach is one of those places, a small stretch looking back toward Crystal Bay. My children love it there and the water is crystal clear, so you can see everything on the lake bed. It's also one of the lake's best places to watch the sunset illuminating the sky and since it's dog friendly, the whole family can come along.

continued from p133

mountain bikers. It's a mix of spectacular views and sometimes technical, generally leg-shaking biking not for the faint of heart. (Note that Marlette Lake is closed until late 2026).

Soak Up the Sun in a Secret Cove

Explore the east shore's hike-in beaches

The best beaches on the Nevada side, Sand Harbor notwithstanding, aren't marked on road signs. Local summer hot spots like **Chimney Beach**, **Secret Harbor Beach** and **Skunk Harbor** are accessed by various official and unofficial trails ranging from 2 to 4 miles (round trip), gaining anywhere from 100ft to 600ft of elevation on the way back up. Most have a designated parking area along Rte 28, but parking legally on shoulders also works. Pack out everything you pack in; these beaches have no amenities. Families should take note of wandering too far astray, as stretches like **Whale Beach** and **Secret Cove** are unofficially clothing optional.

Tour the Home of an Eccentric Billionaire

Learn the secrets of Thunderbird Lodge

Thunderbird Lodge *(thunderbirdtahoe.org; tours $75),* built in 1939, now sits on six lakefront acres. But its eccentric (and exceedingly wealthy) former owner once owned the entire east shore. Tours into his former estate shed light on the history of Tahoe's development and go past unexpected home features, like an opium den, elephant cages and secret tunnels used to keep unexpected guests away. The views are arguably the best on the Nevada side. Tours run from late May to mid-October.

See Tahoe's Most Famous Trees

Kayak or swim to Bonsai Rock

Bonsai Rock isn't technically an island, but rather it's a huge boulder sitting just off the shore. And in the boulder cracks are a series of tiny trees somehow surviving the snow, wind and lack of dirt to grow on top of it, making them look like tiny bonsai trees. There's no formal trail down from the parking area, so just scurry down however you like. You can also take more formal tours with companies like **Clearly Tahoe** *(clearlytahoe.com),* which offers a glass-bottom kayak tour out to the rock.

Places We Love to Stay

$ Budget $$ Midrange $$$ Top End

The South & East Shores

Map p107

Hotel Becket $ Owned by Best Western but dolled up in hipster finishes, Hotel Becket is a good choice for budget-conscious travelers who still want a bit of style.

Camp Richardson $ Tent campsites on a beachfront compound with on-site amenities like a marina, ice-cream parlor and convenience store.

Stardust Lodge $$ A mom-and-pop hotel with clean and functional (if a bit small) rooms just a quick walk from south shore beaches.

Coachman Hotel $$ A renovated roadside motel turned hipster getaway with loads of complimentary perks that'll ultimately save you some dough.

Margaritaville Resort Lake Tahoe $$ A sprawling, newly renovated resort with roomy (and not too over-the-top) tropical-themed suites in an unbeatable location.

Harrah's Lake Tahoe $$ Slightly dated (and oddly colored) rooms, but with fantastic views and walkable to everything in Stateline.

Zephyr Cove Resort $$ Old-school lakeside resort with rustic but comfortable cabins. Fun for families and travelers who value location above all. Budget camping available May to September.

Edgewood Tahoe Resort $$$ A relatively new upscale resort with a private golf course and beach access. Rooms are elegant and minimalist chic; a concierge can arrange VIP experiences.

Landing Tahoe Resort & Spa $$$ Alpine modern meets 1950s rustic chic at this lakefront resort with espresso machines, fireplaces and access to a private beach.

The West Shore

Map p113

evo Tahoe City Hotel $ An adventure-focused hotel with modern rooms and lots of communal social spaces, plus a sauna and cold plunge.

Basecamp Tahoe City $$ A renovated motel whose rooms feel straight out of a trendy glamping resort (only with real walls).

The Inn at Boatworks $$ A revamped lakeside motel near the Tahoe City Marina with free paddleboard, kayak and bike rentals in summer, or snowshoes and sleds in winter.

Granlibakken Resort (p117) **$$** A 74-acre historical resort, with on-site activities, where vintage cabin meets modern wilderness lodge. Some rooms could use updates, but it's a true in-the-woods experience.

The North Shore

Map p121

Village at Palisades Tahoe $$ Hotel rooms up to multiroom condos, lofted above the shops of the Palisades Village. Unbeatable ski access, but don't expect quiet nights.

Cedar Glen Lodge $$ Wood-accented cabins (plus rooms with a cabin vibe) and bigger suites with kitchenettes. The lake is only a short two-minute walk away.

Mourelatos Resort $$ Large suites with classic upscale hotel design. It's slightly dated, but made up for by the beach outside your front door.

Hyatt Regency Lake Tahoe $$$ A luxury resort with a huge private beach, pier bar and an outdoor pool surrounded by pines. Free winter shuttles to Diamond Peak Resort.

Truckee

Best Western Plus Truckee-Tahoe Hotel $ Standard chain-style rooms, but reliably helpful service and a good location. A step above normal chains, with prices that seem like a steal for Truckee.

Gravity Haus Truckee-Tahoe $$ A boutique hotel with luxuriously rustic spaces and unique architectural details. Perks include a fantastic on-site restaurant (Stella), gear storage and on-site bocce.

Martis Valley Lodge $$ A newly opened renovation of a chain hotel with upgrades like an on-site restaurant and ski-rental delivery. The closest location to Northstar without paying slopeside prices.

Donner Lake Village $$ Classically styled lakefront condos with a lakeview lounge, outdoor grills, a dock and other summer-camp-style amenities. Ideal access to Sugar Bowl Resort in winter.

Ritz-Carlton Lake Tahoe $$$ As posh-as-it-gets digs with ski-in/out access to Northstar, private chalets and a high-end lakefront beach club. Everything you expect from a Ritz-Carlton, including the prices.

For places to stay in Yosemite & the Sierra Nevada, see p178

STEPHEN MOEHLE/SHUTTERSTOCK

Above: El Capitan (p147), Yosemite National Park; Right: Bear, Kings Canyon National Park (p159)

Researched by Ashley Harrell

Yosemite & the Sierra Nevada

FORMIDABLE AND EXQUISITE ADVENTURER'S WONDERLAND

Like a backbone rising up over central California, the Sierra Nevada encompasses colossal canyons and some of the highest peaks in the country.

In the Sierra Nevada, everything feels a little less tame, a lot more wondrous and far, far bigger than in other parts of California. The natural environs are ferociously beautiful and brimming with superlatives: the world's biggest trees, the world's oldest trees, the highest waterfall in North America and the highest mountaintop in the contiguous United States.

Formed by tectonic plate crushing against plate and then sculpted by glaciers, this land and its innumerable lakes, meadows, forests and mountains has served as inspiration – and a playground – for people through the ages and from all over the world. To present-day Californians, though, it's something more, too: lifeblood. The melted Sierra snowpack hydrates more than 75% of the state's residents and large swaths of farmland across the Central Valley, which produces a quarter of the nation's food. In addition, the region's national parks inject more than a billion dollars into the economies of nearby communities every year.

Recently, climate change has become a dire threat across the Sierra Nevada, with sizable stretches of the landscape transformed by catastrophic wildfire, drought, floods and severe storms. In addition, the downsizing of the federal government has left the region's public lands increasingly vulnerable to extreme weather, resource exploitation and overtourism. More visitors than ever are recreating in the Sierra Nevada, because at least for now, the inimitable beauty still abounds.

UDDHAVA DAS/SHUTTERSTOCK

THE MAIN AREAS

YOSEMITE NATIONAL PARK
Epic Sierra Nevada scenery.
p144

SEQUOIA & KINGS CANYON NATIONAL PARKS
A vast canyon and humongous trees.
p159

EASTERN SIERRA
Towering mountains and surreal desert landscapes.
p168

Find Your Way

The Sierra Nevada is 400 miles long and around 70 miles wide (covering 25% of California). We've selected the region's three national parks along with its lesser-explored eastern expanse as hubs for you to discover its natural landscapes, history and culture.

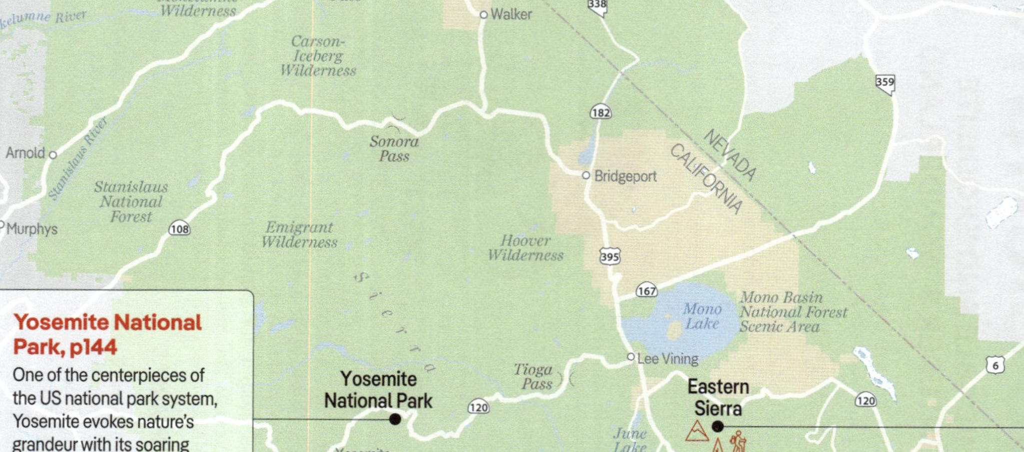

Yosemite National Park, p144

One of the centerpieces of the US national park system, Yosemite evokes nature's grandeur with its soaring granite domes, sky-high waterfalls and lush meadows.

Eastern Sierra, p168

A land of dramatic juxtapositions, where dizzying peaks – many over 14,000ft – rush abruptly upward from the arid expanses of the Great Basin and Mojave Deserts.

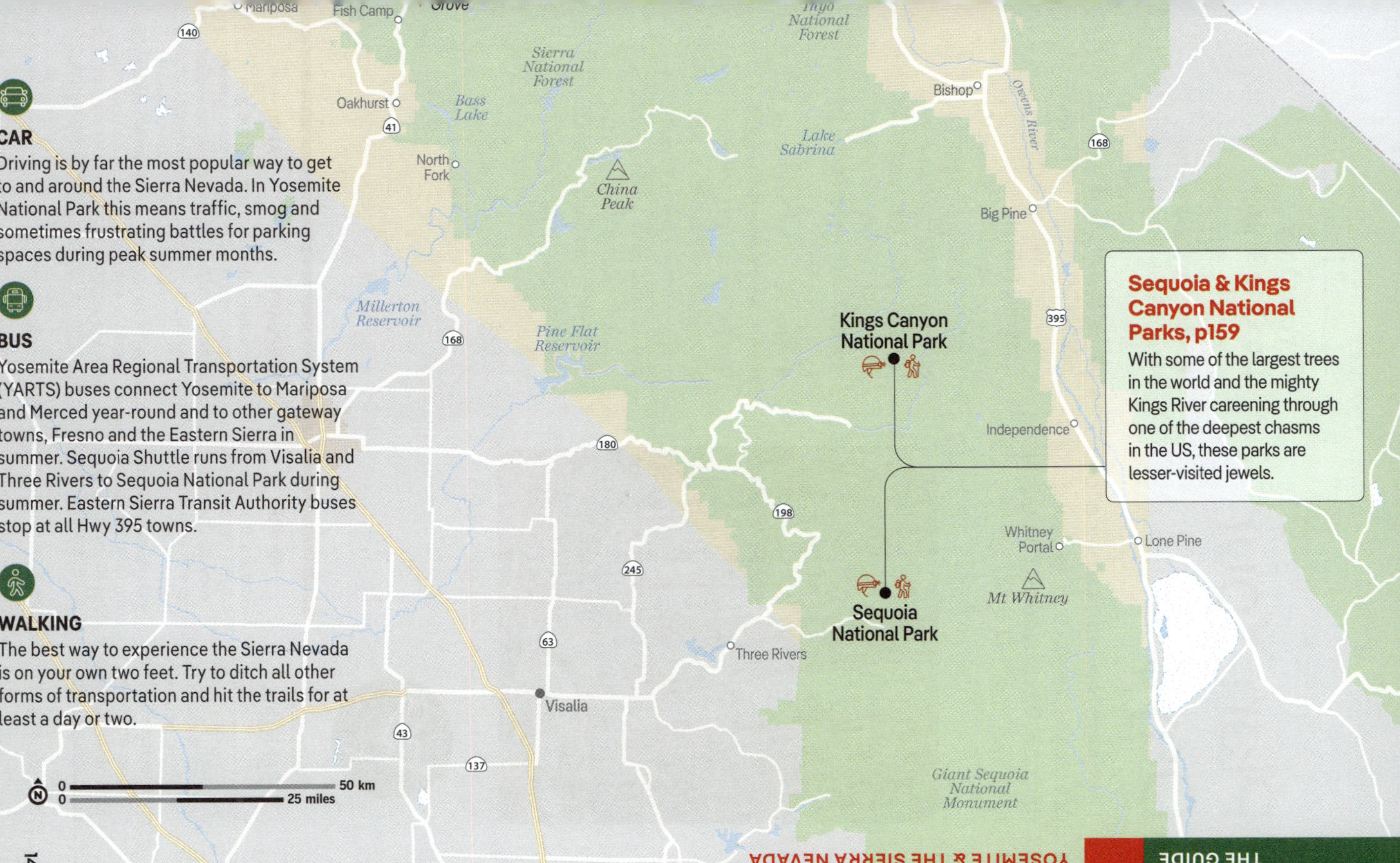

CAR

Driving is by far the most popular way to get to and around the Sierra Nevada. In Yosemite National Park this means traffic, smog and sometimes frustrating battles for parking spaces during peak summer months.

BUS

Yosemite Area Regional Transportation System (YARTS) buses connect Yosemite to Mariposa and Merced year-round and to other gateway towns, Fresno and the Eastern Sierra in summer. Sequoia Shuttle runs from Visalia and Three Rivers to Sequoia National Park during summer. Eastern Sierra Transit Authority buses stop at all Hwy 395 towns.

WALKING

The best way to experience the Sierra Nevada is on your own two feet. Try to ditch all other forms of transportation and hit the trails for at least a day or two.

Sequoia & Kings Canyon National Parks, p159

With some of the largest trees in the world and the mighty Kings River careening through one of the deepest chasms in the US, these parks are lesser-visited jewels.

Plan Your Days

The Sierra Nevada is a place to get close to nature. Hike those trails, ski those slopes, climb that rock and hug that tree.

JORDI C/SHUTTERSTOCK

Sequoia National Park (p159)

If You Only Do One Thing

- Spend the day in Yosemite National Park. To avoid parking or reservation problems, consider a **guided tour of the valley floor** (p150). If DIY is more your style, do the short hike up to misty **Bridalveil Fall** (p149), pull over to admire breathtaking **Tunnel View** (p149) and look for microscopic climbers working their way up the sheer granite of **El Capitan** (p147). Then rent a bicycle to **cruise around Yosemite Valley** (p147).

- In the afternoon, head to the historic **Ahwahnee Hotel** (p153) for a well-deserved cocktail or coffee and lunch before setting out on a longer hike to **Vernal and Nevada Falls** (p149). Reward yourself at **Curry Village Pizza Deck** (p145) and get some restful sleep while camping in a nearby tent cabin.

Seasonal Highlights

There's no bad time to visit. Spring is lovely for wildflowers and waterfalls, summer is great for high-altitude drives and low-altitude hikes, while fall colors and winter snow dustings are pure magic.

JANUARY

Guests gather round resort firepits and **snow sports** reign supreme at Yosemite's Badger Pass Ski Area, along with Mammoth Mountain Ski Area and June Mountain Ski Area in the Eastern Sierra.

FEBRUARY

For two weeks at the end of the month, the thin **Firefall** (p146) becomes Yosemite's most photographed attraction, if the sun's angle and the water flow are just right.

APRIL

By the end of the month, the dogwoods start to bloom and the waterfalls begin to gush with fresh snowmelt. Also, anglers rejoice and pick up their new permits for the start of the fishing season.

Five Days to Travel Around

● Give yourself an additional two days in Yosemite, especially in summer. If you're ambitious, hike Four Mile Trail to **Glacier Point** (p149) and if you prefer taking in jaw-dropping scenery without expending effort, just drive there. On your last day in the park, drive to the Tioga Pass, gaze out at a lunar-looking landscape from the glaciated granite of **Olmsted Point** (p147) and sleep under the stars in **Tuolumne Meadows** (p150).

● Exit the park through the Tioga Pass gate for some adventuring in the Eastern Sierra. Visit **Bodie State Historic Park** (p176), the best preserved ghost town in the West, then mosey around the also-haunting tufas of **Mono Lake** (p175). Don't go home without soaking your weary bones in one of the many **hot springs** (p174).

If You Have More Time

● Keep right on trucking down **Hwy 395** (p172), taking your sweet time hiking around lakes and waterfalls and beholding the wondrous **Devils Postpile** (p175) in summertime, or sliding down **snow-covered mountains** (p174) in wintertime. Hit up the area's best museum near Bishop, **Manzanar National Historic Site** (p171), visit the oldest trees on the planet in the **Ancient Bristlecone Pine Forest** (p171) and take a gander at the blob-like red boulders at the **Alabama Hills** (p172).

● Swing back around to the other side of the Sierra and check out the **world's biggest trees** (p161) at Sequoia National Park, then go spelunking at the wondrous **Crystal Cave** (p161). Finally, wind your way down into neighboring Kings Canyon and set out on some gorgeous **hikes** (p161).

MAY

Cascades continue their magnificent gushing and Bishop celebrates **Mule Days**, a unique week-long event where 'packers' (backcountry cowboys) show off their riding and roping skills in competitions and during an epic parade.

SEPTEMBER

Crowds recede, waterfalls trickle. **Yosemite Facelift** brings climbers and volunteers together for the country's largest trash pickup event, while the **Dark Sky Festival** (p164) graces Sequoia and Kings Canyon National Parks.

OCTOBER

Fall colors light up the Sierra Nevada and nature-obsessed photographers joyride looking for the best shot. The June Lake loop and Mammoth Lakes are particularly stunning at this time of year.

DECEMBER

The parks are frosted and mostly solitary, though diehards often show up to photograph fresh powder. Yosemite's Ahwahnee Hotel throws its extravagant **Bracebridge Dinner** (p153; part feast, part Renaissance fair).

Yosemite National Park

MOUNTAIN SCENERY | WATERFALLS | ABUNDANT WILDLIFE

TOP TIP

Before driving to Yosemite, find out if you'll need a reservation for your visit and secure it through *recreation.gov*. If reservations are sold out, you can enter by booking lodgings within the park, taking a guided tour, obtaining a wilderness permit or Half Dome permit, or riding a YARTS bus.

The crown jewel of California's national parks is defined by its plunging waterfalls, soaring trees, wildflower-dotted valleys and majestic domes. Carved by ancient glaciers, these stunning granite features have been gazed upon by devoted humans for some 8000 years.

The original caretakers, the Ahwahneechee people, were violently displaced in the mid-1800s by white settlers. After roads and inns began springing up, conservationists petitioned Congress to protect the area. In 1864 President Abraham Lincoln signed the Yosemite Grant, which ceded the land to California as a state park. This decision, paired with the efforts of conservationist John Muir, led to a congressional act in 1890 creating Yosemite National Park.

Today, the show-stopping park is also a UNESCO World Heritage Site and is visited by millions of people each year. Look up above the crowds, though and you'll feel awed by the park's unrivaled natural splendors.

GETTING AROUND

Yosemite is accessible year-round from the west (via Hwys 120 W and 140) and south (Hwy 41) and in summer also from the east (via Hwy 120 E). The winding mountain roads are plowed in winter, but snow chains may be required at any time. Rock slides have periodically shut down sections of road for weeks or months and at the time of research, low staffing levels were creating uncertainty around which roads would open when.

Most people drive into the park. During peak visitation periods, there's often standstill traffic in Yosemite Valley. Cycling is a lovely way to move around the valley, as is the free, air-conditioned Yosemite Valley Shuttle Bus. Buses operate year-round from 7am to 10pm at 12- to 22-minute intervals and stop at 19 numbered locations, including parking lots, campgrounds, trailheads and lodges. There's also an East Valley Shuttle that picks up more frequently, every eight to 12 minutes. Shuttle lines can snake around the block in summertime.

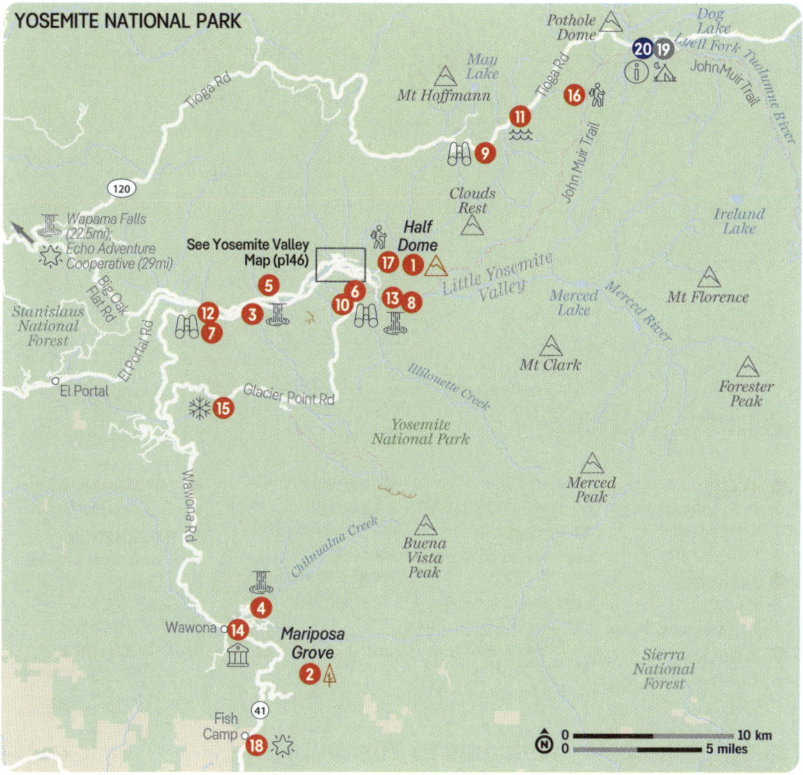

YOSEMITE NATIONAL PARK

Tioga Rd
120
Wapama Falls (22.5mi); Echo Adventure Cooperative (29mi)
Big Oak Flat Rd
Stanislaus National Forest
El Portal Rd
El Portal
See Yosemite Valley Map (p146)
Glacier Point Rd
Wawona Rd
Chilnualna Creek
Wawona
Mariposa Grove
41
Fish Camp
Pothole Dome
May Lake
Mt Hoffmann
Dog Lake
Lyell Fork Tuolumne River
John Muir Trail
Clouds Rest
Half Dome
Little Yosemite Valley
Ireland Lake
Merced Lake
Merced River
Mt Florence
Mt Clark
Illilouette Creek
Forester Peak
Yosemite National Park
Merced Peak
Buena Vista Peak
Sierra National Forest
0 10 km
0 5 miles

HIGHLIGHTS
1 Half Dome
2 Mariposa Grove

SIGHTS
3 Bridalveil Fall
4 Chilnualna Falls
5 El Capitan
6 Glacier Point
7 Inspiration Point
8 Nevada Fall
9 Olmsted Point
10 Sentinel Dome
11 Tenaya Lake
12 Tunnel View
13 Vernal Fall
14 Yosemite History Center

ACTIVITIES
15 Badger Pass Ski Area
16 Cathedral Lakes
17 Mirror Lake
18 Yosemite 360 Tours

SLEEPING
19 Tuolumne Meadows Campground

INFORMATION
20 Tuolumne Meadows

EATING IN YOSEMITE NATIONAL PARK: CASUAL MEALS

MAP P146

Curry Village Pizza Deck: Enjoy tasty pizza at this revamped and buzzing eatery that becomes a chatty après-hike hangout in the afternoon. *11am-10pm* $$

Degnan's Kitchen: In Yosemite Village, this is the spot for salads, pizza, espresso drinks, fresh doughnuts and other baked goodies. *7-11am & 11.30am-6pm* $

Bar 1899: In Curry Village, creative cocktails pair well with a bar-bites menu of tater tots, artichoke dip and foraged Brussels sprouts. *11.30am-10pm* $$

Base Camp Eatery: Yosemite Valley Lodge's casual food court serves staples for all three meals and you can sit indoors or outdoors. *7-10.30am & 11am-8.30pm* $

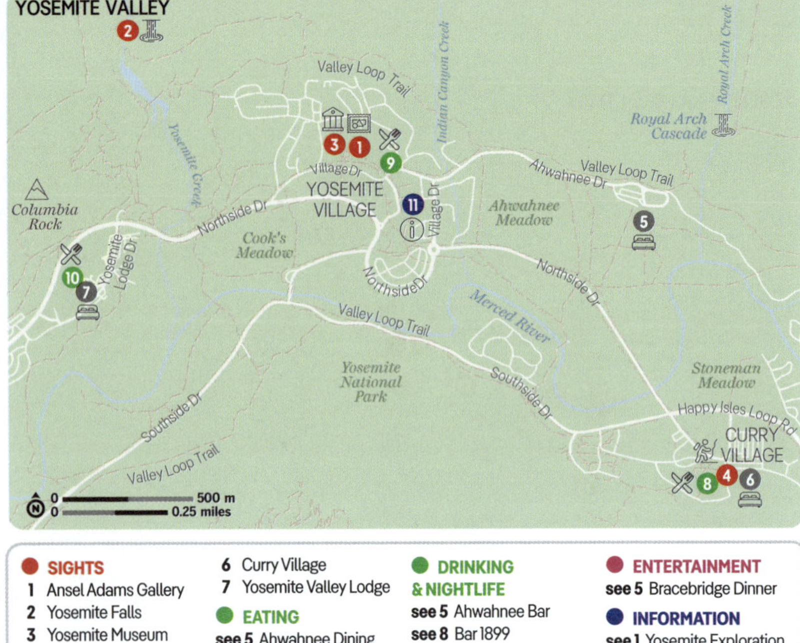

SIGHTS
1 Ansel Adams Gallery
2 Yosemite Falls
3 Yosemite Museum

ACTIVITIES
4 Yosemite Mountaineering School

SLEEPING
5 Ahwahnee Hotel
6 Curry Village
7 Yosemite Valley Lodge

EATING
see 5 Ahwahnee Dining Room
see 7 Base Camp Eatery
8 Curry Village Pizza Deck
9 Degnan's Kitchen
10 Mountain Room Restaurant

DRINKING & NIGHTLIFE
see 5 Ahwahnee Bar
see 8 Bar 1899
see 10 Mountain Room Lounge

ENTERTAINMENT
see 5 Bracebridge Dinner

INFORMATION
see 1 Yosemite Exploration Center
11 Yosemite Valley Welcome Center
see 1 Yosemite Valley Wilderness Center

YOSEMITE FIREFALL

For two weeks in late February, if the sky is clear and the water flow sufficient, visitors can behold a fiery spectacle at Horsetail Fall. As the ribbon of water drops off the edge of El Capitan and catches the sunset, it blazes like a stream of molten lava. Photographers flock to the El Capitan Picnic Area for the best angle and the park service limits visitation and parking to reduce congestion and environmental damage.

Welcome to Yosemite

MAP P146

Exploring the village

Congratulations on arriving in Yosemite Village! You've managed to get through one of the park entrances, drive into the valley and find a spot in the recently expanded parking area near the new $12.5-million **Yosemite Valley Welcome Center**, which opened in 2024. Walk into this 3000-sq-ft state-of-the-art space, where visitors meet with rangers and volunteers to plan their itineraries, shop for guides and maps and learn about safety and stewardship. Then head out to get acquainted with the history, culture and geography of the park.

As you exit the Welcome Center and walk north into the village, you'll soon reach **Degnan's Kitchen** (p145), a cafeteria-style lunch spot. Continue along the path past the post office and the **Yosemite Valley Wilderness Center**, where you can inquire about backpacking trips and permits. Beside it is the famous **Ansel Adams Gallery** *(nps.gov)*, where the black-and-white landscape photographer's original prints are on display. Beyond that building on the right, you'll see the old visitor center, which now contains interactive exhibits on science and history. Behind it, a theater shows a film called *The Spirit of Yosemite* and it's a worthwhile 23-minute introduction to the park.

Next door, a distinctive rustic-style building houses the **Yosemite Museum** (*nps.gov*) and its collection from Miwok and Paiute artists, including hand-woven baskets, beaded buckskin dresses and dance capes made from feathers. There's also an art gallery featuring a permanent collection of paintings and photographs. Behind the museum, a self-guided interpretive trail winds past the reconstructed 1870s Indian Village of Ahwahnee, complete with pounding stones, an acorn granary, a ceremonial roundhouse and a conical bark house. To the west across Village Dr, you'll find the modest and little-visited Yosemite Cemetery, where 65 Native Americans, white settlers and other early contributors to the park's history are buried.

Touring Yosemite Valley

MAP P146 & P147

Natural beauty in every direction

When you're ready to take in the views from the meadows and bridges around the valley floor, the Yosemite Valley Loop Trail awaits. This system of paths is an undeniably great way to get to know Yosemite Valley, although the trail isn't always super clear. In some places it joins the road, while in other places it peters out only to reappear later. Generally, the trail follows alongside Northside and Southside Drs, with some sections tracing the routes of former wagon roads.

For the ambitious, a 13-mile path leads up and down the entire valley. It can easily be cut in half or broken into smaller segments, making the journey manageable for just about any level of hiker. Pick up a free Yosemite Valley hiking map at the **Welcome Center** for easy route-finding and labeled point-to-point distances. Note that parts of the trail are wheelchair- and stroller-friendly and they feature ever-changing views of the valley's most important historic and natural features.

The most famous are, of course, the monumental 7569ft **El Capitan** (El Cap), one of the world's largest granite monoliths and a magnet for rock climbers and 8842ft Half Dome (p151), the park's spiritual centerpiece – its rounded granite pate forms an unmistakable silhouette. Meanwhile, Yosemite's waterfalls mesmerize even the most jaded traveler, especially when the spring runoff turns them into thunderous cataracts. **Yosemite Falls** is the tallest in North America, dropping 2425ft in three tiers. A slick wheelchair-accessible trail leads to the bottom of the cascade or, if you prefer solitude

PARK BASICS

It's $20 per person, or $35 per car, to enter the park for three consecutive days. Activity is concentrated in Yosemite Valley, where most of the iconic slabs of granite reside and Yosemite Village, which has the main visitor center, a museum, eateries and other services. Curry Village is another valley hub with rooms, cabins, dining options and trailheads for popular hikes. Out toward the eastern end of Tioga Rd, Tuolumne Meadows draws hikers to its pristine backcountry in summertime. Glacier Point, another favorite, can be reached on foot or with wheels and offers the park's most spectacular views. Wawona, the park's southern focal point, has a history center and enormous trees. In the northwestern corner, Hetch Hetchy offers waterfall hikes and an up-close look at San Francisco's water supply.

EATING IN YOSEMITE NATIONAL PARK: PICNIC SPOTS

MAP P145

Olmsted Point: Do lunch in an otherworldly landscape with stunning views down Tenaya Canyon to the back side of Half Dome. $

Tenaya Lake: Eat by the shoreline after an easy stroll around one of the park's largest and prettiest natural lakes. $

Inspiration Point: Hike the steep 1.3-mile trail to this gorgeous spot and venture out on a spur trail to feast. $

Tuolumne Meadows: Unpack your picnic beside just about any river bend in Tuolumne Meadows. Don't forget the bug spray, though. $

TOURING YOSEMITE VALLEY ON A BICYCLE

You can bring your own bicycle, rent one ($30/40 per half-/full day) or borrow one through Yosemite Bike Share (free; two hours max).

START	END	LENGTH
Curry Village	Curry Village	7 miles; 2hr

Start your ride in ❶ **Curry Village** with its historic lodgings. Ride east along Happy Isles Loop Rd and make a left at Upper Pines Campground to cross the Merced River. Continue east along the trail until you reach a bicycle parking area near ❷ **Mirror Lake**. If you're here in spring prepare for the splendid sight Mirror Lake is named for: Mt Watkins and Half Dome reflected on its tranquil surface. Take the Mirror Lake Old Carriage Trail back west toward Yosemite Village, down through Backpacker's Campground and on to the Ahwahnee Meadow. Park and enter the ❸ **Ahwahnee Hotel** to admire its soaring ceilings, atmospheric lounges and stone fireplaces.

Pedal west along Ahwahnee Dr, through Yosemite Village, then park just north of the Yosemite Valley Lodge and walk to the ❹ **trailhead for Lower Yosemite Falls**. It's an easy quarter-mile stroll to the base of Yosemite Falls, one of the world's most dramatic natural spectacles. Return to your bike and ride south to cross the Merced River over the Swinging Bridge.

Head northwest through the meadow, parallel to Southside Dr and you'll reach modest ❺ **Yosemite Valley Chapel**, which is listed in the National Register of Historic Places. Designed in 1879, the chapel hosts over 80 weddings a year. Take the Valley Loop Trail back toward ❻ **Curry Village** to return your bike.

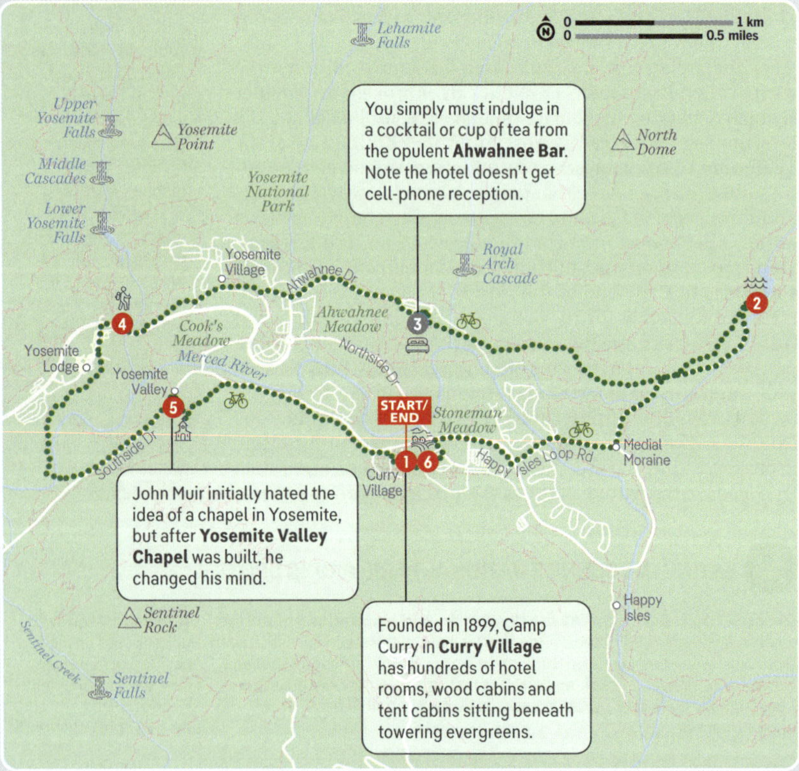

You simply must indulge in a cocktail or cup of tea from the opulent **Ahwahnee Bar**. Note the hotel doesn't get cell-phone reception.

John Muir initially hated the idea of a chapel in Yosemite, but after **Yosemite Valley Chapel** was built, he changed his mind.

Founded in 1899, Camp Curry in **Curry Village** has hundreds of hotel rooms, wood cabins and tent cabins sitting beneath towering evergreens.

and different perspectives, you can also clamber up the Upper Yosemite Falls Trail, which puts you atop the falls after a grueling 3.4 miles.

For those seeking a more tranquil valley trail, the 6.5-mile loop on the west end follows Northside and Southside Drs between the base of El Capitan and the Pohono Bridge. You'll have fabulous views of El Capitan and **Bridalveil Fall**, and can detour to great swimming spots, such as **Cathedral Beach**, along the Merced River. Visit the base of this stunning 620ft waterfall via the half-mile accessible boardwalk starting from a newly expanded parking lot and expect to get misted and see rainbows on the viewing platforms. A short drive west on Wawona Rd, you'll find **Tunnel View**, a mesmerizing spot to drink in vistas of the valley: El Capitan on the left, Bridalveil Fall on the right and Half Dome front and center.

Hiking & Backpacking in Yosemite

MAP P145

Superlative California trails

Over 800 miles of trails cater to hikers of all abilities. You could venture out all day on a quest for viewpoints, waterfalls and lakes, or go camping in the remote outer reaches of the backcountry (for the most up-to-date info on camping and wilderness permits and to make bookings, visit *recreation.gov*).

Some of the park's most popular hikes start right in Yosemite Valley, including the most famous of all: the top of Half Dome (17 miles round trip, see p151 for more). The less ambitious or physically fit can follow the same trail as far as **Vernal Fall** (2.6 miles round trip), the top of **Nevada Fall** (6.5 miles round trip) or idyllic Little Yosemite Valley (8 miles round trip). The Four Mile Trail (9.2 miles round trip) to **Glacier Point** is a strenuous but satisfying climb to a glorious viewpoint.

Along Glacier Point Rd, **Sentinel Dome** (2.2 miles round trip) is an easy hike to the crown of a commanding granite dome. And one of the most scenic hikes in the park, the Panorama Trail (8.5 miles one way), descends to the valley (joining the John Muir and Mist Trails) with nonstop views, including of Half Dome and Illilouette Fall. If you've got kids in tow, easy destinations include **Mirror Lake** (2 miles round trip, or 4.5 miles via the Tenaya Canyon Loop) in the valley and the McGurk Meadow trail (1.6 miles round trip) on Glacier Point Rd, which has a historic log cabin to romp around in. The Wawona area features giant sequoias (the world's largest trees; p152) and one of the park's prettiest – and often overlooked – hikes, to **Chilnualna Falls** (8.6 miles round trip). Best done

PARK ENTRANCES

Arch Rock Entrance: Hwy 140 runs through the Merced River Canyon before entering Yosemite Valley on the western side of the park.

Big Oak Flat Entrance: Hwy 120 W runs east from Groveland through Stanislaus National Forest before entering the park on its west side.

South Entrance: The southern entrance to the park along Hwy 41 is just north of the town of Fish Camp and only minutes to Mariposa Grove.

Tioga Pass Entrance: Hwy 120 E traverses the park as Tioga Rd, connecting Yosemite Valley with the Eastern Sierra.

Hetch Hetchy Entrance: This little-used entrance via Hwy 120 and Evergreen Rd is open during daylight hours with no reservations ever required.

EATING IN YOSEMITE NATIONAL PARK: FANCIER MEALS

MAP P146

Ahwahnee Dining Room: This lavish restaurant was temporarily offering buffet-style meals (including hand-carved prime rib) in 2025. *7-10am & 5.30-9pm* $$$

Ahwahnee Bar: More casual than the nearby dining room, this is the spot for a stiff cocktail, bar bites and tasty seasonal dishes. *11.30am-9pm* $$

Mountain Room Restaurant: Plates of NY strip steak, roasted acorn squash and mountain trout and most seats have killer views of Yosemite Falls. *5-10pm* $$$

Mountain Room Lounge: Wraps and sandwiches accompany craft cocktails, all served beside a Swedish fireplace or on the patio. *5-10pm Mon-Fri, from noon Sat & Sun* $$

WHERE TO TAKE IN PARK HISTORY

Ben Cunningham-Summerfield, born and raised in California, has been a Yosemite park ranger and cultural demonstrator for 30 years. These are his recommendations for places to learn about park history.

Yosemite History Center: In Wawona, this center offers glimpses into the history of Yosemite's early businesses. Cabins from around the park have been moved here and restored and there's even a refurbished Chinese Laundry building.

Yosemite Exploration Center: Opened in 2023, this interactive exhibit hall in Yosemite Village spotlights the park's early geological, human and rock-climbing history.

Yosemite Museum: (p147) Also in the valley, the museum is primarily focused on Native American life. A cultural demonstrator fields questions about park history and museum items.

between April and June, it follows a cascading creek to the top of the dramatic falls.

The highest concentration of hikes lies in the high country of **Tuolumne Meadows**, which is only accessible in summer. One rewarding and popular combo hike is Dog Lake and Lembert Dome (5 miles round trip), but the meadow's best hike has got to be **Cathedral Lakes**, a 7.6-mile jaunt through stunning forests and meadows to a pair of lakes that shimmer beneath the jagged Cathedral Peak (10,911ft). Backpacks, tents and other equipment can be rented from the **Yosemite Mountaineering School** *(travelyosemite.com/things-to-do/yosemite-mountaineering-school-guide-service)*. The school also offers 2-day 'Learn to Backpack' trips for novices *($500 per person, for groups of four or more)* and all-inclusive 3-, 4- and 5-day guided backpacking trips *($500 to $1000 per person)*, which are great for inexperienced and solo travelers. You must bring your own food and water filter.

Guided Tours in Yosemite

MAP P146

Adventure with an expert

Taking a guided tour through the beauty of Yosemite Valley not only helps you dodge the parking issues but also offers an education on the natural splendors. There are lots of options, but one favorite is **Echo Adventure Cooperative** *(echocoop.com)*, an extraordinary worker-owned outdoor company based in Groveland, offering a variety of sightseeing, hiking and backpacking tours. Another great company, **YExplore Yosemite Adventures** *(yexplore.com)*, offers custom tours with experienced local hiking guides based out of Sonora (they have extensive experience taking guests up the Half Dome cables). **Discover Yosemite Tours** *(discoveryosemite.com)* operates bus tours year-round from Oakhurst, Fish Camp and Bass Lake, while **Yosemite 360 Tours** *(visittenaya.com/tours)* is based at Tenaya Lodge, a large family-friendly resort in Fish Camp. They do full-day park tours in luxurious vehicles with retractable roofs and guests of the lodge have priority.

In addition, the park-affiliated nonprofit **Yosemite Conservancy** *(yosemiteconservancy.org)* offers multiday courses, custom trips and seminars that are great alternatives to tours. The **Sierra Club** *(sierraclub.org)* has both paid trips and free activity outings sponsored by local chapters. And the park's concessionaire, **Aramark/Yosemite Hospitality** *(travelyosemite.com)*, runs bus and tram tours, including a wheelchair-accessible two-hour Valley Floor Tour and day trips from the valley to either Glacier Point or Tuolumne Meadows. Visit tour and activity desks at Yosemite Valley Lodge, Curry Village or Yosemite Village; check *travelyosemite.com* or the *Yosemite Guide* for information and pricing.

TOP EXPERIENCE

Half Dome

Just hold on, don't forget to breathe and – whatever you do – don't look down. A pinnacle so popular hikers need a permit to scale it, Half Dome is Yosemite Valley's coveted cocked-top jewel. The hike takes longer than an average work day, with an elevation gain equivalent to 480 flights of stairs and a near-vertical final stretch.

ASHLEY HARRELL/LONELY PLANET

What is Half Dome?

Yosemite's most distinctive natural monument, Half Dome is 87 million years old and has a 93% vertical grade – the sheerest cliff in North America. Climbers come from around the world to grapple with its legendary north face, but good hikers can reach its summit via a 17-mile round-trip trail from Yosemite Valley. The trail gains 4900ft in elevation and has cable handrails for the last 200yd. It's freaky and a few people have fallen and died.

Getting a Permit

The Half Dome cables usually go up at the end of May and come down the first week in October. To stem lengthy lines (and dangerous conditions), the park requires day hikers to obtain a cables permit through a lottery system. For more information, visit *nps.gov/yose/planyourvisit/hdpermits.htm*.

At the Top

The summit is a mostly flat surface with mind-melting views in every direction. Snowfields tend to linger into spring after snowy winters and marmots and chipmunks will approach for a snack (don't comply). Be sure to check out the Diving Board, a prominent rock on the west side of Half Dome where Ansel Adams snapped his famous photograph *The Monolith*.

TOP TIPS

- The hike can be done in a day but is more enjoyable if you camp overnight.
- When a storm's brewing, avoid exposed ridges, summits and granite domes, Half Dome included.
- If hiking during the day, leave at sunrise (or earlier) and have a non-negotiable turn-around time.

PRACTICALITIES

- Scan the QR code to apply for your Half Dome permits
- Application $10, permit $10
- Cables are down May-Oct

TOP EXPERIENCE

Mariposa Grove

In this cathedral of ancient trees, almost 500 hardy sequoias rocket to the sky. Early in the morning or after the crowds have gone, you can explore Mariposa Grove in solitude and contemplate the thousands of years the trees have witnessed. Other highlights include walking through the heart of the still-living California Tunnel Tree and witnessing the girth of the Grizzly Giant.

SARAH_XIE7/SHUTTERSTOCK

TOP TIPS

- The welcome plaza has about 300 parking spaces that fill fast; arrive by mid-morning.
- There are no food services; pack a picnic.
- Bicycles are allowed on Mariposa Grove Rd between the welcome plaza and the Grizzly Giant when the road is open, but not beyond.

PRACTICALITIES

- Scan the QR code for more information on Mariposa Grove.
- Always open, but the access road closes Nov-Apr
- Free with park entrance

The History

In 1864, President Lincoln signed the Yosemite Grant, establishing Yosemite Valley and Mariposa Grove as a state park. This landmark legislation marked the first time in US history that the federal government set aside natural areas to be protected for the benefit of future generations. The Mariposa Grove was formally added to Yosemite National Park in 1906.

Visiting Mariposa Grove

A visit begins with either a 2-mile shuttle ride from the welcome plaza or a 2-mile hike along the Washburn Trail. On the right as you enter the lower grove, the Fallen Monarch tree and its exposed roots illustrate the sequoias' shallow but diffuse life-support system, while many wind-toppled, weakened and scarred trees nearby offer evidence of a changing climate. Keeping walking and a half-mile up you'll encounter the 800-year-old Grizzly Giant, a monster of a tree. The walk-through California Tunnel Tree, the favored spot for photos, is close by. In the upper grove is the more famous Fallen Wawona Tunnel Tree. It's about a mile round trip from the Fallen Wawona Tunnel Tree to the wide-open overlook at Wawona Point (6810ft), which takes in the entire area.

An Ahwahnee Experience

MAP P146

The Sierra's stylish side

Dating back to 1927, the **Ahwahnee Hotel** *(travelyosemite.com)* was built from granite, cement and steel to attract wealthy guests. These days, though, all park visitors have the right to wander beneath the soaring ceilings, relax in atmospheric lounges and peer through massive windows at Glacier Point, Half Dome and Yosemite Falls. Those less inclined to stay the night may enjoy a meal in the baronial dining room or a casual drink in the piano bar, admiring the leaded glass, sculpted tiles, Native American trappings, German Gothic chandeliers and Turkish rugs. At Christmas the hotel hosts the **Bracebridge Dinner**, a combination of banquet and Renaissance fair. Book early and for high season and holidays book rooms a year ahead.

Going Wild

MAP P145

Outdoor adventure in Yosemite

There are a great many ways to adventure within this outdoor wonderland and the **rock climbing** in particular is legendary. The park's sheer spires, polished domes and soaring monoliths attract climbers from all over the world, including famous ones and they often stay at Camp 4 near El Capitan in spring and fall. In summer, another base camp springs up at Tuolumne Meadows Campground. Climbers looking for partners post notices on bulletin boards at both campgrounds.

In early summer, floating down the Merced River is a leisurely way to soak up valley views. Raft rentals for a 3-mile trip are available in Curry Village and include a shuttle ride back to the rental kiosk. Down in Wawona, the South Fork of the Merced offers some of the best stream **fishing** in the park and on a hot summer day, of course, nothing beats **swimming** in the cool river. Whatever you do, don't jump in near a waterfall, or even pretend you're going to. People have died that way.

The onset of winter opens up a different set of options, as the valley becomes a quiet, frosty world of snow-draped evergreens, ice-coated lakes and gleaming white mountains. Popular winter sports include cross-country **skiing** on 350 miles of trails and roads and the family-friendly **Badger Pass Ski Area** *(travelyosemite.com/winter/badger-pass-ski-area; adult/child lift ticket $64/38.50; half-day adult/child $56/33.50)* has been beckoning skiers since 1935. You'll also find opportunities around the park for snowshoeing, ice skating, snow camping, sledding and tubing.

YOSEMITE'S DREAMIEST WATERFALLS

Yosemite Falls: The tallest waterfall in North America, dropping 2425ft in three tiers; it's a brutal hike to the top.

Bridalveil Fall: In the valley, gusts blow this 620-footer side to side – the Ahwahneechee called it Pohono (Spirit of the Puffing Wind).

Vernal & Nevada Falls: These two Merced River beauties fall 317ft and 594ft respectively and are the highlights of the Mist Trail.

Chilnualna Falls: These falls plummet into a deep chasm and can be taken in on an appealing Wawona day hike.

Wapama Falls: By the Hetch Hetchy reservoir, this 1000-footer is reached on a 5-mile hike from O'Shaughnessy Dam.

Beyond Yosemite National Park

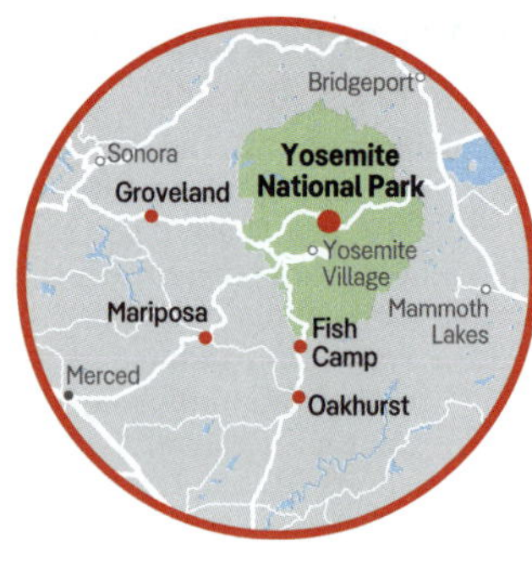

The gateway towns to Yosemite National Park are worth more than a passing glance out the car window.

Places

GETTING AROUND

It's ideal to have your own wheels, but there's also the **YARTS** *(yarts.com)* bus. It has three routes west of the park: Fresno through Oakhurst and Fish Camp on Hwy 41 (May to September); Sonora through Groveland on Hwy 120 (May to September) and Merced on through Mariposa and the Merced River Canyon on Hwy 140 (year-round). Tickets cost $10 to $22 one-way. Buy them online or pay with exact change or credit card on the bus. Schedules vary.

Southwest of the national park along Hwy 140, Mariposa is the largest and most interesting of the gateway hubs. The old mining and railroad town has loads of Old West character and a couple of good museums dedicated to the area's heritage, plus rollicking nightlife. Heading toward the park on Hwy 140, the Merced River tumbles through the Merced River Canyon, offering stunning views and recreational opportunities.

To the north along Hwy 120 W perches Groveland, a little town with restored gold-rush-era buildings and loads of old-timey charm. Down south along Hwy 41, travelers can ride a historic steam train in Fish Camp and just south of there, quotidian Oakhurst offers a few fun surprises.

Mariposa

TIME FROM YOSEMITE NATIONAL PARK: **45MIN**

A town for time travel

This no-stoplight former gold-rush town packs quite the cultural punch. Dive in with a wander around the historic downtown. Then hit up the **Mariposa Museum & History Center** *(mariposamuseum.com; adult/child $10/5)*, where the town's past comes to life with old menus, train tickets, photos and the like and a Miwuk exhibit features expertly woven baskets, jewelry, arrowheads and more. At the county fairgrounds, rock hounds will dig the **California State Mining & Mineral Museum** *(parks.ca.gov; adult/child $4/free)*, where the 13lb 'Fricot Nugget' (the largest crystalized gold specimen from the California gold-rush era) is displayed.

Get your climb on

Climbing enthusiasts should pop over to the **Yosemite Climbing Museum** *(yosemiteclimbing.org/museum; suggested donation $5)*, which contains memorabilia stretching back to when the sport's pioneers were making their own gear. There's also the **Yosemite Boulder Farm**, a B&B with climbing and disc-golf on the town's outskirts. The property offers 6 acres of

Gold panning, Merced River

granite, with 20 boulders and climbs for every level. Father-and-son owners Dean and Willie Pollard spent three years clearing brush, leveling landings and power washing the boulders and Willie and his wife Amanda operate the B&B (guests must stay here to use the park). The vibe is super-convivial.

An outdoor smorgasbord

The fine folks who live in Mariposa are there for a reason: these adrenaline junkies love the outdoors. Big wall climber and journalist Chris Van Leuven is one such person and his side gig is **Yosemite E-biking** *(yosemiteebiking.com)*. He'll lead you on some truly exhilarating Sierra Foothills roads. Half-/full-day tours cost $200/325 per adult, with a minimum of two.

For high-flying adventurers, **Skydive Yosemite** *(skydiveyosemite.com; dives from 10,000/12,000/14,000ft cost $209/259/309)* is near the Mariposa-Yosemite Airport. Jumps include views of Half Dome and El Capitan. Rumor has it that Paul Wignall, a former model who co-owns the company, was an inspiration for the 'Blue Steel' look in the film *Zoolander*.

River fun

Declared a Wild and Scenic River by Congress in 1987, the Merced has twisting and tumbling white water that's best experienced on a raft. In spring, the exhilarating trip takes

BEST DAY TRIPS FOR HISTORY BUFFS

Hornitos: An old gold-mining settlement 30 minutes' drive west of Mariposa, with a still operational bar, objects of intrigue and possibly ghosts.

Coulterville: Historic buildings line the streets of this charming former gold-rush supply town 25 miles north of Mariposa.

Columbia State Historic Park: A mini gold-rush theme park where volunteers dress in 19th-century garb and parade around blacksmith shops, theaters and saloons.

Hite Cove: Hike to a true ghost town on this 4.5-mile trail (one way) along the Merced River. Rock walls and heavy machinery remain.

Gold-panning with Ira Estin: This long-time local *(209-966-7262)* takes you gold-panning along the Merced, teaching about the history and tools of the gold rush.

EATING IN MARIPOSA: OUR PICKS

Happy Burger: Burgers, fries and shakes served with a heavy dose of Americana kitsch. The prices are small and the menu's enormous. *6am-8pm* $

Savoury's: Beloved upscale eatery specializing in bacon-wrapped dates, duck breast, steak and grilled rack of lamb. *5-9pm Sun-Thu, to 10pm Fri & Sat* $$

1850 Brewing Company: Atmospheric spot that brews its own beer and also serves up yummy steaks, burgers and small plates like nachos. *11am-9pm Wed-Sun* $$

Little Shop of Ramen: From-scratch ramen with complex broth and handmade noodles. The owner's partner runs a delightful wine bar in the same space. *hours vary* $$

OTHER OAKHURST ACTIVITIES

Thrift shopping: Wander a collection of thrift, antique and gift shops in Coarsegold Historic Village, a short drive south of Oakhurst.

Lake fun: Some consider Bass Lake a mini Lake Tahoe, only warmer. You can swim, canoe, fish, hike and more.

Mountain biking: Oakhurst has easy access to singletrack trails and fire roads and Pedal Forward Bikes & Adventure has rentals and guided tours.

Throwing axes: World champion axe-thrower Nate Hodges owns Yosemite Axe Throwing, a chill spot for tossing weapons around.

Seeing big trees: When Yosemite's famous groves are packed, Nelder Grove off Sierra Sky Ranch Rd has 60 giant sequoias and plenty of solitude.

you down Class III and IV rapids, whereas things get a lot more relaxed in summer after most of the snowmelt has run its course. **Zephyr Whitewater Expeditions** *(zrafting.com)* has been running trips on the Merced since 1973 and the large, reputable company has experienced guides and a seasonal office across from Yosemite Bug near Briceburg. Half-day trips cost $113 to $128; full-day trips range from $176 to $191 and include lunch.

If white water feels too extreme, head up the road to the **Merced River Recreation Management Area** *(blm.gov/visit/merced-river)* in Briceburg, where there's an **information center**, a picnic area, an extension bridge over the river, some campgrounds and a trail system. Depending on the time of year, it's an ideal spot for fishing, camping, hiking or just watching the rafts drift by.

Fish Camp & Oakhurst

TIME FROM YOSEMITE NATIONAL PARK: **45MIN**

Riding the Sugar Pine Railroad

From mid-March through late November, the historic steam train of the **Yosemite Mountain Sugar Pine Railroad** *(ymsprr.com; per person from $31.80)* chugs from Fish Camp

DRINKING IN MARIPOSA: BEST NIGHTLIFE

Grove House: In the evenings, grab some farm-to-table fare and a craft beer and catch live music with the locals. *4-9pm Mon-Thu, to 10pm Fri & Sat*

Alley: A cozy beer and wine bar ideal for a slice of pizza, with occasional trivia and live music on weekends. *4-10pm Tue-Thu, to midnight Fri & Sat*

Hideout Saloon: A rough-and-tumble late-night bar with dollar bills hanging from everywhere and a regular cast of surly patrons. *noon-2am Mon-Thu, from 11am Fri-Sun*

Twisted Cedar Taphouse: A sweet little bar serving up a delicious variety of craft mead and cider, plus super tasty barbecue from an adjoining business. *11.30am-10pm*

ALUN REECE/ALAMY

Yosemite Mountain Sugar Pine Railroad

through Sierra National Forest on a 4-mile loop used for lugging lumber at the turn of the 20th century. It's a classic family adventure with some good history woven in and you can even bring the dog at no charge. There's also a small museum, a gift shop and a sandwich shop, plus gold-panning tours *($10/15 per person online/on-site)* with a prospector.

A virtual visit

Those who stay in Oakhurst can fly around Yosemite National Park without ever leaving their seats at **Yosemite Cinema** *(yosemitecinema.com; adult/child $35/23)*. The theater's marquee VR film, *Experience Yosemite,* uses state-of-the-art chairs that tap into all the senses to make it feel like you're flying up the face of El Capitan alongside Alex Honnold, accompanying Ansel Adams on a photo expedition and hovering over the historic campfire chat between John Muir and President Teddy Roosevelt.

Groveland

TIME FROM YOSEMITE NATIONAL PARK: **45MIN**

Strolling in Groveland

Kick off a stroll through Groveland at the **Iron Door Saloon** *(irondoorsaloon.com),* California's oldest continuously running saloon, where taxidermied heads and an estimated

NEARBY SPLASHES

Sierra Mac: The company offers day and multiday trips on the Tuolumne and Merced Rivers as well as the experts-only Cherry Creek.

ARTA River Trips: A nonprofit running trips on the Tuolumne and Merced Rivers (day and multiday) that emphasize untouched scenery.

Rainbow Pool: If you prefer water that isn't fast moving, visit this popular swimming hole 15 miles east of Groveland in the Stanislaus National Forest.

Carlon Falls: Off Evergreen Rd near the Big Oak Flat Yosemite entrance, a well-maintained trail leads to cascading water and swimming holes.

Diana Pool: This lesser-known waterfall and swimming hole is reached via a 1.5-mile hike along the North Fork of the Merced River. Get directions from a local.

EATING & DRINKING IN OAKHURST: OUR PICKS

South Gate Brewing Company: Popular Oakhust brewpub serving primo steaks (the smoked ribeye is to-die-for), pizzas, sandwiches and salads. *hours vary* $$

Elderberry House: The Californian-French restaurant at Château du Sureau in Oakhurst serves haute cuisine in what looks like a castle. *5-8pm* $$$

Idle Hour Winery & Kitchen: Indoor-outdoor spot to drink good wine that pairs well with the Mediterranean-inspired cuisine. *11am-8pm Wed-Sat, 10am-2pm Sun* $$

Ducey's on the Lake: Lakefront locals' favorite with a 6pm early bird special and music and dancing upstairs. *7am-8.30pm Mon-Thu, from 7.30am Fri-Sun* $$

GRAHAM JEPSON/ALAMY

Iron Door Saloon (p157)

$4000 (in $1 bills) adorn the walls. Then head west on Main St to **Motherlode Made**, a one-of-a-kind gifts and souvenirs market hawking the wares of more than 40 local artists and craftspeople. Across the street at the **Grove Mercantile**, pick up more gifts in the boutique and sample the artisanal homemade ice cream. If it's outdoor gear you're after, saunter along to **Yosemite Basecamp Outfitter** one block over, on Ponderosa La. This socially and environmentally sustainable adventure shop sells outdoor gear and clothing; the owners also run an excellent guiding company, **Echo Adventure Cooperative** *(echocoop.com)*.

GOLD-RUSH HISTORY

Eureka! Read more about the **California gold rush** and how it shaped the land and culture of the state on **p199**.

EATING & DRINKING IN & AROUND GROVELAND: OUR PICKS

Lucky Buck Cafe: Quirky Buck Meadows diner serving large portions of comfort food, with lots of vegetarian options, good pie, a full bar and a great gift shop. *7am-9pm* $$

Priest Station Cafe: A longstanding family-run roadside restaurant boasting delicious sandwiches on a great deck overlooking the mountains. *8am-8pm* $$

Mountain Sage: Adorable Groveland cafe serving fair-trade coffee and delicious baked treats. It also contains an art gallery, a nursery and a thrift store. *7am-2pm* $

Around the Horn Brewing Company: A gold-rush–themed brewery with innovative craft beer, tasty bar food and a super-fun patio. *11am-9pm Thu-Mon, from 4pm Tue* $

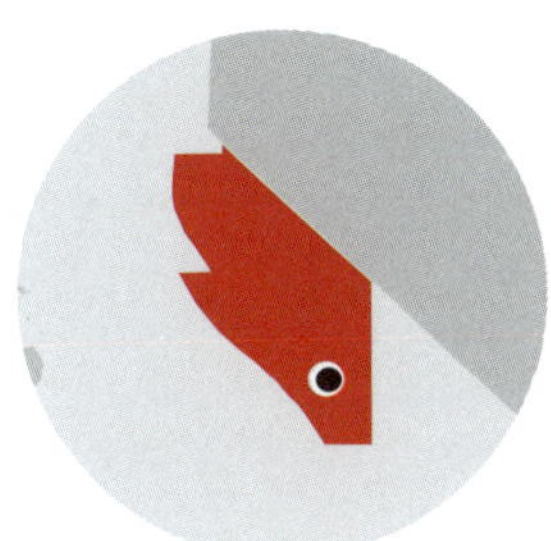

Sequoia & Kings Canyon National Parks

BIG TREES | COOL CAVES | MESMERIZING HIKES

Far from the hubbub of Yosemite Valley, some 200 miles to the southwest, these side-by-side parks comprise a quieter stretch of the Sierra. Here it's easy to find solitude within wildflower-strewn meadows or by an alpine lake, to unwind before a gushing waterfall or pull off a deserted highway and gaze into a dramatic gorge. People mainly visit, however, for the parks' forests, which feature some of the planet's largest giant sequoias. If you've ever wanted to see these magnificent trees, now is the time.

Over the last few years, climate change has threatened these groves like never before. In 2020 and 2021, two incredibly intense fires scorched thousands of sequoias living within the parks, killing 20% of species. While some impacted areas have remained off-limits to visitors, other areas such as Crystal Cave have reopened and the undeniable beauty of the parks endures.

TOP TIP

Although administered as a single unit by the National Park Service (NPS), Sequoia and Kings Canyon National Parks are actually two national parks. Sequoia has more famous sequoias (including General Sherman, the world's largest tree), while Kings Canyon is better known for its canyons, valleys, waterfalls and mountain peaks.

GETTING AROUND

The easiest way to get around these parks is with your own vehicle. But from late May to early September, Sequoia Shuttle runs buses four times daily between Visalia, Three Rivers and the Giant Forest Museum in Sequoia National Park *($15 per person round trip, reservations required).* All buses are wheelchair-accessible and equipped with bicycle racks. Sequoia National Park also has four free shuttle routes within the park (operating during the summer and over some holidays); Kings Canyon has no shuttles.

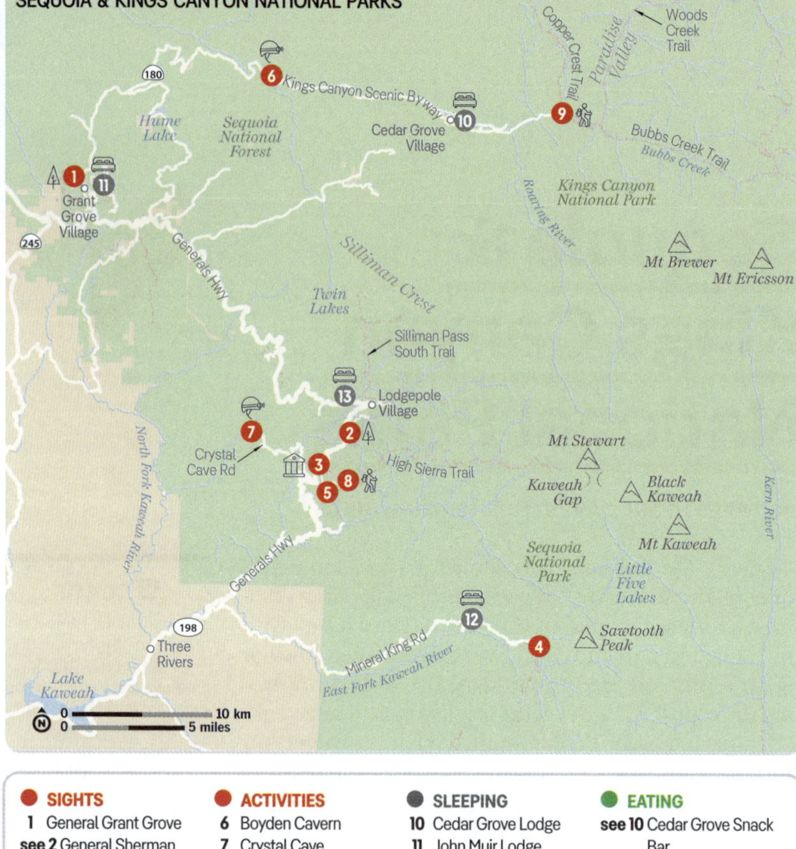

SIGHTS
1 General Grant Grove
see 2 General Sherman Tree
2 Giant Forest
3 Giant Forest Museum
4 Mineral King
5 Moro Rock

ACTIVITIES
6 Boyden Cavern
7 Crystal Cave
8 High Sierra Trail
9 Rae Lakes Loop

SLEEPING
10 Cedar Grove Lodge
11 John Muir Lodge
12 Silver City Mountain Resort
13 Wuksachi Lodge

EATING
see 10 Cedar Grove Snack Bar
see 11 Grant Grove Restaurant
see 13 Peaks Restaurant
see 12 Silver City Mountain Resort Restaurant

Superlative Sequoias

Visiting the world's biggest trees

Build your big tree anticipation with a primer on their intriguing ecology and history at the **Giant Forest Museum** off the Generals Hwy within Sequoia. Hands-on exhibits teach about the life stages of the trees, which can live for more than 3000 years and the fire cycle that releases their seeds and allows them to sprout on bare soil. The museum is housed in a historic 1920s building designed by Gilbert Stanley Underwood, famed architect of the Ahwahnee.

Now you're ready for the big time. Jump on the shuttle (recommended) or drive five minutes up the highway to

Giant Forest, a 3-sq-mile grove that protects around half of the world's most gargantuan tree specimens. Among them is the world's biggest by volume, the **General Sherman tree**, rocketing 275ft into the sky. Pay your respects then consider doing the Congress Trail, a paved 2-mile pathway that begins near the General Sherman tree and takes in the Washington Tree (named in honor of George Washington) and the see-through Telescope Tree.

For even more big tree action later in your trip, there's the **General Grant Grove** over in Kings Canyon. Take the paved half-mile General Grant Tree Trail, an interpretive walk that visits a number of mature sequoias, including the 27-story General Grant Tree. This giant holds triple honors as the world's second-largest living tree (by trunk volume), a memorial to US soldiers killed in war and the nation's official Christmas tree since 1926.

PARK BASICS

Sequoia and Kings Canyon National Parks *(nps.gov/seki; per person/car for 7 days $20/35)* are both accessible by car only from the west via Hwy 99, from Fresno or Visalia. It's 46 miles east on Hwy 198 from Visalia into Sequoia National Park – you pass through the gateway town of Three Rivers before entering the park. From Fresno, it's 57 miles east on Hwy 180 to Kings Canyon. The two roads are connected by the Generals Hwy, inside Sequoia. There is no access to either park from the east. There are five main regions of the parks to explore: Foothills, Mineral King and the Giant Forest (and Lodgepole area) within Sequoia and Grant Grove and Cedar Grove within Kings Canyon.

Hit the Trails

All the iconic hikes

More than 850 miles of maintained trails await your footsteps in both national parks. From sun-bleached granite peaks soaring above alpine lakes to wildflower-dotted meadows and roaring waterfalls, this is a hiker's paradise.

Which day hikes appeal most will largely depend on your preferences and stamina. Are you the sort who appreciates a quick ascent to the tippy-top of a granite dome to enjoy panoramic views over 150 miles of mountain range? Then do **Moro Rock**, just south of the Giant Forest. If you'd prefer a more secluded jaunt to a glacially carved tarn, Mineral King's Eagle Lake has you covered. For anyone craving a satisfying 9-mile walk along a riverside and up a natural granite staircase to the park's largest waterfall, Cedar Grove's Mist Falls Trail is perfect.

For those more interested in overnight hikes, you too have come to the right place. Mineral King, Lodgepole and Cedar Grove offer the best backcountry trail access, while the Jennie Lakes Wilderness in the Sequoia National Forest boasts pristine meadows and lakes at lower elevations. The most popular multiday trek in Kings Canyon is **Rae Lakes Loop**, which skirts a chain of jewel-like lakes over 41 glorious miles. And the **High Sierra Trail**, a 49-mile stunner along a dramatic ridge, offers epic views and river crossings, concluding at Mt Whitney.

Campsites and wilderness permits must be booked at *recreation.gov*. Park-approved, bear-proof food canisters are mandatory for wilderness trips.

Spelunking

A cave and a cavern

In the summer of 2025 one of Sequoia National Park's prime attractions, **Crystal Cave** *(visitsequoia.com/sequoia-national-park-attractions/crystal-cave; tour adult/child $20/10)*, reopened for the first time in four years (previously, the road

PARK HISTORY

For millennia, the Mono, Yokuts, Tüba-tulabal, Paiute and Western Shoshone people lived and thrived in the region's foothills, forests and canyons. Trappers began to arrive in 1827 and miners followed during the California gold rush, decimating the indigenous communities and damaging the region with dams, logging, mining and ranching.

Conservationists pushed the government to intervene, and in 1890 Sequoia became the second national park in the US (after Yellowstone). A few days later the 4 sq miles around Grant Grove were declared General Grant National Park and, in 1940, absorbed into the newly created Kings Canyon National Park. In 2000, vast tracts of land in the surrounding national forest became the Giant Sequoia National Monument.

leading to the cave had been closed after fires and winter storms damaged it).

The cave is stunning and was carved over millennia by an underground river with marble formations estimated to be up to 100,000 years old. Milky-white formations take the shape of ethereal curtains, domes, columns and shields. The cave is also a biodiverse habitat for spiders and bats. Tickets for the 50-minute tour are only sold online in advance, not at the cave. You'll definitely want to bring a jacket.

There are hundreds of other caves in and around Sequoia and Kings Canyon National Parks, but the only other one you can tour is privately owned **Boyden Cavern** *(boydencavern.com)*, accessed via the Kings Canyon Scenic Byway. Although it's smaller than Crystal Cave, this one was also carved out by an underground river and was known to Native American tribes in the early 1800s. After a survey crew found it later in the century, a Hume Lake logger named Putnam Boyden decided he wanted to open it for sightseers. He bought the cave, moved in and offered tours for 5¢.

The experience hasn't changed much since, but regular tours now cost between $17 and $23, depending on the day. Visitors hike a short but incredibly steep trail to the entrance before ducking into the cave, where the temperature quickly drops to 55°F (13°C). Stalactites hang like daggers from the ceiling and white marble takes the shape of pancake stacks and 'cave bacon,' as the guides call it. There's also a **flashlight tour** *($35 per person)* that lasts a bit longer and a private extended tour for up to five adults *($250)*.

Enjoy poking around the ancient wonder and keep your eyes peeled for the shrews, spiders, scorpions and (of course) bats, but try not to touch the sensitive formations. Book tickets in advance on the website.

Adventuring in Mineral King

Seclusion in the Sierra

A scenic subalpine valley at 7500ft, **Mineral King** is Sequoia's backpacking mecca and a good place to find solitude. Gorgeous and gigantic, its glacially sculpted valley is ringed by massive mountains, including the jagged 12,343ft Sawtooth Peak. The area is reached via Mineral King Rd – a winding, steep and narrow 28-mile road not suitable for recreational vehicles (RVs) or speed demons; it's usually open from late May through October, but there will be intermittent road construction through 2027. Consult the park website for more information about possible delays.

Scattered along the last 6 miles of road are two first-come, first-served park campgrounds, a ranger station and the private **Silver City Mountain Resort** *(silvercityresort.com)*. This rustic, old-fashioned place rents everything from cute and cozy 1950s-era cabins to modern chalets and the restaurant's burgers and pies are delicious.

Hiking from any of the valley's three trailheads involves steep climbs along strenuous trails. Be aware of the altitude, even on short popular hikes to places like Crystal, Monarch,

KINGS CANYON SCENIC BYWAY DRIVING TOUR

This drive enters one of North America's deepest canyons, traversing the forested Giant Sequoia National Monument and shadowing the Kings River to Road's End.

START	END	LENGTH
Grant Grove turnoff	Road's End	35 miles; 1hr

Begin at the ❶ **Grant Grove turnoff** and drive about 3 miles up Hwy 180, then pull over to drink in the mountain panorama at ❷ **McGee Vista Point**. Continue winding downhill through the Sequoia National Forest past the ❸ **turnoff for Converse Basin Grove**. Head downhill, deeper into the canyon, as the road serpentines past chiseled rock walls laced with waterfalls. Stop for superb scenery at ❹ **Junction View**, about 10.5 miles from Grant Grove and ❺ **Yucca Point**, another 3.5 miles further.

Continue around ear-popping curves for 5 miles and you'll reach the entrance to ❻ **Boyden Cavern**, a privately owned marble wonder filled with curious rock formations and bats. Continuing, the road bottoms out and runs parallel to the Kings River, its roar ricocheting off granite cliffs soaring high above. Soon you'll reach the parking lot for ❼ **Grizzly Falls**, often a torrent in late spring.

The scenic byway reenters the national park just over 2.5 miles further along, passing the Lewis Creek bridge and a riverside beach. At Cedar Grove Village, you can stop at the visitor center and market before continuing to the Roaring River Falls and pretty Zumwalt Meadow trailheads. More hiking and swimming holes (like Muir Rock) await at ❽ **Road's End**, where the only way to keep going across the Sierra Nevada is on foot.

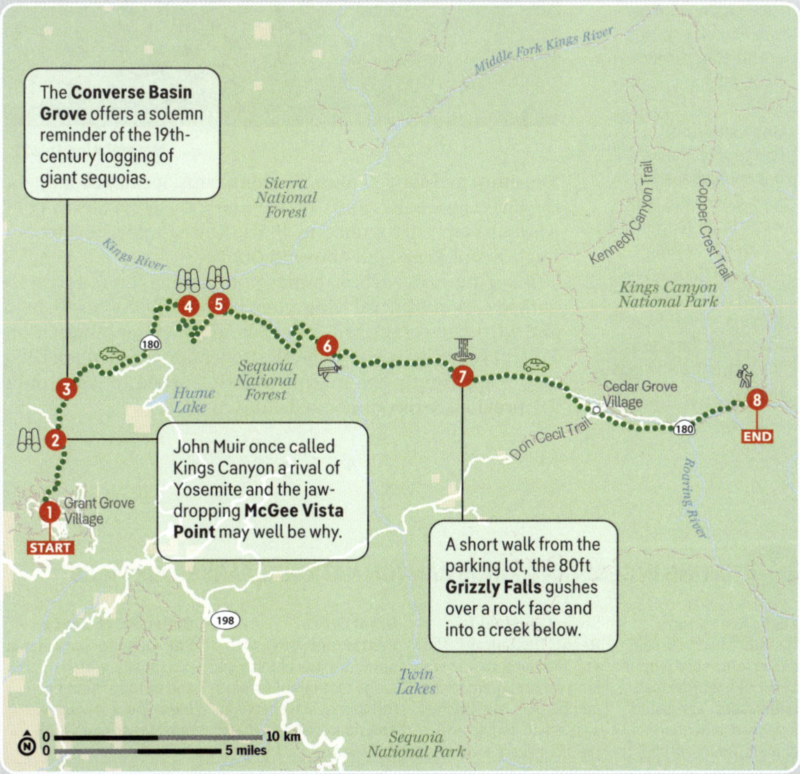

The **Converse Basin Grove** offers a solemn reminder of the 19th-century logging of giant sequoias.

John Muir once called Kings Canyon a rival of Yosemite and the jaw-dropping **McGee Vista Point** may well be why.

A short walk from the parking lot, the 80ft **Grizzly Falls** gushes over a rock face and into a creek below.

Middle Fork Kings River
Sierra National Forest
Kings River
Kennedy Canyon Trail
Copper Crest Trail
Kings Canyon National Park
180
Sequoia National Forest
Hume Lake
Cedar Grove Village
Don Cecil Trail
Roaring River
START
END
Grant Grove Village
198
Twin Lakes
Sequoia National Park
0 10 km
0 5 miles

BEST OUTDOOR ACTIVITIES IN SEQUOIA & KINGS CANYON NATIONAL PARKS

Stargazing: The annual Dark Sky Festival includes star parties, ranger programs, solar viewing and NASA astronaut talks.

Horseback riding: Summer rides from Grant Grove Stables and Cedar Grove Pack Station in Kings Canyon and Horse Corral Pack Station in Sequoia.

Rock climbing: Sequoia and Kings Canyon's most popular climbing routes are Obelisk, Grand Sentinel and Chimney Rock.

Snowshoeing: Lodgepole Market has snowshoes for rent. Check the park website for ranger-led snowshoe walks.

River rafting: When the white water is flowing, several outfitters run trips down the Kaweah and Kings Rivers.

SEBASTIEN BUREL/SHUTTERSTOCK

Mineral King (p162)

Mosquito and Eagle Lakes. For long trips, locals recommend the Little Five Lakes and, further along the High Sierra Trail, Kaweah Gap, surrounded by Black Kaweah, Mt Stewart and Eagle Scout Peak – all above 12,000ft.

In spring and early summer, hungry marmots terrorize parked cars at Mineral King, chewing on radiator hoses, belts and wiring to get the salt they crave after winter hibernation. Protect your car by wrapping the underside with a diaper-like tarp – apparently the marmots have learned to get around the previously recommended chicken wire.

EATING IN SEQUOIA & KINGS CANYON NATIONAL PARKS: OUR PICKS

Peaks Restaurant: Wuksachi Lodge's main dining room serves up an excellent breakfast buffet, soup-and-salad lunch fare and gourmet dinners. *hours vary* $$$

Silver City Mountain Resort Restaurant: The only restaurant in Mineral King serves lip-smacking hamburgers, sandwiches, salads and homemade pie. *hours vary* $

Grant Grove Restaurant: Grab an outdoor table at this solid lodge restaurant serving traditional and seasonal American dishes. *7-10am & 11.30am-8pm* $$

Cedar Grove Snack Bar: Open for light meals seasonally, with indoor and outdoor seating. *11am-3pm & 4-9pm mid-/late May to mid-Oct* $

Beyond Sequoia & Kings Canyon National Parks

Lesser known than Yosemite's gateways but growing in popularity with travelers, Visalia and Three Rivers punch above their weight.

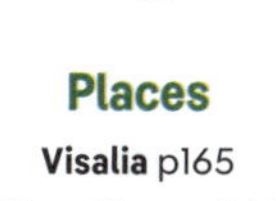

Places

When park lodgings fill up in summertime, visitors are relegated to the gateway towns. And they often like it! The agricultural prosperity and well-maintained downtown of Visalia, in the foothills of the Sierra Nevada, make it a convenient stopover and its old-town charm offers a reason to stay and stroll among original Victorian homes, cute shops and buzzing brewpubs.

A half-hour's drive closer to the park and named for the convergence of three Kaweah River forks, Three Rivers is a quirky village increasingly populated by retirees and other newcomers. It's also a jumping-off point for rafting trips on the Kaweah and the main drag, Sierra Dr (Hwy 198), is lined with cozy lodgings, outstanding coffee shops and casual restaurants.

Visalia

TIME FROM SEQUOIA & KC NATIONAL PARKS: **45MIN**

Wander a majestic oak forest

The main draw in the area is the **Kaweah Oak Preserve** *(sequoiariverlands.org),* about 7 miles east of Visalia. The preserve features 344 acres of majestic oak trees, which once stretched from the Sierras to (long-gone) Tulare Lake in the valley. A gorgeous setting for easy hikes, it's a glimpse of the valley ecosystem before orchards and vineyards took over and more than 300 plant and animal species inhabit the preserve, including bobcats, great horned owls and woodpeckers.

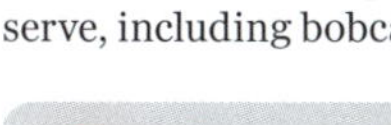

GETTING AROUND

Hwy 198 runs northeast from Visalia through Three Rivers to Sequoia National Park's Ash Mountain Entrance. The road to remote Mineral King veers off Hwy 198 at the northern end of Three Rivers, just south of the park's Ash Mountain Entrance.

Your own wheels will allow for the most freedom, but there's also the Sequoia Shuttle bus, which run four times daily between Visalia and the Giant Forest Museum ($15 round trip, 2½ hours) via Three Rivers. Reservations are required.

UNSUNG FORESTS & RIVERLANDS

Aaron Collins of Sequoia Riverlands Trust says travelers who stick to the national parks are missing out. *sequoiariverlands.org*

Just outside the park is some of California's most overlooked beauty – oak-studded foothills and working lands, full of wildlife, native plants and wide-open skies. One of my go-to trails is the loop at Dry Creek Preserve. Once a gravel quarry, it's been restored into one of the few remaining sycamore alluvial woodlands in the world.

Short on time? Dry Creek and neighboring Homer Ranch Preserve are both easily accessible from Hwy 198. But if you're staying longer, it's worth driving out to Blue Oak Ranch Preserve. With sweeping views of the Sierra Nevada, a quiet pond and ancient blue oaks, this place reminds you why land conservation matters.

HAYK_SHALUNTS/SHUTTERSTOCK

For travelers interested in some hands-on experience, the preserve offers stewardship opportunities, with no long-term commitment necessary. You can work in the native plant nursery or help with trail maintenance. Email *education@sequoiariverlands.org* for more info.

Three Rivers

TIME FROM SEQUOIA & KC NATIONAL PARKS: **15MIN**

Riding white water

Thundering along the **Kaweah River** by raft is an exhilarating endeavor, especially in spring when the river is charged with snowmelt. The rapids are Class III and IV (intermediate and advanced), so frothing currents and pulse-quickening spins are guaranteed. Time to get drenched!

Local operators lead excursions between March and July when the current cooperates and it is swiftest around Memorial Day. Outfitter **Sequoia Adventures** *(sequoiaadventures.com)* is based at the Three Rivers Hideaway campground and

EATING & DRINKING IN VISALIA: OUR PICKS

Component Coffee: Artful coffee lab grinding the best beans in town and serving burritos, açai bowls and avocado toast. *7am-5pm* $

Brewbakers Brewing Company: Stained-glass lamps and gleaming beer vats herald a delightfully retro brewpub. Grab a booth and tuck into comfort food. *11am-9pm* $$

Elderwood: The chefs here serve locally sourced food, while mixologists shake up novel cocktails. Perched on the art deco Darling Hotel's roof deck. *7am-9.30pm* $$$

Mulligan's Sports Bar: Pair some craft cocktails and tasty bar bites with a tee time at Visalia's first indoor golf simulator. *hours vary* $$

Kaweah River

has a put-in right on the property, along with decades of experience guiding adventurers through these foaming waters. Their trips vary from one to five hours and range from $50 to $150 per person.

Mountain Descents *(mountaindescents.com)* also has decades of experience and runs trips of varying length and price, from $50 to $216 per person. Their short, family-friendly rides allow time to paddle and swim in calm waters, or you can choose challenging trips that hit rapid upon rapid. Make a day of it by booking the 10-mile trip: you'll shimmy past pine-lined riverbanks and shriek at sudden splashes and lunch is included.

EATING & DRINKING IN THREE RIVERS: OUR PICKS

Three Rivers Brewing Co: Run by an award-winning craft-beer maker, with tasty reds, IPAs, sours and stouts on tap. *11am-10pm Thu-Sat, to 9pm Sun & Mon* $$

River View Grill & Bar: River-view honky-tonk with occasional live music. Overpriced food, though the bar's a hoot in summer. *11am-9pm Fri & Sat, to 8pm Sun-Wed* $$

Sierra Subs & Salads: Friendly roadside eatery with a riverside back deck and beloved, from-scratch sandwiches and salads. *10.30am-5pm Tue-Sat* $

Gateway Restaurant: Classy indoor-outdoor establishment with gorgeous river views, a large selection of booze and tasty steaks and seafood. *8am-9pm* $$$

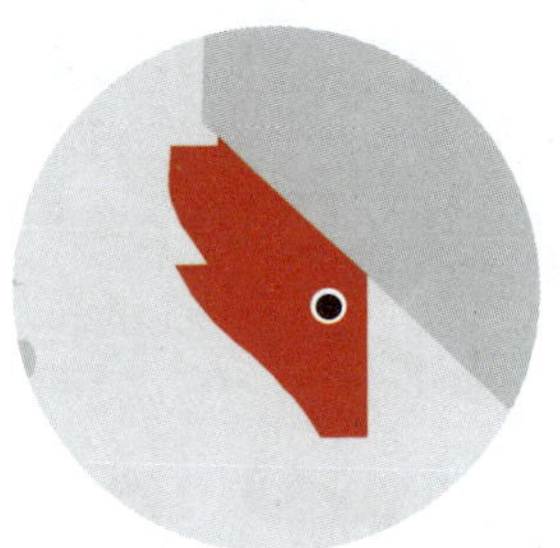

Eastern Sierra

SHEER MOUNTAINS | SURREAL DESERTSCAPES | QUIETUDE

TOP TIP

Be prepared for the elements when you're exploring the Eastern Sierra, particularly if you're visiting outside of the summer months. Snow often regularly blankets higher-elevation areas and mountain passes, so you'll want to check **Caltrans** *(quickmap.dot.ca.gov)* for road updates. Bring layers but also water and sunscreen, as the high desert sun is intense.

The lesser-explored side of the Sierra is a compelling amalgam of high desert, rural towns and blissfully empty space, backed by some of the tallest mountains in the contiguous US. Many are over 14,000ft and frequently snow dusted, shooting skyward from the arid Great Basin and Mojave Deserts. It's a dramatic juxtaposition and a landscape far less accessible than its western counterpart. But those who make the journey are rewarded with said beauty, plus pine forests, lush meadows, ice-blue lakes, hot springs and glacier-gouged canyons.

The Eastern Sierra Scenic Byway (Hwy 395) runs the entire length of the range. Turnoffs dead-ending at the foot of the mountains deliver you to pristine wilderness and countless trails, including the famous Pacific Crest Trail, John Muir Trail and the main Mt Whitney Trail. Add two ski areas, the hauntingly gorgeous Mono Lake and California's best-preserved ghost town and it's no wonder that the Eastern Sierra is on everybody's to-do list.

Hiking Mt Whitney

MAP P169

One majestic monolith

The mystique of **Mt Whitney** (14,505ft) captures the imagination and conquering it becomes an obsession for many. The main Mt Whitney Trail (the easiest and busiest one) leaves

GETTING AROUND

The Eastern Sierra is easiest to explore under your own steam. Keep in mind that some mountain roads close in winter, as do most of the passes that take you over the Sierras from east to west, including Tioga Rd (Hwy 120) to Yosemite. In the summertime, a twice-a-day bus with **YARTS** *(yarts.com)* connects Mammoth Lakes, June Lake and Lee Vining with Yosemite destinations along Hwy 120 and Yosemite Valley. See the website for prices.

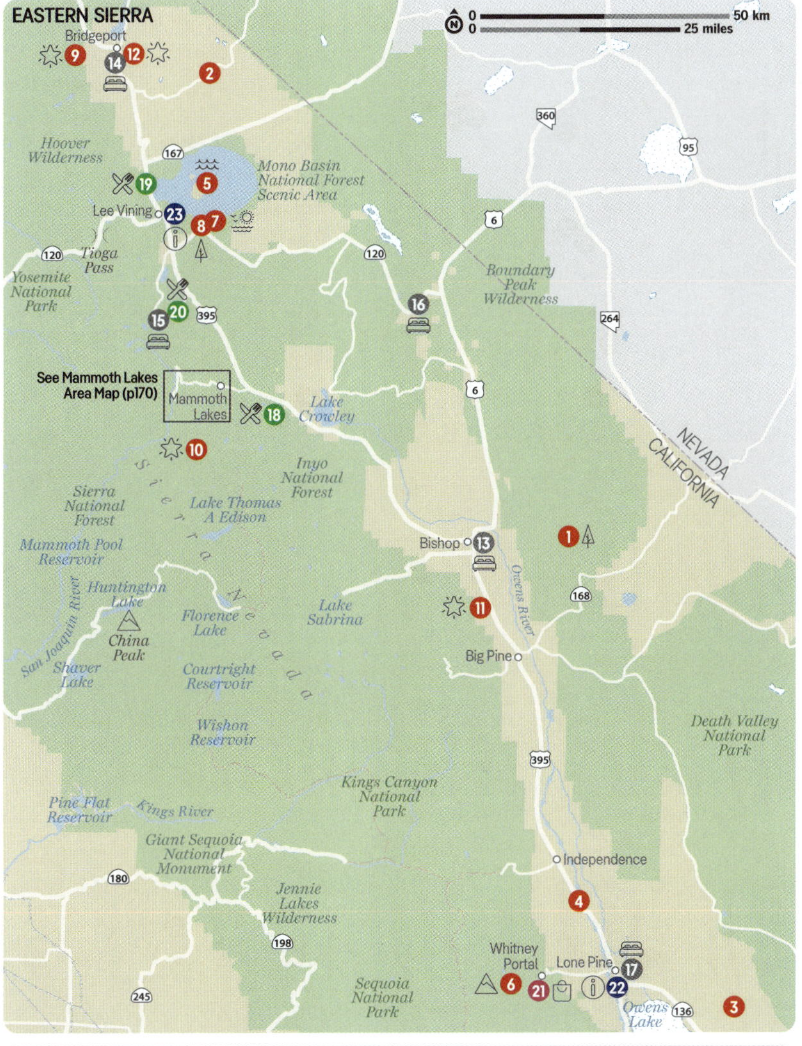

SIGHTS
1 Ancient Bristlecone Pine Forest
2 Bodie State Historic Park
3 Cerro Gordo
4 Manzanar National Historic Site
5 Mono Lake
6 Mt Whitney
7 Navy Beach
8 South Tufa

ACTIVITIES
9 Buckeye Hot Spring
see 1 Discovery Trail
10 Iva Bell Hot Springs
11 Keough's Hot Springs
12 Travertine Hot Spring

SLEEPING
13 Bishop Creekside Inn
14 Bodie Hotel
15 Double Eagle Resort & Spa
16 Inn at Benton Hot Springs
17 Whitney Portal Hostel & Hotel

EATING
see 17 Alabama Hills Cafe
18 Convict Lake Resort Restaurant
19 Mono Inn
20 Pino Pies
see 23 Whoa Nellie Deli

DRINKING & NIGHTLIFE
see 20 June Lake Brewing

SHOPPING
21 Whitney Portal Store

INFORMATION
22 Eastern Sierra Interagency Visitor Center
23 Mono Lake Committee Information Center
see 1 Schulman Grove Visitor Center

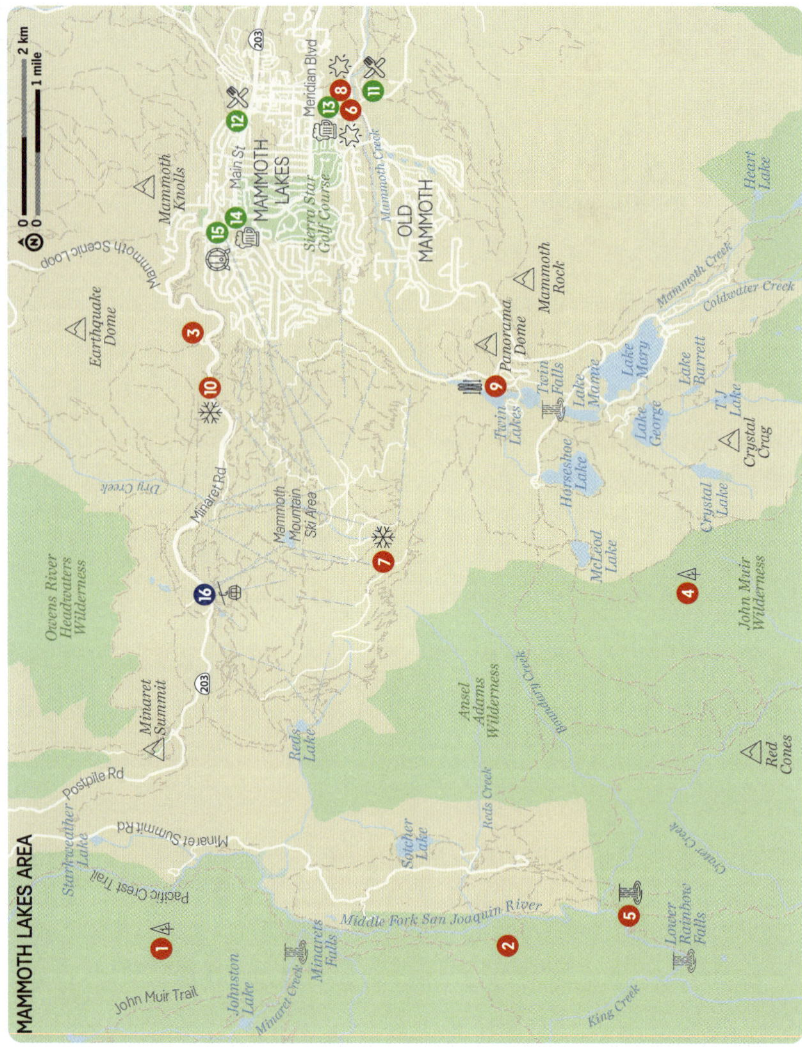

SIGHTS

1 Ansel Adams Wilderness Area
2 Devils Postpile National Monument
3 Earthquake Fault
see 7 Eleven53 Interpretive Center & Café
4 John Muir Wilderness Area
5 Rainbow Falls

ACTIVITIES

6 LA Kings Ice at Mammoth Lakes
7 Mammoth Mountain
8 Mammoth Rock 'n' Bowl
9 Tamarack Cross-Country Ski Center
10 Woolly's Adventure Summit

SLEEPING

see 9 Tamarack Lodge

EATING

11 Dos Alas
see 9 Lakefront Restaurant
12 Skadi

DRINKING & NIGHTLIFE

13 Distant Brewing
14 Mammoth Brewing Company
15 Shelter Distilling

TRANSPORTATION

16 Panorama Gondola

from Whitney Portal, 13 miles west of Lone Pine via Whitney Portal Rd (closed in winter) and climbs about 6000ft over 11 miles. It's a super-strenuous, really long walk that'll wear out even experienced mountaineers, but it doesn't require technical skills if attempted in summer or early fall. Earlier or later in the season, you'll likely need an ice axe and crampons and to stay overnight.

Many people in good physical condition make it to the top, although only superbly conditioned, previously acclimatized hikers should attempt this as a day hike. Breathing becomes difficult at these elevations and altitude sickness is common. Rangers recommend spending a night camping at the trailhead and another at one of the two camps along the route: Outpost Camp at 3.5 miles or Trail Camp at 6 miles.

Permits *($15)* are hard to come by, particularly for summer. If you're lucky enough to snag one in the February lottery, you'll receive it by email from *recreation.gov* about a week before your hike. Print it yourself or at the **Eastern Sierra Interagency Visitor Center** *(fs.usda.gov/r05/inyo/recreation)* in Lone Pine, where you can also get info on weather and trail conditions and pack-out kits. If you don't get a lottery permit, you can try to capitalize on cancellations. Or you can hike the first three miles to Lone Pine Lake and back (in one day) without a permit. Near the trailhead, the **Whitney Portal Store** *(whitneyportalstore.com)* sells groceries and snacks. It also has public showers and a cafe serving enormous, delicious pancakes.

Walk in the World's Oldest Forest

MAP P169

Respect your elders

For encounters with some of the earth's oldest living things, plan at least half a day at the **Ancient Bristlecone Pine Forest** *(fs.usda.gov/inyo)*. These otherworldly-looking trees are found above 10,000ft on the White Mountains' slopes where almost nothing grows, allowing the bristlecones to thrive.

To reach the groves, take Hwy 168 east 12 miles from Big Pine to White Mountain Rd, then turn north and climb the curvy road 10 miles. Park at the solar-powered **Schulman Grove Visitor Center** *(open mid-May to October)* and see if there are any ranger talks during your visit. Then set out on the 1-mile **Discovery Trail** through the Schulman Grove, a fantastic introduction to these gnarled and wind-battled stalwarts.

Interpretative panels explain how Dr Edmund Schulman's curiosity about old trees led him to this grove in 1953, where he found the world's first known 4000-year-old tree. He later found Methuselah, the world's oldest (known) living tree, at around 4700 years. Stay on the trail to avoid damaging the fragile root systems.

A second grove, the Patriarch Grove, is set within a dramatic open bowl and reached via a 12-mile graded dirt road. Four miles on you'll find a locked gate: the departure point for hikes to 14,246ft White Mountain Peak (California's third-highest mountain).

UNDERSTANDING MANZANAR

A shameful chapter in the nation's history is memorialized at the **Manzanar National Historic Site** *(nps.gov/manz)*, where between 1942 and 1945, 11,070 people of Japanese ancestry were incarcerated by the US government. Little remains of the dusty war relocation center, but a stark wooden guard tower alerts drivers to veer off Hwy 395 and enter the camp's only remaining building, the former high-school auditorium. Inside, a superb interpretive center tells the heartbreaking stories of the former residents who languished here yet managed to create a thriving community. There's also a 22-minute documentary and a self-guided 3.2-mile driving tour, where visitors can explore a recreated mess hall and barracks, a reconstructed women's latrine, restored gardens and the haunting camp cemetery. A visit is one of California's historical highlights and should not be missed.

ROAD TRIP

Cruising Highway 395

This is the ultimate California road trip, a south–north route tracing the eastern escarpment of the mighty Sierra Nevada. The road passes near the highest and lowest points in the continental US (Mt Whitney and Death Valley), plus three national parks and the back entrance to Yosemite (summer only). Highlights also include massive blue lakes, an important historical site and a ski mountain that families will adore.

1 Lone Pine

Start in Lone Pine at the Museum of Western Film History, investigating paraphernalia from hundreds of movies. Then head to the nearby orange, round-earthen mounds of the Alabama Hills, where many of the Old West Hollywood movies were shot. Even if you don't climb Mt Whitney, the drive to the Whitney Portal is gorgeous.

The Drive: Wind back down the mountain and through the sage-speckled desert, then turn left and head north on Hwy 395.

2 Manzanar National Historic Site

Near the tiny town of Independence is **Manzanar National Historic Site** (p171), a museum focusing on one of the darkest chapters in US history. On this windswept land, a WWII-era concentration camp incarcerated thousands of Japanese Americans between 1942 and 1945. Also noteworthy is the Eastern California Museum, with exhibits on the area's Native American history.

The Drive: Hop back on Hwy 395 and keep on truckin' north. It's about a 55-minute drive to Bishop.

FELIX LIPOV/SHUTTERSTOCK

Rainbow Falls, Devils Postpile National Monument

❸ Bishop

You could spend a few days hiking, cycling, fishing and climbing in the Eastern Sierra's second-largest town. Set aside time for the Laws Railroad Museum & Historic Site, to sift through Old West relics and explore antique railcars.

The Drive: Return to Hwy 395, then veer off west through Inyo National Forest on Rte 203, which becomes Mammoth's Main St.

❹ Mammoth Lakes

In the year-round resort town of Mammoth Lakes, the mountain's ski season can run into June, with backcountry hikes galore and a massive mountain-biking park. Don't miss Reds Meadow, west of Mammoth Mountain and the surreal 10,000-year-old **Devils Postpile National Monument** (p175).

The Drive: Back on Hwy 395, head north for 20 miles to the scenic June Lake Loop.

❺ June Lake Loop

The June Lake Loop drive traces the eponymous lake and meanders through a horseshoe canyon under the shadow of Carson Peak. Especially scenic in fall, the road is backed by the Ansel Adams Wilderness Area and its high-country trails. The June Mountain Ski Area pops off in winter and in summer the lake beach becomes quite the party scene.

The Drive: Cross Hwy 395 and head east for 14 miles on Rte 120 to Mono Lake's South Tufa area.

❻ Mono Lake

North America's second-oldest **lake** (p175) is a quiet and mysterious 70-sq-mile expanse of deep blue water. The glassy surface reflects jagged Sierra peaks, young volcanic cones and the unearthly tufa towers that make the lake so distinctive.

BEST HOT SPRINGS IN THE EASTERN SIERRA

Keough's Hot Springs: Historic complex featuring a tepid outdoor pool and a hotter soaking pool. Locals bathe nearby in complimentary 'hot ditches.'

Buckeye Hot Spring: Secluded piping-hot spring with several pools beside Buckeye Creek – handy for a cooling dip. Clothing optional.

Travertine Hot Spring: Natural pools amid impressive rock formations just outside of Bridgeport. Can become kind of a scene after dark.

Inn at Benton Hot Springs: A historic resort outside of already-remote Benton, with antique-filled rooms and campsites featuring private soaking tubs.

Iva Bell Hot Springs: True hot-springs diehards get permits to hit the 24-mile out-and-back Fish Creek Trail to these remote, incredible pools.

ALEJANDROAMBITE/SHUTTERSTOCK

Mammoth Mountain

Playing Outside on Mammoth Mountain

MAP P170

WHEEEEEEEEEE!

Mammoth Lakes is a famous mountain-resort town endowed with larger-than-life scenery – active outdoorsy folks worship at the base of its imposing 11,053ft **Mammoth Mountain** *(mammothmountain.com; lift ticket adult/child from $109/49)*. It's a skiers' and snowboarders' dream resort, with sunny skies, a reliably long season (usually November to June) and more than 3500 acres of fantastic tree-line and open-bowl skiing. When the snow finally fades, the area is an outdoor wonderland of mountain-biking trails and endless alpine hiking.

At any time of year, you can take the **Panorama Gondola** *(adults $49, two children per adult ride free)* to the top to visit the **Eleven53 Interpretive Center & Café**, with intriguing exhibits on the region's landscapes and wildlife, along with friendly docents to answer questions. The views are astounding and visitors love taking photos with the mountaintop's famous sign.

Walking in Wilderness

MAP P170

Mammoth Lakes offers trails galore

Mammoth Lakes rubs up against the **Ansel Adams Wilderness** and **John Muir Wilderness Areas**. Both are laced with fabulous trails leading to shimmering lakes, rugged peaks and hidden canyons. Major trailheads leave from the Mammoth Lakes Basin, Reds Meadow and Agnew Meadows; the last is accessible from June through September and for the most part only by shuttle.

From various spots along the Reds Meadow area, long-distance backpackers with wilderness permits and

RESPONSIBLE TRAVEL

For more tips on how to travel lightly in California and help conserve the state's precious natural resources, see p190.

bear canisters can easily jump onto the John Muir Trail (to Yosemite to the north and Mt Whitney to the south) and the Pacific Crest Trail (fancy walking to Mexico or Canada?).

Get Down with the Devil

MAP P170

The strange things volcanoes do

The rawness and relative newness of the Eastern Sierra's volcanic formations are reminders of the region's active and ongoing evolution. And the most astounding landmark formed in the current era of volcanic activity is the **Devils Postpile National Monument** *(nps.gov/depo; adult/child $15/7)*, west of Mammoth Lakes.

To reach it, visitors must park near Mammoth Mountain Inn and hop on the shuttle bus in front of the Adventure Center, which transports you to one of the region's most beautiful and varied landscapes. Exit the shuttle at the Devils Postpile Ranger Station and take the easy half-mile trail around the feature, which is perched atop a hill. As you walk, consider that about 80,000 to 100,000 years ago, a violent volcanic vent filled the river canyon in which you stand with lava 400ft deep. The lava cooled so quickly that it formed one of the world's most impressive examples of columnar basalt, reaching up to 60ft high. These multisided columns are virtually symmetrical and their honeycomb formation can be viewed up close by taking a short trail up the hill.

From the monument, continue on a 2.5-mile hike through fire-scarred forest to awe-inspiring **Rainbow Falls**, where the San Joaquin River gushes over a 101ft basalt cliff. The chances of seeing a rainbow forming in the billowing mist are highest at midday. The falls can also be reached via an easy 1.5-mile walk from the Reds Meadow area, which has a cafe, store, campground, pack station and shuttle stop.

Diving into Mono Lake

MAP P169

And other ways to enjoy it

After drinking in the glassy blue-green expanse of **Mono Lake** while driving along Hwy 395, you'll likely want an immersion. The Mono Basin Scenic Area Visitor Center is a

WATER FIGHT

In the 1930s Los Angeles expanded and bought up water rights in the Mono Basin, diverting streams feeding Mono Lake. The lake water dropped, doubling its salinity and threatening its ecological balance. In 1976 environmentalist David Gaines found that, if left untouched, Mono Lake would dry up within 20 years. To avert disaster he formed the Mono Lake Committee. Years of legal action followed and in 1994 the city was forced to reduce its diversions to allow the lake to rise by 20ft. Unfortunately, that hasn't happened. The lake is still low, creating dust and other environmental issues and conservationists have continued fighting. To learn more, visit the **Mono Lake Committee Information Center** *(monolake.org)* in Lee Vining.

EATING IN THE EASTERN SIERRA: OUR PICKS

MAPS P169 & P170

Whoa Nellie Deli: Mobil gas-station restaurant famous for Mono Lake views, live bands and amazing mahimahi tacos. *7am-8pm* $$

Convict Lake Resort Restaurant: Impress your date at this classy, beloved establishment for beef Wellington or fresh rainbow trout. *5-8.30pm* $$$

Lakefront Restaurant: Incredibly romantic French-Californian restaurant in the delightful Tamarack Lodge on the Twin Lakes. *5-9pm* $$$

Alabama Hills Cafe: The breakfast portions are big, the bread is freshly baked and the soups are hearty. Also, the owners have opened a bar nearby. *5am-3pm* $

Dos Alas: In a frontier-style timber building with stunning mountain views; Cuba's flavors come alive in Mammoth Lakes. *5-9pm Wed-Sun* $$

Skadi: Inside the Empeiria High Sierra, Chef Ian Algerøen's 'fine alpine dining' is inspired by his Norwegian heritage and techniques. *5-9pm Wed-Sun* $$$

Mono Inn: Within a restored 1922 lodge, this elegant restaurant features a farm-to-table tasting menu and lovely Mono Lake views. *5-9pm Fri-Mon* $$$

Pino Pies: Originally located in Bishop, these New Zealand–style meat pies became a hit when the owner moved the business to June Lake. *7am-5pm Wed-Sun* $

FAMILY-FRIENDLY MAMMOTH ACTIVITIES

Woolly's Adventure Summit: A mountain coaster! Snow tubing! A bungee trampoline! A climbing wall! A ropes course! A zipline! Do it all for $50.

Earthquake Fault: It's not every day you can gaze into an earthquake's aftermath: a sinuous fissure half a mile long with a crevice 20ft deep. Kids dig it.

Tamarack Cross-Country Ski Center: Amid magnificent scenery around Twin Lakes and the Lakes Basin are 20 miles of groomed tracks.

Mammoth Rock 'n' Bowl: Stylish 12-lane bowling complex with foosball, ping-pong and darts, plus a sports bar.

LA Kings Ice at Mammoth Lakes: An Olympic-sized recreation center operating as an ice rink from October to April and as a three-court gymnasium the rest of the year.

short drive north of Lee Vining, where you'll find exhibits on the lake's history, wildlife and geology and an interpretative trail overlooking the lake.

Rangers normally give patio talks on weekends and they also lead excellent walking tours about 20 minutes away at the **South Tufa area** on the lake's rim. (In 2025 it was unclear if these would continue, as President Trump was gutting the federal government.)

You can visit South Tufa on your own though and that's where you'll find the largest number of limestone towers, which resemble tall, thin sandcastles, rising from the lake. They form when minerals are released from subterranean springs and a mile-long loop trail meanders through these bizarre formations, with interpretative signage for hikers. Looking out over the lake, you may notice that the brackish water teems with buzzing alkali flies and brine shrimp, both considered delicacies by dozens of migratory bird species that return each year. So do about 60% of the state's population of California gulls, which nest on the lake's volcanic islands in spring and summer.

If you want more activities, rent water toys or take a guided tour that gets you out on the water. In summer and early fall, visitors put in at **Navy Beach**, a short drive or hike from South Tufa, with kayaks, canoes and paddleboards. Gliding among the tufa is a quintessential California experience and swimming is also quite memorable thanks to the salty, buoyant water. Just be sure you don't have any open cuts and avoid menacing the tufa.

Time Traveling in Bodie

MAP P169

An authentic ghost town

At **Bodie State Historic Park** *(parks.ca.gov/bodie; adult/child $8/5)* a gold-rush ghost town is preserved in a state of 'arrested decay.' Weathered buildings sit frozen in time on a dusty, windswept plain where gold was first discovered in 1859. Within 20 years the place grew from a rough mining camp to an even rougher boomtown with a population of 10,000 and a reputation for lawlessness. Fights and murders were commonplace, the violence no doubt fueled by liquor dispensed in the town's 65 saloons, some of which did double duty as brothels, gambling halls or opium dens. The hills disgorged some $34 million worth of gold and silver in the 1870s and '80s, but when production plummeted, so did the population and eventually the town was abandoned to the elements.

DRINKING IN THE EASTERN SIERRA: BREWERIES & DISTILLERIES

— MAP P169

June Lake Brewing: A top draw, this open tasting room serves around 10 drafts and brewers swear the June Lake water makes the difference. *noon-8pm*

Mammoth Brewing Company: The highest West Coast brewery, at 8000ft, this place has more than a dozen brews on tap and serves tasty bar food. *10am-10pm*

Distant Brewing: Popular brewery and tasting room featuring craft beer made with local ingredients. The IPAs are killer. *noon-9pm Sun-Thu, to 10pm Fri & Sat*

Shelter Distilling: An après fave in Mammoth's village; spirits and beer are made with alpine snowmelt and foraged ingredients. *11am-10pm Sun-Thu, to 11pm Fri & Sat*

MARIUSZ S. JURGIELEWICZ/SHUTTERSTOCK

Bodie State Historic Park

To get here, head east through the sage-dappled hills for 13 miles (the last 3 miles are unpaved) on Hwy 270, about 7 miles south of Bridgeport. Allow two hours to wander the abandoned town, peering through the windows of weather-beaten buildings. You'll see stocked stores, furnished homes, workshops filled with tools and a schoolhouse with homework assignments still scrawled on the chalkboard. The jail is still here, as are the fire station, a bank vault and many other buildings. The former Miners' Union Hall houses a museum and visitor center and ranger talks take place at the museum and a church. There's also a tour of the stamp mill, where quartz rock containing gold and silver was crushed with iron rods. To complete the experience, spend the night at the Bodie Hotel, a former boarding house and brothel that was transported to nearby Bridgeport in the 1800s.

THE CURSE OF CERRO GORDO

In 2018, social-media influencer Brent Underwood bought **Cerro Gordo** *(store.cerrogordomines.com)*, an abandoned silver-mining town 20 miles east of Lone Pine. He paid $1.4 million for the 360-acre property and 22 structures, including the American Hotel and its intact saloon. Intent on preserving the history, Underwood moved here and began revamping it to attract visitors. Then things started going wrong: the pandemic hit, the hotel burned down, a '1000-year flood' took out the road. Underwood has pressed on, rebuilding the seven-room hotel, installing a movie theater and exploring abandoned mine shafts. The place seems to be a cursed work in progress, but it can be visited at no charge every day from 9am to 5pm. Get here on an 8-mile dirt road; 4WD recommended.

Places We Love to Stay

$ Budget $$ Midrange $$$ Top End

Yosemite National Park

Maps p145 & p146

Curry Village $ A collection of motel rooms, wood cabins and canvas tent cabins in the heart of Yosemite.

Tuolumne Meadows Campground $ At 8600ft and the biggest campground in the park, it has 329 sites and was revamped in 2025.

Yosemite Valley Lodge $$ Low-slung complex of rustic lodgings, eateries, a lively bar and a pool; a short walk from the base of Yosemite Falls.

Ahwahnee Hotel (p153) **$$$** Sumptuous historic property in the valley with killer views, a famous dining room and a heated pool.

Just Outside Yosemite

Yosemite View Lodge $$ Two miles from the park entrance, this modern complex has hot tubs, a restaurant and pools.

Evergreen Lodge $$$ A classic, nearly century-old resort with comfy cabins and pre-furnished glamping tents spread among the trees.

Rush Creek Lodge $$$ Luxe, country-chic resort and mountain-adventure destination with hot tubs and a fabulous Yosemite-inspired spa.

Firefall Ranch $$$ Built in 2024 on 300 verdant acres, with 55 posh cottages surrounding a tranquil lake, three good restaurants and amenities galore.

Mariposa & Around

Yosemite Bug Rustic Mountain Resort $ Budget-friendly oasis with eclectic accommodations, a beloved restaurant and a spa.

Mariposa Hotel Inn $$ An atmospheric, creaky 1901 building filled with old photos, mirrors, newspaper clippings and vintage everything.

Wildhaven Yosemite $$$ A classic new glamping experience, with charming cabins and platform tents featuring firepits, expansive decks and yoga.

Fish Camp & Oakhurst

Sierra Sky Ranch $$ Former 14-acre ranch with cozy, homespun rooms, shady verandas and old Western furnishings.

Tenaya Lodge $$$ Sprawling family-friendly resort and activity hub near Yosemite's south entrance.

Narrow Gauge Inn $$$ A 26-room inn near the Sugar Pine Railroad with a down-home vibe and fine restaurant.

Château du Sureau $$$ Luxe Relais & Châteaux property with discreet service and lavish European style throughout. Amenities suitable for royalty.

Groveland

Yosemite Basecamp $$ An 'adventure loft' and 'basecamp bunkhouse' in Groveland with boot dryers and soaking tubs.

Hotel Charlotte $$ An elegant historic hotel featuring a classy restaurant and buzzy back patio.

Groveland Hotel $$$ This well-run, historic and tasteful property dates from 1850. Subtle nods to the Old West abound. Great back patio.

Sequoia & Kings Canyon National Parks

Map p160

John Muir Lodge $$ Stone-and-timber retreat in Grant Grove Village with homespun rooms, a cozy fireplace and tent cabins.

Cedar Grove Lodge $$ The only indoor sleeping option in the canyon, this riverside lodge offers 21 simple motel-style rooms.

Silver City Mountain Resort (p162) **$$** Cozy, rustic cabins in remote Mineral King offering a unique mountain experience.

Wuksachi Lodge $$$ The parks' most upscale option, with stone fireplaces, forest views and generic motel-style rooms.

Visalia & Three Rivers

Three Rivers Hideaway $ A friendly campsite and RV park with easy access to rafting and walking trails.

Lamp Liter Inn $$ Revamped, family-owned establishment in Visalia with country cottages facing an outdoor pool.

Buckeye Tree Lodge $$ Hotel rooms and cabins, some with river views, just south of the park in Three Rivers.

The Darling $$$ Modern rooms in a sleek building overflowing with art deco style in downtown Visalia.

Eastern Sierra

Maps p169 & p170

Whitney Portal Hostel & Hotel $ The perfect launchpad for Mt Whitney trips, with dorms and modern motel rooms with views.

Bodie Hotel $$ Experience an 1800s boardinghouse transported to Bridgeport from Bodie in all its rickety (but restored!) glory.

Bishop Creekside Inn $$ Get a room with a patio on Bishop Creek, which flows through the elegant grounds of Bishop's fanciest stay.

Tamarack Lodge $$ A cozy resort on Lower Twin Lake with a classy bar and an excellent restaurant. Stay in a rustic-style room or a cabin.

Double Eagle Resort & Spa $$$ Fancy for June Lake, these two-bedroom log cabins and balcony hotel rooms exude rustic elegance. Great spa.

JLPHOTOWORX/SHUTTERSTOCK

Tuolumne Meadows Campground

TOOLKIT

The chapters in this section cover the most important topics you'll need to know about in Lake Tahoe, Yosemite & Central California. They're full of nuts-and-bolts information and valuable insights to help you understand and navigate these areas and get the most out of your trip.

South Lake Tahoe (p106)

BRANISLAV_ZVADA/SHUTTERSTOCK

Arriving

Sacramento and Reno-Tahoe airports primarily receive US internal flights. To fly into either of these destinations, you'll likely be changing planes in New York or LA. The train from LA makes for a leisurely route into Sacramento, while the 99 and 5 highways link Southern and Northern California.

Visas

Check travel.state.gov for rules for the US Visa Waiver Program (VWP), whereby citizens of 42 countries can stay up to 90 days with an approved passport and Electronic System for Travel Authorization (ESTA).

Cash

ATMs are easily located at major transport hubs. It's a good idea to carry a small amount of cash with you, as card payments are almost (but not quite) ubiquitous.

SIM Cards

Buy a prepaid SIM card for US connectivity. Ask for advice about the best mobile coverage if you're headed to a remote mountain destination.

Wi-fi

It's very easy to stay connected in the region, as hotels, restaurants and public spaces abound with free network connections. An exception is remote mountain locations.

From Transport Hubs to Popular Destinations

FROM	TO	DURATION	FROM	TO	DURATION
SACRAMENTO	LAKE TAHOE	2hr 10min	RENO-TAHOE	SACRAMENTO	2hr 20min
SACRAMENTO	YOSEMITE	2hr 50min	RENO-TAHOE	LAKE TAHOE	1hr 20min
SACRAMENTO	CHICO	1hr 25min	RENO-TAHOE	NEVADA CITY	1hr 35min
SACRAMENTO	BAKERFIELD	4hr 10 min	RENO-TAHOE	YOSEMITE	2hr 40min

CROSS COUNTRY TRAINS

Arrive in style in central California by taking the train. Sacramento is served by the **Coast Starlight** service, which links Seattle and Portland to the north with Los Angeles to the south, via snowy peaks, dense forests and a gorgeous sweep of Pacific Ocean coastline. The equally enticingly named **California Zephyr** – following an equally enticing route – takes the course of the first Transcontinental Railroad over the Rockies before climbing up into the high Sierras: you can arrive in the mountain town of Truckee from Chicago or Denver.

FROM LEFT: FUSE/GETTY IMAGES, GOGLIK83/GETTY IMAGES

Getting Around

Many people opt to drive in the region, but bear in mind that trains, buses and even hikes can provide you with a more relaxed alternative.

TRAVEL COSTS

Car rental per day from **$30**

Train ticket from LA to Sacramento **$144**

EV charging **$0.25/KWh**

Bike rental per day **from $27**

Carbon Considerations

For remoter destinations you'll be reliant on driving. Consider hiring an EV to lighten your impact on the environment, or take a train to a major hub such as Sacramento and drive from there. The 5 and 99 highways that cut through the state make for gruelling driving, and are best avoided – either by taking the train or opting for the coastal highway if you're driving from LA to Sacramento.

Parking

In this car-focused country, parking is relatively easy, and nearly all accommodation and eating places will have their own lots. For city parking, look out for meters (where you can use a bank card) or park for free on residential streets: just be aware of signs which list potential parking restrictions.

TIP

Download the Amtrack app to buy tickets and check routes. Consider purchasing a Rail Pass if you have extensive travel plans – promotional deals can make this a great bargain.

SOME ROAD RULES

Drive on the right, pass on the left. Only pass on the right if you're on an open highway with two or more lanes of travel on your side. If you meet a vehicle on a steep, narrow incline, the vehicle facing downhill must reverse to allow the other to pass. A left turn at a red light can only be made from one one-way street into another.

DRIVING ESSENTIALS

Drive on the right

Speed limit is usually 65mph on freeways, 55mph on two-lane highways and 35mph in cities

.08

Blood alcohol limit is 0.08%

Hiking

The area around Lake Tahoe is particularly well served by hiking trails. Lace up your boots, put on your backpack and explore this stunning area the slow way. A good place to start your research is alltrails.com, or call into the nearest tourist office for maps and advice on conditions.

Train Routes

For short hops between central California towns, check out the Amtrack *(amtrak.com)* website. You can take in the views from an upper deck, and arrive at your destination refreshed. As well as the coastal service, there is a line that links Bakersfield with Stockton and Sacramento via Fresno and other valley towns; Truckee and Sacramento are also connected by train.

Cycling

The high mountain ranges are only for the hardiest of cyclists, or those powered by e-bikes. But this is a relatively cycle-friendly region: in the university town of Davis, bikes outnumber cars. One excellent dedicated cycle route is the 32-mile American River Bike Trail which links Sacramento with Folsom.

Money

CURRENCY: US DOLLAR ($)

Cards & Cash

In California you'll find ATMs everywhere, at banks, gas stations, supermarkets, train stations and airports. Nearly all vendors accept cards, but there are exceptions where you'll need cash. Visa and Mastercard are the most widely accepted cards, American Express and Discovery less so. You may have to enter your pin for card payments.

Tipping

Tipping is very much the norm in California. Aim to tip 15–25% for waiting staff, and have some dollars ready for housekeeping staff: leave around $5 when you depart your room. When making a card payment in a restaurant, cafe or bar, the option to add a percentage tip to the total is usually given.

Contactless Payment

After a surprisingly slow start, the tech-savvy state has caught up, and you can now use your phone or smart watch to make payments rather than with a card. Some farmers market stalls, for example, are cash only, so be prepared.

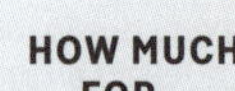

HOW MUCH FOR...

Museum entry
$10–25

ATM fees
$3

Driving Hwy 99
Free

Parking
Free–$10

HOW TO... Save Money on Your Journey

It's tempting to fly into one city and out of another to maximise on your trip time and travel more widely across California or the wider US. But you often get more economical deals flying into and out of the same destination, so weigh this up against the cost of returning to your starting point for the trip home.

SKIP THE SUV

Car rental companies may want to upgrade you to a gas-guzzling SUV. Just stay no, and drive a smaller, more fuel-efficient vehicle. They're easier to park, too!

SALES TAX

Be aware of a little sting in the tail when you make a purchase: sales tax. With the exception of groceries, the state of California adds a tax of 7.25% to goods and services, which isn't marked up on the item – tax is added when purchases are made. Local sales taxes may add an additional 2%, and accommodation taxes are variable, but can be up to 14% in larger settlements. There are no tax refunds for international visitors.

Accommodations

B&Bs

Often located in historic homes with private gardens or flower-decked balconies, B&Bs are good for those wanting a more intimate experience and recommendations for the locale; they provide a more personal alternative to private short-term rentals. Many hosts also cook up wonderful breakfasts and, it being California, they will likely use farm-to-fork organic produce. Multiple-night stays may be required, and in some establishments small children are not hosted.

Hostels

Budget-friendly HI-affiliated and independent options, offering anything from single-sex and/or mixed dorms, to private en suite rooms. Hostels are often located in key locations, including city centers, and many are in impressive and even landmark historic buildings. Hostels are always convivial places to meet other travelers or to chinwag with knowledgable staff, and many have excellent doubles for couples.

Hotels

You'll find everything from luxe boutique resorts to hip city hangouts and cookie-cutter chains. Rooms are often priced by the size and number of beds in a room, rather than the number of occupants. Note that many properties add 'resort fees' to the daily room rate. Service is generally excellent, and breakfasts are on the generous side.

Motels

Handy for road-trippers and less expensive than hotels; some have swimming pools and rooms with kitchenettes. While facilities can be basic, motels often have low-key charm and 50s or 60s design features which fits the California road trip aesthetic nicely. As well as along the highways, you'll find motels on the city fringes.

HOW MUCH FOR A NIGHT IN A...

B&B
$150–250

Hostel
$30–45

Campsite pitch
$20–50

Camping

Not just a cheap sleep, but a great way to truly connect with central California's great outdoors, be it on a lake shore, under pine trees or by a rushing river. Many sites cater to tents, trailers and RVs, and are open year-round. Book ahead during high season when the mountain areas are a magnet for rafters and hikers.

BEST PRICES

Accommodation prices usually vary according to demand, or there may be different rates for online, phone and walk-in bookings. B&B rates are more consistent, but virtually every other accommodation will charge wildly different rates depending on the time of year and even your negotiating skills. Generally, midweek rates are lower except at urban hotels geared to business travelers, which lure leisure travelers with weekend deals. Discount cards (eg AAA, AARP) may get you about 10% off standard rates at participating hotels and motels. Bargaining may be possible for walk-in guests without reservations, especially at off-peak times.

CLOCKWISE FROM TOP LEFT: SHARPNER/SHUTTERSTOCK, IVONNE WIERINK/SHUTTERSTOCK, KONSTANTINOS69/SHUTTERSTOCK, PIRTUSS/SHUTTERSTOCK

Family Travel

Central California makes for an excellent destination for families: welcoming, well organized and with bountiful experiences to entice kids, from gold panning at a Sacramento museum to rafting the rivers. The downside is: 'are we there yet?' Driving through the center of the state can be a long and dull affair, so consider trains for at least part of your trip.

Family Accommodation

Hotels often apply a small surcharge for the third and fourth person, but children under a certain age (this varies) may stay free. Cribs or rollaway cots usually cost extra. Beware that suites or 'junior suites' may be simply oversized rooms; ask about the layout when booking. Renting a multi-bed hostel room with bunk beds is a good family option, as is getting kids under canvas in the great outdoors.

Feeding the Kids

Casual eateries typically have high chairs and children's menus, and some break out paper place mats and crayons for drawing. Even restaurants without special kids menus can usually whip up something. Supermarket chains such as Trader Joe's, Whole Foods and Gelson's have healthy takeout food. Baby food, infant formula and other necessities are also widely sold at supermarkets and pharmacies.

Discounts

These are available for everything from museum admission and movie tickets to bus fares. The definition of a 'child' varies from 'under 18' to age six. A limited number of venues offer student discounts for older children and university students.

Car Safety

Children aged under six or weighing less than 60lb must be buckled up in the back of the car in a safety seat. Be sure to book a safety seat ahead when you reserve your car.

BEST ATTRACTIONS FOR FAMILIES

Kayaking
Kayak on **Lake Tahoe** (p98), or take a dip from a sandy beach

Cable-car thrills
Ride the high cable car at **Palisades Tahoe** (p124)

Ghost hunting
Look for ghost town spooks at **Bodie State Historic Park** (p176)

Get splashed by a waterfall
Take a trail to a **Yosemite cascade** (p153)

Roundhouse life
Explore the roundhouse and mortar holes at **Indian Grinding Rock** (p84)

Pan for gold
Try some gold panning and explore underground streets in **Old Sacramento** (p47)

AFFORDABLE CALIFORNIA

In hotels and motels, look out for 'kids stay free' and 'free breakfast' promotions. And bear in mind that sometimes no organized activity is needed. We've seen young kids thrill at catching their first glimpse of a sequoia tree, and teens with sophisticated palates bliss out over their first taste of heirloom tomatoes at a farmers market or shrimp dumplings at a dim-sum palace. It's a good idea to pack a cooler bag with lunch and snacks for day trips, to avoid tempting but pricey cafes at visitor attractions.

Health & Safe Travel

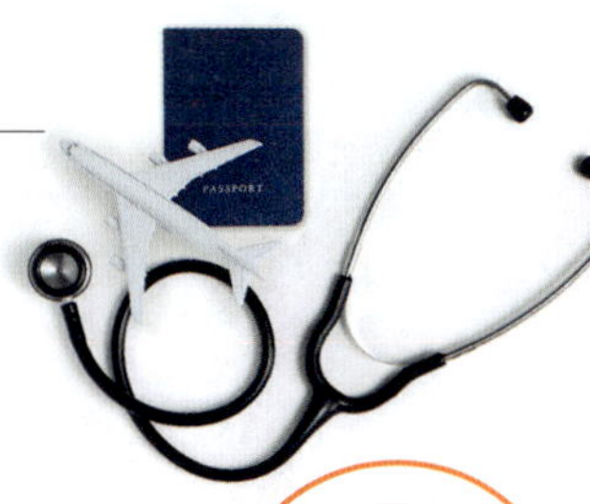

INSURANCE

Travel insurance to cover theft, loss and medical problems is essential, especially for international visitors. Domestic visitors should confirm they have proper coverage. Some policies do not cover 'risky' activities such as diving, motorcycling and skiing, so be sure to read the fine print.

Earthquakes

Earthquakes happen all the time, but most are undetectable. If you're caught in a serious tremor:

- Stay in an open outdoor space, if possible.
- Get under a desk or table or stand in a doorway, if indoors.
- Protect your head and stay clear of windows or anything that may fall.
- Don't head for elevators or go running into the street.

Drinking Water

It's fine to drink water from the tap anywhere in California, except at some wilderness campgrounds where the water may not be potable (look for signs or ask the campground host). Bring a water bottle on your trip, as drinking water fountains are widespread in cities, parks and remoter spots.

VACCINES

Currently there are no vaccination requirements for visiting the USA. California has recently had outbreaks of measles and whooping cough, since fewer children are being vaccinated.

FIRE SAFETY

LOW
Control of fires is generally easy

MODERATE
Fires can start from accidental causes

HIGH
Fires can start easily from most causes

VERY HIGH
Fires start easily and spread rapidly

EXTREME
Fires start quickly, burn intensely and are hard to control

Wildfires

The wildfire season gets ever longer and more perilous (at least June through November but it can now happen at any time). Fires limit access to roads and parks, and can cause vacationers and residents to flee for their lives. At the time of research, fires have affected Chico, Yosemite National Park, Lake Tahoe and all the national forests.

STAY COOL

Take it easy as you acclimatize to central California's high temperatures, especially north of the area around Chico and Red Bluff. A minimum of 3L of water per person per day is recommended when you're active outdoors. Be sure to eat a salty snack, too, as sodium is necessary for rehydration.

FROM LEFT: PIXEL-SHOT/SHUTTERSTOCK, AMEDEOEMAJA/SHUTTERSTOCK

Food, Drink & Nightlife

When to Eat

Breakfast Usually 7am–11am. Residents most often grab this meal on the go.

Brunch 11am–3pm weekends. Often accompanied by a glass of California white wine.

Lunch Generally served noon–2:30pm. Lunch out tends to be for social or business purposes. Alcohol is rarely consumed.

Dinner 5pm–9pm, and later in the cities.

Where to Eat

Whether you're into fine dining at a destination vineyard or you're searching for the ultimate roadside taco joint, the state will spoil you. As well as restaurants, cafes and diners, look out for food trucks, often located in parking lots, and fabulous weekend farmers markets where you can put together a stellar picnic. Make reservations online at least a month ahead for top tables. Apart from at the very-high-end restaurants, the dress code is California casual.

MENU DECODER

Corkage You can bring your own wine to most restaurants; a 'corkage' fee of $15 to $30 usually applies.

Farm-to-fork Fresh local produce (often organic) with a reassuringly short supply chain.

Entree Always confusing to non-Americans – this is the word for a main course.

Heirloom Hip term for types of produce meant to evoke varieties grown in the past.

Split-plate If you ask the kitchen to divide a plate between two (or more) people, there may be a small split-plate surcharge.

Allergies and dietary restrictions Travelers that have food allergies or dietary restrictions are in luck – both vegetarian and vegan fare is all the rage in California and nearly all restaurants are sensitive to and can cater for most specific dietary needs.

HOW TO... Order

California cooking methods often celebrate old traditions with modern twists, and menus prefer 'small plate' dining, the latter concept encouraging the ordering and sharing of numerous dishes at the table, similar to Spanish tapas or family feasting. When it comes to wine, order Californian: the Golden State bottles more than 600 million gallons of vino annually, making it the world's fourth-largest producer after France, Italy and Spain. Excellent drops are produced up and down the length of the state, with more than 117 varietals grown in its soils. And don't be afraid to pair a beer with your meal. Innovation, seasonality and experimentation are common themes running through the taps, whether it's a barrel-aged red ale, an apricot-infused sour or a Yuletide choc-peppermint stout. Waiter staff are almost always expert in assisting with your order. Just don't forget to tip!

FROM LEFT: JULIA PAVALIUK/SHUTTERSTOCK, IMPACT PHOTOGRAPHY/SHUTTERSTOCK, RAM RIDER/SHUTTERSTOCK, RUSLAN SEMICHEV/SHUTTERSTOCK

HOW MUCH FOR A...

Coffee
$3–5

Glass of local wine
From $7

Craft beer
$5–9

Burrito
$10–14

Basque meal in Bakersfield
$20–30

Açaí bowl
$7–10

Cup of artisanal ice cream
$6

HOW TO... Eat & Drink Like a Local

Start your morning with a coffee. Some have it black, but most add something like oat milk and various flavorings. Breakfast might be a Greek-style yogurt or something simple from an artisanal bakery; fare like omelets and hash browns is saved for a special occasion or weekend brunch.

Food trucks are popular for lunch; Mexican food trucks are the most frequented, and are often superb and relatively cheap. Lunch may also be something light, like a salad. And, while many won't admit to this, the long lines outside In-N-Out Burger prove that not all California meals are healthy.

After-work drinks at a brewery while sitting outside on a patio are popular year-round. Sure, sometimes temperatures might drop into the 50s, but that's what overhead heaters are for.

Dinner at home might feature whatever is fresh at the local farmers market (many are open year-round). Favorite dining-out choices are Vietnamese, Japanese, regional Chinese, Italian (pasta is favored over pizza), the catch-all Mediterranean (which is a lot like Californian!), regional Mexica, other Central American cuisines and regional American. A trendy cocktail or a local wine is a favorite accompaniment.

Restaurants are casual and many feature year-round outside dining. Bars tend to close early, so even in cities streets can be quiet by midnight.

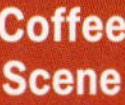

Coffee Scene

The specialty coffee scene continues to expand, with local roasters and specialty coffee bars taking a more artisanal approach to their Joe. The emphasis is on single-origin, seasonal beans, lightly roasted in small batches.

TASTING THE VINTAGES

Clutch your wallet The days of free tastings are long gone, and a 45-minute tasting can cost $30 or more.

Swirl Before tasting a just opened bottle of wine, swirl your glass to oxygenate the wine and release the flavors.

Sniff Dip your nose (without getting it wet) into the glass for a good whiff. This sniff prompts your senses and your salivary glands to fully appreciate the wine.

Swish Take a swig, and roll it over the front of your gums and sides of your tongue to get the full effect of complex flavors and textures on all your taste buds. After you swallow, breathe out through your nose to appreciate the finish.

If you're driving or cycling, don't swallow Sips are hard to keep track of at tastings, so perfect your graceful arc into the spittoon.

Take it easy There's no need for speed, even if the winery seems to be hurrying you along. Plan to visit three wineries a day maximum.

No need to buy No one expects you to buy – but it's customary to purchase a bottle before winery picnics, and tasting fees are sometimes refunded with purchases.

Join the club? Many wineries push their own 'wine clubs' with promises of free future tastings and discounts. Before plunking down the dough, ask yourself: 'Will I ever come here again?'

Responsible Travel

Climate Change & Travel

It's impossible to ignore the impact we have when traveling; Lonely Planet urges all travelers to engage with their travel carbon footprint, which will mainly come from air travel. While there often isn't an alternative, travelers can look to minimize the number of flights they take, opt for newer aircrafts and use cleaner ground transport, such as trains. One proposed solution – purchasing carbon offsets – unfortunately does not cancel out the impact of individual flights. While most destinations will depend on air travel for the foreseeable future, for now, pursuing ground-based travel where possible is the best course of action.

The **UN Carbon Offset Calculator** shows how flying impacts a household's emissions.

The **ICAO's carbon emissions calculator** allows visitors to analyse the CO_2 generated by point-to-point journeys.

Eat Veggie or Vegan

There is a superb choice of veggie and vegan food across the state – once you've seen the vast cattle farms on Hwy 99 you'll be even more inclined to reach for a salad or a veggie burrito.

Fill Your Bottle

Save money and cut down on plastic waste by bringing a water bottle and filling it at one of the myriad public drinking fountains.

Take a Straw

A certain someone has issued an order to ban paper straws. Consider bringing a washable straw so you can sip your drink with a clear conscience.

Zero Waste Stores

If you're self-catering, head to a zero waste store and save on the plastic packaging that is ubiquitous at otherwise conscious California groceries and supermarkets.

Take the Train

Central California is pretty well served by train, so get out of the gas guzzler and put your feet up (maybe not literally) on one of the state's double-decker trains.

Car rental companies have embraced hybrid and electric vehicles. You usually have a choice of vehicles at California locations. The state has thousands of charging stations; see *afdc.energy.gov/fuels/electricity_locations.html*.

Central California has dozens of wineries committed to sustainable practices – important, given the amount of water, pesticides and herbicides that some others use. Ask before you book a tour how ecofriendly the winery's methods are.

EAT FARM-TO-FORK

The region's organic producers have long been pondering the environmental impact of our shopping habits. Organic farmers markets produce means no insect-killing chemicals, and it's low carbon in terms of transportation.

GET UNDER CANVAS

Campers mostly use very little electricity – much less than hotel stays necessitate. Switch off that torch, have a look at the stars and feel a little closer to nature.

Hop on a Bike

Bikes, e-bikes and e-scooters are easily rented at all of California's main tourist areas. CalBike *(calbike.org)* has dozens of links to online and downloadable maps of bike routes, lanes and paths statewide.

Save Water

California's near permanent drought means that everybody can help save water, including visitors. Take shorter showers, and turn off the tap when brushing your teeth, shaving or washing your face.

There's no need for new threads: the region excels in vintage clothing stores.

If you're staying a while, connect with the local community and do some volunteering.

Life-giving Forests

California relies on its national forests for half of its water supply. Forest protection and sustainable recreation isn't just desirable: it's essential to life in this thirsty state.

RESOURCES

greenbusinessca.org
Search for green businesses by categories.

happycow.net
Vegetarian and vegan restaurants in California and beyond.

saveourshores.org
Sponsors events to improve Monterey Bay National Marine Sanctuary's beaches.

CLOCKWISE FROM TOP LEFT: ISEN STOCKER/SHUTTERSTOCK, ROCKET GLASS/SHUTTERSTOCK, NETRUN78/SHUTTERSTOCK, ANDREW IVAN/SHUTTERSTOCK

LGBTQ+ Travelers

Inclusivity tends to be the norm in California, and its embrace of all things LGBTQ+ is cause for both admiration and ridicule in other parts of the USA. But it's a large and diverse state in terms of demographics and culture, and though largely progressive, attitudes vary from region to region. To generalize, the agricultural parts of the state are less tolerant.

Wedding Bells

Though it's now legal across the USA, many LGBTQ+ couples have a preference for marrying in a state known for its queer welcome. When he was mayor of San Francisco, current California governor Gavin Newsom defied the then law by instructing his officials to grant marriage licenses to same-sex couples. In today's California, you needn't be a citizen or take a blood test. Just fill out a form at a county clerk's office, pay a fee and get a license. Then get hitched!

LGBTQ+ RESOURCES

Advocate *(advocate.com/travel)* News, LGBTQ+ travel features and destination guides.

Damron *(damron.com)* Long-running, advertiser-driven gay travel guides and app.

LGBT National Help Center *(lgbthotline.org)* Counseling, information and referrals for people of all ages.

Out Traveler *(outtraveler.com)* Free online magazine articles with travel tips, destination guides and resort reviews.

Purple Roofs *(www.purpleroofs.com)* Gay-owned and -operated online directory of LGBT+-owned and -friendly accommodations.

Misterb&b

If you're looking for actively friendly LGBTQ+ accommodation, have a browse of Misterb&b (misterbandb.com). There are some particularly lovely options in Sacramento, including historic homes. They can also connect you to local communities and resources, as well as parties, exhibitions, restaurants and more.

THE LAW

Be aware of your rights if you're living or working in California. The California Fair Employment & Housing Act makes it illegal for an employer to fire, demote, fail to hire, harass or otherwise discriminate against anyone due to their sexual orientation, gender identity and/or gender expression.

Pride

Sacramento knows how to throw a party, and its June Pride events are unmissable. Chico rivals the state capital with its Pride celebrations, including a big downtown party, Drag Storytime and a queer board game night.

PINK NEIGHBORHOOD

The epicentre of gay life in Sacramento is Lavender Heights, which sits pretty in the Midtown area: just look for the rainbow crosswalk. From May through October the district hosts legendary block parties and second Saturday celebrations each month. As well as the fun times, you'll find community resources here: the Sacramento LGBT Community Center and the Lavender Library with its queer literature, documents, zines and films.

NITO/SHUTTERSTOCK

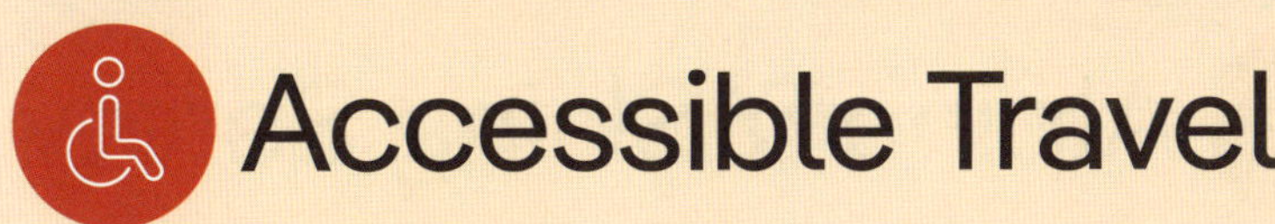

Accessible Travel

More populated areas of California are reasonably well equipped for travelers with disabilities, although older properties may have limitations.

Getting Around

Most intersections have dropped curbs; some have audible crossing signals. The Americans with Disabilities Act (ADA) requires public buildings built after 1993 to be wheelchair-accessible, including restrooms.

Airports

California's airports comply with accessibility laws. Assistance is available through your airline.

Accommodations

Motels and hotels built after 1993 must have at least one ADA-compliant accessible room; state your specific needs when making reservations. Holiday rentals and vintage properties may not be accessible.

RESOURCES

Access Northern California *(accessnca.org)* Extensive links to accessible-travel resources, including outdoor recreation opportunities, lodgings, tours and transportation.

California State Parks *(parks.ca.gov)* Searchable online map and database of accessible features at state parks.

Yosemite National Park Accessibility *(nps.gov/yose/planyourvisit/accessibility.html)* Detailed information for Yosemite, including services for deaf visitors.

TRAVELING

Major airlines, Greyhound buses, FlixBuses and Amtrak trains accommodate people with disabilities, usually with 48 hours of advance notice required. Major car-rental agencies offer hand-controlled vehicles and vans with wheelchair lifts at no extra charge, but reserve these well in advance.

The Outdoors

Most national and many state parks, and some other outdoor recreation areas, offer paved or boardwalk-style nature trails accessible by wheelchairs.

Phones & ATMs

Telephone companies will provide relay operators (dial 711) for those who are hearing impaired. Many banks provide ATM instructions to customers in Braille.

PARKING

US residents with a permanent disability quality for a free lifetime pass, which waives entry fees to all national parks. California State Parks' disabled discount pass ($3.50) gives 50% off parking and camping fees.

Seeing-eye dogs are permitted to accompany passengers traveling on public transportation.

ERIC ISSELEE/SHUTTERSTOCK

Alpine & Skiing Safety

California's marvellous mountains are mostly safe, but there are a few warnings to heed and precautions to take to ensure you avoid danger. If you're taking to the slopes to ski or snowboard, check your insurance policy to make sure you're covered.

Avalanches

As you marvel at all the snowy peaks in the Sierra Nevada, be aware that deadly avalanches can occur at any time and even on terrain that seems relatively flat. It's vital that people venturing off groomed slopes check avalanche conditions first. Whether you're backcountry ski-touring or simply hiking or snowshoeing, rent a homing beacon.

Heat Exhaustion & Heatstroke

On hot days, drink plenty of water. A daily minimum of 3L per person is recommended when you're active outdoors. Dehydration can cause heat exhaustion, often characterized by heavy sweating, fatigue, lethargy, nausea, etc. Continuous exposure to high temperatures can lead to possibly fatal heatstroke. Immediate hospitalization is essential. Meanwhile get out of the sun, douse with cool water and fan continuously. Sun lotion with SPF 30 blocks 97% of dangerous solar rays; SPF 50 blocks 98% and SPF 100 blocks 99%.

Hypothermia

Mountain temperatures can quickly drop below freezing. Rain or high winds can lower body temperatures fast. Symptoms of hypothermia include exhaustion, numbness, shivering, stumbling and cramps. For mild hypothermia, get dry and change into warm clothing. Drink hot liquids (no caffeine or alcohol) and eat. For severe hypothermia, seek immediate medical attention.

Packing for Mountain Hiking

Instead of cotton, wear synthetic or woollen clothing that retains warmth even when wet. Carry waterproof layers and high-energy snacks.

Mountain Lions

Attacks on humans by mountain lions are rare, but can be deadly. If you encounter a mountain lion on a hiking trail, stay calm, pick up small children, face the animal and retreat slowly. Make yourself appear larger by raising your arms or grabbing a stick. If the lion becomes menacing, shout or throw rocks. If you are attacked, be sure to fight back aggressively.

DON'T TOUCH THE WILDLIFE

Never feed or approach wild animals – it causes them to lose their innate fear of humans, which in turn makes them dangerously aggressive. Many birds and mammals carry serious diseases that can be transmitted through bites. Disturbing or harassing protected species is a crime, subject to enormous fines. Watch for signs indicating natural areas that have been declared off-limits for bird nesting in spring. Always look inside your shoes for snakes and spiders before putting them on when camping. Snake bites are rare, but occur most often when a snake is stepped on or provoked. Antivenom is available at most hospitals. For more on bears, see p207.

SKI SAFETY TIPS

- Have your equipment safety checked by a pro.
- Wear goggles or sunglasses and apply sunscreen at all times.
- Helmets are recommended.
- If you're feeling unconfident on the slopes, take a lesson, and don't push yourself physically.
- If you are becoming tired, stop skiing.
- Avoid closed and roped areas.
- Steer clear of snow vehicles.
- Be aware of your surroundings.
- Observe difficulty ratings for ski runs, and don't go beyond your experience level.
- Control your speed, and ensure that you can stop at any given moment.
- Stay hydrated.
- If you are injured, contact Ski Patrol.
- Do not ski or take the lifts if you have consumed drugs or alcohol.
- On the lifts, remove pole straps from your wrists and hold them in one hand.
- Backpacks should be carried in your lap on the lifts.
- Never jump from a lift.

Nuts & Bolts

OPENING HOURS

Some restaurants and shops in tourist areas may close a little earlier than this, particularly in the winter off-season (an exception being the ski areas).

Banks 9:30am–5pm weekdays

Bars 4pm–2am

Restaurants 11am–3pm and 5:30pm–10pm daily, some with longer hours Friday and Saturday

Shops 10am–7pm Monday–Saturday, 11am–6pm Sunday (convenience stores 24/7)

Water

All towns have water fountains where you can keep your bottle topped up.

Restrooms

Public facilities are generally clean and well maintained.

Weights & Measures

Imperial (except 1 US gallon equals 0.83 imperial gallons).

GOOD TO KNOW

Time zone
Pacific Standard Time (GMT/UTC −8 hours)

Country calling code
+1

Emergency number
911

Population
40 million

PUBLIC HOLIDAYS

On these holidays, banks, schools and post offices are closed. Museums and transport services may operate a Sunday schedule. If a holiday falls on a weekend, it's usually observed on a Monday.

New Year's Day January 1

Martin Luther King Jr Day Third Monday in January

Presidents' Day Third Monday in February

Cesar Chavez Day March 31

Memorial Day Last Monday in May

Independence Day July 4

Labor Day First Monday in September

Indigenous Peoples' Day Second Monday in October

Veterans Day November 11

Thanksgiving Day Fourth Thursday in November

Christmas Day December 25

Electricity 120V/60Hz

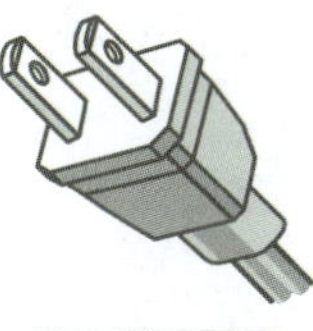

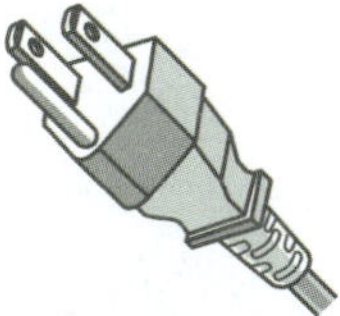

STORYBOOK

Our writers delve deep into different aspects of life in Lake Tahoe, Yosemite and Central California.

Yosemite Valley (p147)

SUZIE DUNDAS

A HISTORY OF SIERRA NEVADA IN 15 PLACES

This region was once home to Native American peoples living in close relationship with nature and the landscape, who left literal impressions on the rocks in the form of mortar holes. In the middle of the 19th century California was swept by Gold Rush fever. Prospectors, miners, hustlers, settlers and eccentrics – all have since left their mark here.

THE DEEP HISTORY of the area is still discernible, in fragile crafts and monuments created by the first inhabitants, and in the magnificent landscapes they once lived in harmony with. The area's population once comprised people from the Miwok, Nisenan and Yokuts tribes, as well as smaller indigenous groupings. Pre-Gold Rush sites are few, but from the 1850s onward there was a crazed flurry of digging and building. The mines themselves, as well as melancholy post-boom ghost towns, make for some of the most intriguing sights. Many settlements conjure the archetype of the one-street town familiar from Western movies, though several owe their existence to immigrant workers and prospectors from China. Central California, like the rest of the US, is defined by the labor of immigrants. The city of Sacramento, capital of the state of California, has a bold grid of streets studded with historic and modern buildings, over-arched with trees that help to cool a region that is increasingly feeling the heat in summer. From diverted rivers to near-bursting dams, central California is shaped by thirst, and by hunger for the bounty of the fruit and nut trees that march in neat, seemingly never-ending rows across the valleys.

1. Indian Grinding Rock State Historic Park

FIRST NATIONS

Throughout central California there are traces of the pre-colonial life that was present here for millennia, and no sight is more poignant and evocative than Grinding Rock. The rock in question features hundreds of mortar holes, where acorns were ground to produce nutritious porridge, as well as petroglyphs – carvings of animal and human tracks and circles – dating back more than 2000 years. You'll also see a handsome reproduction of a traditional Miwok roundhouse. Grinding Rock remains a sacred place for the Miwok people, who celebrate the acorn harvest here each September.

For more on Indian Grinding Rock State Historic Park, see page 84

2. Sutter's Fort

COLONIAL BEGINNINGS

Failed businessman and would-be colonizer John Sutter was a Swiss immigrant who built an adobe fortress in New Helvetia (New Swizerland) back in 1841. The fort promoted Sutter's power-grab in the region, and was the place from which he carried out murderous raids on those Native American villages that refused to comply with him. The buildings you see now are later 19th-century reconstructions – they were abandoned during the Gold Rush and soon deteriorated. It was from this contested, blood-soaked fortress that the city of Sacramento grew, a painful history now acknowledged at a site where the noble pioneer myth long held sway.

For more on Sutter's Fort, see page 48

3. Nevada City

BIRTH OF A GOLD TOWN

Entrancingly pretty and surrounded by pine-cloaked hills, Nevada City was once a Nisenan village named Ustumah. Gold was found in the surrounding area in the mid-19th century: in 1849 the town was founded to house the miners, and a wave of gold-fueled construction began, resulting in the beautiful wrought-iron and brick buildings that you see today. Another outcome of the mining was the poisoning of the nearby Yuba River due to mercury used in the extraction process; opposition to this kickstarted a tradition of environmental activism that continues in NorCal to this day.

For more on Nevada City, see page 85

Sutter's Fort State Historic Park (p48)

KIT LEONG/SHUTTERSTOCK

4. Empire Mine State Historic Park

GOLD IN THEM THAR HILLS

The state's fortunes turned in the waters of the American River, with the discovery by James Marshall of a tiny nugget of gold in 1848. But it was at places like the 1850 Empire Mine where the process of extraction and the accretion of enormous wealth reached a peak. From 1850 to 1956 the miners here, mostly Cornish, produced 5.8 million troy ounces of gold (worth about $8 billion today). The handsome and genteel English-style manor house that adjoins the mine illustrates how some of the money was spent, its refined air a stark contrast to the mining frenzy that occurred below the earth.

For more on Empire Mine State Historic Park, see page 87

5. Kingsburg

SWEDEN IN CALIFORNIA

The first two Swedes arrived in this small railway settlement in 1872, and by 1921 nearly all of the town's residents were of Swedish origin. Today Kingsburg trades on its Scandi past with numerous kitschy stores featuring stylised dala horses, and cinnamon wafts emanating from the bakeries. The sense of a living history is hard to discern, outside of the Swedish Festival held in May and the lighting of the town's Christmas tree. Kingsburg remains though, one of many places that illustrate California's rich immigrant diversity.

For more on Kingsburg, see page 64

6. Locke

TUMBLEDOWN CHINESE TOWN

The Delta town of Locke was built by and for Chinese workers who constructed the surrounding levees, and its story is one of prejudice, and of the resilience of central California's immigrants. The workers' homes were destroyed by arson in 1912, and the community came together to build a new town. Still inhabited, though scarcely, Locke feels like a miraculous survival, the wonky swollen wooden buildings on the main street housing the Dai Loy gambling museum, a Chinese medicine practitioner, a couple of stores and a surprisingly raucous bar.

For more on Locke, see page 53

7. Forestiere Underground Gardens

SUBTERRANEAN CITRUS

In the early 1900s, Sicilian immigrant Baldassare Forestiere was feeling the cold of the Fresno winters, and the intense heat of the summers. Intertwining his knowledge of Italian citrus groves with his experience as an East Coast subway tunneler, he began to dig. The result is a fantastical underground garden, with lemon, orange and grapefruit trees as well as vines reaching from below-ground planters towards apertures that let in the light. You can also see the cave-like living quarters that Forestiere excavated. Only a portion of this magical creation survives, a tribute to both imagination and industry.

For more on Forestiere Underground Gardens, see page 63

8. Reno Arch

NEON GLORY

Lake Tahoe is one of the natural marvels of central California, but its Nevada side has long had a more urban aspect, with the good times rolling just north of the lake in Reno. The fabulously retro neon Reno Arch welcomes visitors to the city's casino strip and proclaims the place to be 'The Biggest Little City in the World' – a slogan chosen by competition in 1929. The earliest neon sign was erected here in 1926, with the current iteration echoing the Deco vibe of times past.

For more on Reno, Nevada, see page 126

9. Manzanar National Historic Site

WARTIME HORRORS

A stark wooden guard tower alerts drivers to one of US history's grimmest chapters, which unfolded on a barren, windy sweep of land some 5 miles south of Independence. Little remains of the infamous war concentration camp, a dusty square mile where more than 10,000 people of Japanese ancestry were corralled during WWII.

The camp's lone remaining building, the former high-school auditorium, houses a superb interpretive center. Thought-provoking exhibits chronicle the stories of the families who languished here, yet managed to build a vibrant community. Otherwise, vestiges of buildings, gardens, and the haunting camp cemetery remain.

For more on Manzanar National Historic Site, see page 171

10. Palisades Tahoe

OLYMPIC GOLD

In 1960, this gorgeous valley west of Lake Tahoe beat the favorite Innsbruck and was chosen to host the Winter Olympics; at the time it labored under the racist appellation of Squaw Valley, but the name was changed in 2020 following pressure from the Washoe tribe. The relatively undeveloped resort was swiftly overhauled, and its successful hosting of the Olympics put the region on the international skiing map. As attractive for its après-ski scene as it is for its extremely challenging chutes, bowls and cornices, this glamorous destination still pulls in eager skiers come winter time.

For more on Palisades Tahoe, see page 124

11. Davis Farmers Market

BIRTH OF A MOVEMENT

The ultimate weekend occupation in the region is to mosy around the stalls of neighborhood farmers markets, which allow growers to sell direct to the public. From farm fresh eggs to abundant fruit and veg to local honey and nuts and scrumptious baked goods, the produce is top quality. This trend started in Davis way back in 1976, when five UC Davis students came together through activism and the agrarian movement to support small-scale and organic farming; eventually a parking lot was purchased by the town council to give the market a permanent home, where it continues to flourish and inspire.

For more on Davis Farmers Market, see page 55

12. Buck Owens' Crystal Palace

COUNTRY MUSIC MAGNET

Originally from Texas, singer-songwriter and guitarist Buck Owens revived country honk-tonk and defined the 'Bakersfield Sound' in his adopted home. His long-time dream was the creation of the Crystal Palace, which he opened in 1996 – it's a fantastical assemblage of pastel-painted wood that looks like a country shack on steroids. Buck and his Buckaroos performed there at weekends, playing intimate gigs that took him back to his pre-fame days; he used the venue to nurture the

Manzanar National Historic Site (p171)

careers of young singers, as well as showcasing established stars. Crystal Palace remains a big draw for country music lovers.

For more on Buck Owens' Crystal Palace, see page 65

13. Museum of Western Film History, Lone Pine

MOVIE MYTHS

More than 400 movies, not to mention numerous commercials (mostly for rugged SUVs and Jeeps), have been shot in the area. This fascinating museum contains paraphernalia from locally set films, not just Westerns (as the name of the museum suggests). One of the most fascinating pieces in the collection is the 1928 Lincoln camera car – mounted cameras caught the action while cars drove alongside galloping horses. See items from Django Unchained, Tremors, Star Trek and other memorabilia in engaging exhibits.

For more on the museum and Lone Pine, see page 172

14. Oroville Dam

WATERS RISING

In February 2017, Oroville made national headlines when a dam east of town threatened catastrophe. After heavy rains, several flood control measures failed and the swollen waters of Lake Oroville – California's second-largest reservoir and the water source for farms of the Central Valley and 23 million people – threatened disaster. In a chaotic evacuation, 188,000 people were given just an hour to leave their homes, while news helicopters live streamed the traffic jam. The dam held, but the crisis caused millions in damage and added another hot-button issue to the complex debate about California's water management, climate change and crumbling infrastructure.

For more on Oroville, see page 59

15. El Capitan

BODACIOUS CLIMB

The visual icon of Yosemite National Park, El Cap is a 3000ft granite cliff which rises dramatically from the valley floor. It has been ascended many times by roped climbers, but in 2017 Alex Honnold decided to climb the rock unaided. Preparation involved making the climb multiple times while roped, locating tiny protrusions that would allow for micro foot- and hand-holds. With great perseverance and strength, Honnold free climbed El Capitan in just under four hours, his achievement documented in edge-of-the-seat documentary Free Solo. To date nobody has repeated this ultra-dangerous feat, though El Cap sees regular attempts at breaking the speed climbing record.

For more on El Capitan, see page 147

MEET CALIFORNIA'S MOUNTAIN RESIDENTS

CLOCKWISE FROM TOP LEFT: VAWILEY/GETTY IMAGES, SUZIE DUNDAS, DIMA BRINZA/SHUTTERSTOCK, CHRISTER DABU/SHUTTERSTOCK

The California dream still thrives in the Sierra Nevada – but it's one of catching every powder day and never missing a mountain sunset, not one of striking it rich in Hollywood (though you'll find plenty of wealthy residents here, too). Suzie Dundas introduces her people.

FROM HIGH-ALTITUDE SKI towns to almond country, those who live in the Sierra Nevada are a study in contrasts, from liberal, tree-hugging hippies and off-the-grid libertarians and homesteaders to the mega-rich.

Some say Northern Californians are laid-back and low-key to a fault, always late, never working as hard as they could, and glued to their reusable water bottles – but that's a surface read. In outdoor towns like Truckee, Mammoth and Bishop, people are up early to be first on the ski lift on powder days. Schedules are based on trail conditions and having time to enjoy the outdoors, not on 9-to-5 commitments – something that has gotten significantly easier with the growth in tech work and remote jobs.

Mountain communities can be tight-knit, but tourism is their bread and butter. While locals may complain about crowds, tourists have long been a fixture in towns around Yosemite, Mt Whitney and Lake Tahoe. Towns aren't as reasonably priced as they used to be, and residents are usually either well-off enough to own a home, or may share one of the few available rental homes with four or five other hospitality industry workers or outdoor guides. Either way, most have a rescue dog, gear closet and mountain bike. Even on Saturday nights out, function beats fashion, and you won't find locals wearing designer ski jackets or fur-topped leather boots (though the ski jackets may be even pricier).

Outside of tourism centers, communities across the Central Valley remote parts of Northern California tend to be more conservative and agricultural. In towns like Merced or Paso Robles, you'll find more pickup trucks than Priuses, as well as larger lots and farms, often with horses roaming or wine growing out back. Some communities may be more traditional and resistant to an influx of younger residents – though with so many mountain bikers and hikers realizing the appeal of more rural towns, attitudes are slowly changing.

But while the population in the Sierra Nevada may be piddly when compared with coastal cities, it still has depth, and most residents don't fit neatly into one box. You'll find farmers who run their own social media accounts, and tech workers anxious to live off-grid and raise chickens. One thing most residents have in common is a respect for the land and support of environmentalism, though not always for the same reasons. While ski town residents may demonstrate in favor of aggressive strategies to fight climate change, rural residents may worry more about the loss of agricultural income caused by hotter temperatures. Still, they'll both tell you the state's natural resources are worth protecting.

Complicated as it may be, one thing remains the same: with the exception of Indigenous Americans like the Washoe, Paiute, Miwok, Nisenan and Shoshoone, among others, everyone in the Sierra Nevada came from somewhere else. And most stay for a reason: the mountains are home, and no beachfront cottage in San Diego or high-rise in San Francisco could replace the joy of the trails, fresh air and world-class recreation just minutes away. After all, as residents here love to say: we live where you vacation.

Population

Only a fraction of California's 39-million-plus population live in the Sierra Nevada. The largest towns include South Lake Tahoe (21,000), Truckee (17,000) and Auburn (14,000); even popular tourist towns like Mammoth Lakes have less than 10,000 full-time residents.

WE'RE USED TO CHALLENGES

If there's one unifying trait among Northern and Central Californians, it's resilience. Life in this part of California is more demanding and more extreme, for everything from driving in blizzard conditions to suffering through the combination of wildlife smoke and no air-conditioning. Few towns have escaped crises like wildfires, droughts, floods and housing shortages. People who stay more than a few years are willing to endure a little extra hardship (and extra expenses) for the privilege of living near some of the best recreation in the country.

But that doesn't mean those challenges go undiscussed, or don't cause problems. Most of the Sierra Nevada hurts for diversity, to a noticeable degree when visiting. Debates over land use, climate change, immigration and social issues are ongoing. The Sierra Nevada's small towns, like many in the US, are wrestling with balancing growth, gatekeeping and environmental protection.

Mountain biking, Truckee (p127)

SUZIE DUNDAS

PRESSURE ON THE REGION

Mountain and foothills towns have long depended on tourism. But overtourism, along with a host of other ongoing concerns, is becoming a tricky balancing act. By Suzie Dundas

MANY OF THE mountain towns of the Sierra Nevada that once started as mining outposts and railroad stops are now celebrated recreation destinations, thanks primarily to tourism. Towns like Truckee and Mammoth Lakes boomed with the popularity of skiing in the 1960s and '70s, and the gateway communities ringing Yosemite, Lake Tahoe and Sequoia-Kings Canyon National Park have long been interwoven with the tourism industry.

Today, however, these towns are grappling with a range of ongoing challenges, many of which are intensified by the rising demand to live and vacation in the mountains. Tourism keeps these towns' economies afloat, but it can quickly tip into overtourism – a phenomenon that brings both prosperity and significant challenges to otherwise small communities. Add in broader threats facing California, such as climate change, high costs of living and wildfires, and it becomes clear that life in the region's snow-covered mountain towns is far from as idyllic as it may appear.

Be the Right Kind of Visitor

Local businesses from hotels to restaurants and outdoor outfitters depend on the spending of millions of visitors that flock to California's eastern stretches each year, but it comes at a cost. Popular towns and their surrounding trails, lakes and campgrounds have been overwhelmed, especially during peak seasons. Overflowing parking lots, piles of litter outside stuffed trash cans and hundreds of styrofoam coolers and beer cans left behind on beaches have become frequent sights after holiday weekends. Sensitive habitats near lakes and along trails are damaged by trampling and erosion, and the region's wildlife suffer as visitors – often unaware – leave food out, drawing animals dangerously close to roads and homes.

Pressures also impact full-time residents. Increased traffic congestion, overtaxed stores and a shortage of long-term housing are persistent problems throughout the Sierra Nevada. When locals can't afford to live where they work, labor shortages follow, making it difficult for small business owners to stay afloat.

It's an issue seen in mountain towns throughout the West, but fortunately, it's one the Sierra Nevada has made progress in addressing. Many ski resorts and state parks around Lake Tahoe now require reservations, alleviating traffic and reducing emissions as cars idle in roads and parking lots. Campaigns like Take Care Tahoe *(takecaretahoe.org)* and Take Care Sierra *(takecaresierra.org)* promote responsible recreation, and organized beach cleanups let visitors and residents alike give back.

The solution for visitors is simple: be a thoughtful guest in the mountains. Educate yourself before arriving and consider how your plans may impact the community.

Prioritize staying in hotels, rather than private home rentals, and take public transportation when you can. Respect trail and beach closures, and consider spending an afternoon volunteering wherever you visit, whether that's assisting in building mountain bike trails or participating in a Yosemite National Park cleanup. It's also worth planning a shoulder-season trip rather than traveling in the busy season (which means smaller crowds and more affordable prices, too). If you are visiting in the busy season, consider spending a day in a smaller community, like Downieville (for bikes and beers) or Murphys (for wine tastings), or explore national parks in the early morning and evening, when crowds are smaller.

Wildfires are the New Normal

Wildfires are an increasing threat to communities in the foothills and mountains alike, driven largely by decades of poor forest management and unchecked development rather than climate alone. Historically, Sierra forests experienced frequent natural fires that thinned trees and maintained open, fire-resistant forests. However, years of a fire suppression policy that prioritized extinguishing all blazes as quickly as possible impacted that natural cycle, and now, forests are packed with dense trees and growth – and worsened by unpredictable cycles of drought and snow.

This unnatural buildup of fuel has set the stage for catastrophic fires. The 2021 Dixie Fire was the first to burn completely through the Sierra, and the 2024 Park Fire destroyed more than 700 structures and cost $351 million to fight.

Overdevelopment compounds this crisis. Wildfires have been started by power lines, by unattended fires and dropped cigarettes, and even by car exhaust pipes parked on dry leaves. When development is dense, evacuations are slower and vehicles block critical firefighting equipment and personnel from getting to the front lines.

It's easy for visitors to help. Stay on top of fire warnings at fire.ca.gov/incidents, and reschedule travel to any towns in or near evacuation zones. Pay close attention to campfire, outdoor grilling and parking regulations, and call out any dangerous behavior you observe, like tossing cigarettes out of car windows or shooting fireworks or crackers.

Tahoe's Changing Climate

Climate change is a very real, very immediate issue for all Californians, from residents of the Central Coast whose homes are eroding beneath them to residents of Far North California suffering from unseasonable heat waves. But the impacts of climate change are even more pronounced in the mountains and foothills – not only because changing weather makes recreation- and weather-based businesses hard to predict, but because climate change exacerbates many of the issues towns are already facing.

More unpredictable snow and drought patterns cause financial instability for the ski industry, including restaurants, rental companies and guiding companies. A low snow year means snowmobile tours can't run, visitors don't come to town and employees can't find stable work. And since the mountains get most of their moisture in the winter, a low snow year makes the forests dry and full of brush, which makes wildfires burn hotter and faster.

Warmer temperatures also make it easier for invasive species to thrive. The region's sugar pine trees have been decimated by a Mountain pine beetle infestation, and New Zealand mud snails are thriving in Tahoe's waters, taking food from native species needed to support healthy fish populations.

There are some specific things you can do when visiting the Sierra to help. Keeping the environment strong enough to fight these challenges is a key priority, which is easy to do. Never litter or leave anything outdoors (including toilet paper and food scraps). Always camp at least 200ft from bodies of water, and use reef-safe sunscreens to help keep chemicals out of waterways. Don't blaze your own trails, don't mark or damage plants or trees, and bring a reusable water bottle and coffee cup with you.

It may sound minor, but it's making a difference. In the early 2020s, Tahoe reversed a nearly 30-year trend of declining water clarity, and new bike-share programs in places like Yosemite, Truckee and South Lake Tahoe are making it easier and easier to leave the gas guzzlers at home.

CLOCKWISE FROM TOP LEFT: EUGENE MOERMAN/SHUTTERSTOCK, LISA PARSONS/SHUTTERSTOCK, JONATHAN SUDDUTH/GETTY IMAGES, ANNA39/GETTY IMAGES

BEARS OF THE SIERRA NEVADA

Everything you need to know about California's number one spokescreature. By Ashley Harrell

THE SIERRA NEVADA brims with enchanting wild animals, but most revered of all is the American black bear. You'll see bears on hats, T-shirts and other souvenirs throughout the region, from Yosemite National Park to the Lake Tahoe Basin. But before you set eyes on the real thing, it helps to have some background.

Meet the Black Bears

The first thing to know about the bears in the Sierra Nevada is that they aren't grizzlies. These bears, *Ursus americanus,* are commonly known as black bears, but here's where things get a little confusing: they aren't always black. Some are cinnamon or off-white, and others just look brown. Do not call them brown bears, though. Because that is the common name for grizzlies *(Ursus arctos horribilis).*

Grizzlies are much larger and more aggressive, and although they grace California's state flag, they no longer exist in the Golden State. Once roaming throughout California, grizzlies were driven out by hunting and habitat loss as European

Clockwise from top left: Black bear, Sequoia National Park (p159); Black bear and cub, Lake Tahoe (p98); Black bear, Mammoth Lakes (p173); Black bear, Sierra Nevada

settlers moved west, and the last confirmed sighting of a wild California grizzly was in 1924.

Black bears, while smaller and generally less dangerous, still require a wide berth and plenty of respect. Adult males weigh between 150lb and 400lb, and females range from 100lb to 300lb. All black bears have powerful bodies, dexterous limbs and sharp claws; they can climb trees, walk upright and run up to 35 miles per hour (the fastest human runs 27 miles per hour).

No, black bears don't consider you a meal, as they're far too busy feasting on berries, nuts, acorns, grasses, insects and the occasional small mammal. They have an excellent sense of smell, so while they usually try to avoid humans, sometimes their noses lead them into our vicinity. It's important to remember, though, that the bears aren't the problem: instead, it's humans being careless about the disposal of their garbage.

How We Harm Bears

The problems people have created for bears began a very long time ago. It's hard to believe, but in places like Yosemite National Park, staff and visitors were once actively encouraged to feed bears. Up until the 1970s, Yosemite rangers put on evening 'bear shows,' drawing the animals in by dumping trash at designated feeding sites so the tourists would watch. It was as reckless and unsustainable as it sounds.

While direct feeding has long been outlawed, a more subtle but still significant problem has persisted: garbage. When visitors leave food or trash unsecured, bears capitalize. Once a bear learns that humans are an easy source of calories, it becomes what wildlife officials call 'food conditioned.' From there, it's a short leap to 'habituated,' meaning the bear loses its natural fear of humans. That often ends badly: in the name of safety, wildlife managers oftentimes relocate or even euthanize bears.

Sequoia National Park (p159)

FROM LEFT: KAVRAM/SHUTTERSTOCK, ART WOLFE/GETTY IMAGES

This cycle – people leaving food out, bears learning to associate humans with meals, and then being labeled as dangerous – is a tragedy that's played out time and again across the Sierra Nevada.

The Problem in Lake Tahoe

Lake Tahoe is ground zero for humans making trouble for bears. Essentially, the region's expanding residential areas, large number of visitors and abundant short-term rentals have created a perfect storm, to the point where it's usual to see bears wandering neighborhoods, raiding garbage bins and even breaking into homes.

Some bears in Tahoe have adapted so thoroughly to this lifestyle that they've stopped hibernating altogether, remaining active through the snowy winter months to take advantage of year-round garbage. One high-profile example is 'Hank the Tank,' a massive black bear accused of breaking into dozens of homes in the South Lake Tahoe area. Hank became a media sensation in 2022 when reports emerged of his 500lb frame and uncanny knack for entering houses. While it was later revealed that several large bears were responsible, the story highlighted how serious the situation had become.

Enter the BEAR League, a nonprofit based in the Tahoe Basin that works to protect both bears and people. They educate the public, help respond to bear incidents and advocate for more bear-aware policies. Volunteers with the Bear League have even helped rehabilitate orphaned cubs and installed bear-proof trash systems in problem areas.

How We Help Bears

Whether you're renting a cabin in Tahoe or hiking through the backcountry of Yosemite, you have a role to play in protecting the Sierra Nevada's black bears.

The most important thing you can do is store your trash properly. If you're staying in a rental property, never leave trash outside unless it's in a bear-resistant container, and be sure to lock all doors and windows at night. If you're at a campground, make sure your garbage is locked up in a bear-resistant container, and never leave food, wrappers, coolers or even toiletries outside or in your car. Bears can open car doors, break windows and smell through packaging. Improper food storage in bear country can result in fines of up to $5000.

Black bear

If you're lucky enough to see a bear, do not approach, not even to take a photo. Use binoculars or a zoom lens if you want a close look. If you're driving in bear country, don't speed, and if you're hiking, make noise as you walk to give bears time to move away from your path. If you see a bear on a trail, give it space and back away slowly – do not run.

Lastly, don't be shy about talking with fellow travelers about bear safety. If you see someone leaving food out or getting too close to a bear, speak up. It could save a bear's life.

INDEX

Map Pages **000**

Map Pages **000**

M

N

O

P

'A hike through oak-studded hills leads you to Hidden Falls (p77), a secluded 30-foot waterfall that feels like a secret garden.'

'The historic river port next to downtown, Old Sacramento (p47) is the city's top visitor draw. The kitschy gold-rush-era atmosphere makes it good for a stroll.'

FROM LEFT: FIIPHOTO/SHUTTERSTOCK, CHRIS ALLAN/SHUTTERSTOCK

Mapping data sources:
© Lonely Planet
© OpenStreetMap http://openstreetmap.org/copyright

THIS BOOK

Destination Editor Melissa Yeager

Production Editors Ursula O'Sullivan-Dale, Jennifer McCann

Image Editors Jo-anne Riddell, Megan Cassidy

Coordinating Editor Gabrielle Innes

Cartographers Alison Lyall, Corey Hutchison

Assisting Editors Soo Hamilton, Hannah Cartmel

Cover Researcher Katelyn Perry

Thanks Alison Killilea

Paper in this book is certified against the Forest Stewardship Council™ standards. FSC™ promotes environmentally responsible, socially beneficial and economically viable management of the world's forests.

Published by Lonely Planet Global Limited
CRN 554153
1st edition – Jan 2026
ISBN 978 1 83758 815 2

10 9 8 7 6 5 4 3 2 1
Printed in China